'R'

JAVA™ DESIGN

JAVA™ DESIGN

Objects, UML, and Process

Kirk Knoernschild

✦ Addison-Wesley

Boston • San Francisco • New York • Toronto • Montreal
London • Munich • Paris • Madrid
Capetown • Sydney • Tokyo • Singapore • Mexico City

Many of the designations used by manufacturers and sellers to distinguish their products are claimed as trademarks. Where those designations appear in this book, and Addison-Wesley, Inc. was aware of a trademark claim, the designations have been printed with initial capital letters or in all capitals.

The author and publisher have taken care in the preparation of this book, but make no expressed or implied warranty of any kind and assume no responsibility for errors or omissions. No liability is assumed for incidental or consequential damages in connection with or arising out of the use of the information or programs contained herein.

The publisher offers discounts on this book when ordered in quantity for special sales. For more information, please contact:

Pearson Education Corporate Sales Division
201 W. 103rd Street
Indianapolis, IN 46290
(800) 428-5331
corpsales@pearsoned.com

Visit AW on the Web: www.aw.com/cseng/

Library of Congress Cataloging-in-Publication Data

Knoernschild, Kirk.
    Java design : objects, UML, and process / Kirk Knoernschild.
        p.   cm.
    Includes bibliographical references and index.
    ISBN 0-201-75044-9
       1. Java (Computer program language) 2. UML (Computer science) I. Title.

    QA76.73.J38 K57 2002
    005.13'3—dc21

                                                        2001053552

Copyright © 2002 Kirk Knoernschild

For information on obtaining permission for use of material from this work, please submit a written request to:

Pearson Education, Inc.
Rights and Contracts Department
75 Arlington Street, Suite 300
Boston, MA 02116
Fax: (617) 848-7047

ISBN 0-201-75044-9
Text printed on recycled paper
1 2 3 4 5 6 7 8 9 10—MA—0504030201
First printing, December 2001

To Grandma Maude

Mom and Dad, I love you and want to thank you for your guidance, support, and constant love that have made everything possible.

Nickie, your eternal love and understanding have enabled me to pursue my passion and realize a dream. I love you, Nickie.

CONTENTS

PREFACE

This book emphasizes the utilization of Java, the Unified Modeling Language (UML), object-orientation, and software process as a cohesive whole. This book will help you

- Understand how to apply proven object-oriented design principles and patterns to develop resilient, robust, and extensible software systems using the Java programming language
- Gain insight into how to adopt and take advantage of the most useful aspects of the UML on a Java development project, while ignoring those less often used
- Do the preceding within the context of a well-defined, repeatable, and predictable software development process, ensuring that the software artifacts that are created are used

This book documents my experiences developing enterprisewide software applications. It contains input from literally hundreds of developers I've instructed and worked with throughout my years of teaching and applying these concepts. It answers these developers' most frequently asked questions in a format that I've found to be understandable by those developers. The approach taken in presenting these answers is one of clear and concise directions, followed by elaborating how various technologies can be used together to realize resilient results. I hope that the information in this book can save you both time and energy in your development efforts.

Intended Audience

This book discusses how the UML can be used during an implementation stage of the software development lifecycle. With its emphasis on object orientation, problem solving, and communication, this book will give developers a deeper understanding of how to design cleaner Java applications. Much of the discussion is focused on refactoring or cleaning up the design of existing code. Using these concepts, developers can become more efficient in discovering more resilient solutions sooner.

Designers and architects can benefit by gaining a deeper understanding of how the UML can be used to create a system of checks and balances when establishing architectural restrictions and designing subsystems. These individuals will gain insight into how our models serve as the mechanism to validate our systems' architectures. The numerous principles and guidelines discussed also will help contribute to more resilient systems, as well as serve as a measuring stick of our existing object-oriented designs.

Project managers, IT managers, and project sponsors can benefit by obtaining a deeper understanding of the importance of these key technologies. No longer will we view each of these technologies as separate entities, but we'll see them as a set of complementary tools that can be used together to contribute to a lower-risk development effort.

Feedback

I'm always interested in obtaining feedback from individuals reading this book. Feel free to e-mail me the information you found most useful. But more importantly, I'm interested in hearing how you feel this book could be improved. Such feedback can ensure future readers obtain the knowledge needed to enhance their software development efforts. I'll post additional information on this book at www.kirkk.com/JOUP.html.

Acknowledgments

A very special thanks goes out to all of the thoughtful reviewers who contributed significantly in helping to ensure the material in this book was both useful and accurate. Most significantly, I would like to extend a personal thank you to Adam Brace, John Brugge, Levi Cook, and David Williams. Their thoughtful reviews and contributions played significant roles in my ability to complete this work.

In addition, I would like to thank Paul Becker, my editor. Without his constant encouragement and patience, I no doubt would have been unable to complete this work. Thank you to Debbie Lafferty, without whom I would not have been a part of the Addison-Wesley family. I would like to thank Tyrrell Albaugh, my production manager, for her careful guidance through the final editing stages of the manuscript. And, of course, without the patience of Nancy Crumpton, some of my ill-formed sentences and grammatical errors might not have been caught. Finally, I want to thank the rest of the Addison-Wesley family, most of whom I did not have the honor of meeting. They made significant contributions in making this book a reality.

Last, I thank those individuals, too many to name, who have contributed, no matter how small, to my life. You know who you are!

Kirk Knoernschild
joup@kirkk.com
www.kirkk.com

INTRODUCTION

The convergence of a suite of technologies into a cohesive whole represents a significant advantage over the same technologies standing independently. Java, object orientation, the Unified Modeling Language (UML), and software process are prominent technologies that contribute significantly to the success of software development efforts. Yet used independently, their true power may not be realized. Each of these four unique, yet complementary, technologies has a distinct form and can be studied and applied independently. However, when used together as a set of supporting technologies, we increase the likelihood of developing higher-quality, on-time, and on-budget software that meets our business needs.

Our goal is to discuss the concepts that enable developers to use the UML, objects, and software process to solve complex problems encountered during design and implementation of enterprisewide Java development. We must ensure we realize the maximum benefit of each of these powerful technologies by assembling and applying the best practices as a cohesive whole. In addition, we must ignore, or at least use more judiciously, those aspects that lack significant and immediate value. Mechanisms that enable us to prove our systems are resilient, extensible, and maintainable are sorely needed.

Unfortunately, the complexity of a single technology can be overwhelming. Regardless, we must utilize a combination of complementary technologies that ensures that the software we build is more robust. Hence, our goal throughout this book is to emphasize convergence—the convergence of Java, object orientation, the UML, and software process, and to describe how each can be used as part of a cohesive whole.

The Power of Convergence

Throughout my travels as a corporate developer, professional instructor, consultant, and mentor, I've found that software developers everywhere consistently struggle with the same fundamental challenges. In essence, these challenges are centered on software design. Whether accommodating scope creep, managing a constant evolution in requirements when developing a new system, or attempting to add new features into an existing system, the architectural mechanisms utilized in each of the situations are vital in determining the success or failure of the software development effort. Systems that support change will grow with the businesses they support; those that don't inevitably will crumble beneath their own weight, eventually resulting in a new development effort.

On a theoretical front, when considering a software system with an ultimately flexible architecture, the possibilities are endless. Simply plugging new components into the system could easily accommodate changing requirements and scope creep. Older rules no longer supported could be dealt with by removing those components from the system. This Promised Land currently exists only in theory; pragmatically speaking, it is almost impossible to achieve, but that isn't to say that we shouldn't strive to achieve it. By putting forth the effort, we're assured of making it one step closer.

Taking this next step is not easy. It involves changes throughout the entire software development lifecycle. By utilizing today's best-of-breed technologies, methodologies, and principles, we can create the set of complementary tools to take our efforts to this next level. Using these complementary tools creates a development effort with an implicit system of checks and balances. These help ensure that our systems will, in fact, be more flexible and resilient to change.

In *The Timeless Way of Building*, Christopher Alexander discusses an aesthetically pleasing feeling associated with architecture called "The Quality Without a Name" [ALEXANDER79]. He describes various aspects of a garden, a storefront, or a room that create a feeling of warmth. The cause of this feeling can't be attributed to any singular aspect of the surroundings but is the result of how each atomic element works together to create this quality. This description can be applied to software architecture as well. In my discussions with students and clients, I often ask if they've had similar feelings when developing software. Most developers can remember when they've felt proud of their work. They see that the system is flexible, performs well, and is bug free. They have achieved "Quality Without a Name" in software development.

What This Book Is

With this book, we intend to provide solid insight into using the UML and object orientation to develop Java applications within the context of a well-defined software process. We concentrate on the most frequently used aspects of the UML, highlighting best practices of software process as we progress.

Because this book is centered around the full lifecycle, various guidelines are presented that can help ensure adherence to the best practices of solid design.

It is highly unlikely that any organization can successfully adopt a technology overnight. With the rampant emergence of recent technologies such as Java, including Java 2 Enterprise Edition (J2EE), the UML, object orientation, and various software processes, an adoption strategy is critical to success. We discuss practices that can help ensure that a successful integration takes place.

Once integrated, however, proven practices must be adhered to. The object-oriented structure of our system, and the manner in which it is implemented, will contribute significantly to the success of our software. We also discuss many of the important decisions that development teams make when architecting object-oriented software.

In general, the intent is to emphasize the more significant elements of these technologies, while ignoring the elements that are less often employed. As such, this book serves as a guide through many of the most common and most significant decisions made on all software development efforts.

Our approach to discussion is pragmatic. Discussions of theory take place only in situations where such discussion is warranted and where it can provide deeper insight.

What This Book Is Not

This book is not an exhaustive resource on UML syntax. Spending valuable time understanding the use of technologies in only a small percentage of application development is purely academic. Therefore, UML syntax is discussed only where it is warranted.

This book is not an in-depth study of all of the UML diagrams. We focus on those diagrams that are used most often in the development lifecycle and those that contribute most to application development. These diagrams often are incorporated into a development environment that is adopting the UML for the first time.

This book is not a comprehensive Java resource. A general understanding of Java syntax is assumed. While all examples use Java, and some of our discussions are specific to Java, an understanding of another object-oriented language most likely will suffice for those developers without an in-depth understanding of Java.

This book doesn't present a formal software development process. Instead, we glean best practices from a suite of proven software development processes. As such, while our discussion constantly considers process, we're not interested in a particular software development process, but instead those practices embodied within software processes that focus on success.

High-Level Book Organization

This book can be conceptually broken into two parts. The first four chapters present the UML, object-orientation, and software process as independent entities. This helps clarify the purpose and the value of each of the powerful technologies in an independent fashion. The remaining chapters emphasize convergence in a practical and example-laden manner. Our discussions in the latter chapters emphasize applying the concepts discussed in the first four chapters.

How to Read This Book

It's recommended that the chapters in this book be read in order. The concepts in each chapter build as the book progresses. If reading the chapters in order is not a viable option for you, consider the following:

- For those most interested in Java and object orientation, Chapters 1 and 3 and 7 through 11 will be of most interest.
- Those readers wishing to explore software process and its relation to the UML will find Chapters 4 through 6 most interesting.
- Those who desire to explore strictly the UML will find Chapters 2, 3, and 6 most applicable. What follows is a brief overview of the topics covered in each chapter.

Chapter Synopsis

Chapter 1 introduces objects and the goal of object-oriented system design. Some of the contents of this chapter may surprise you. We don't spend a lot of time introducing the most fundamental concepts; instead, we discuss concepts such as *polymorphism* and *inheritance* in terms of principles and patterns that serve as the context for much of the discussion later in this book.

Chapter 2 provides a brief history of the UML, which we strongly feel is necessary in order to fully understand it. We also introduce the primary goals of the UML and the problems the UML helps to solve.

Chapter 3 introduces the Java programming language and its mappings to the UML. We don't attempt to teach Java; instead, we focus on how various UML constructs can be mapped to the Java programming language. We discuss modeling from a conceptual level to form the basis for this discussion.

Chapter 4 discusses the important role that software process plays in the software development effort. We discover the benefits associated with structuring our diagrams in a way that enables us to more easily identify the problem we're trying to solve. We introduce the best practices that any software development process should promote and explain how the UML fits into these set of best practices.

Chapter 5 stands out in that we take a reprieve from our emphasis on the UML, Java, and objects and discuss the many factors that contribute to the adoption of each of these complementary technologies as a cohesive whole. This chapter examines many of the considerations that should be taken into account for any team or organization contemplating pragmatic integration of these newer technologies into their development environment.

Chapter 6 begins our journey in the convergence of Java, the UML, objects, and software process. In this chapter, we discuss some of the basic artifacts associated with establishing our system's requirements. This chapter serves as the basis for later discussions. While we don't elaborate in detail on the methods and practices used to elicit and manage requirements, we do present a simple set of requirements and one alternative to their formatting.

Chapter 7 works toward identifying the first set of analysis artifacts. By analyzing the requirements presented in the previous chapter, we identify our initial analysis classes. We categorize these as either boundary, entity, or control classes, which are used to organize our abstractions according to their behavior. The result is a first attempt at our system's design.

Chapter 8 emphasizes the dynamic aspects of our system. We introduce in more detail the UML sequence diagram, and in addition to the syntactic elements on this diagram, we also discuss many of the important decisions associated with allocating behavior to our initial classes identified in Chapter 7.

Chapter 9 presents a discussion on the static aspects of our system. Based upon the behaviors allocated to our objects, discussed in Chapter 8, and the object collaborations, we're now better prepared to design our system's structure. The UML class diagram is used throughout the majority of this chapter, and many important design decisions are discussed. This chapter not only discusses the relations between classes, but also presents package diagrams, which describe the relationships that exist between the packages that compose our system.

Chapter 10 discusses the important role that software architecture plays in contributing to more resilient, maintainable, and extensible systems. In addition to discussing the significance of software architecture, common architectural mechanisms and patterns are introduced and discussed in the context of our ongoing example. In addition, this chapter provides more detailed elaboration on the importance of our package relationships.

Chapter 11 introduces subsystems and their unique nature. We also introduce the important characteristics of a subsystem.

Appendix A presents the Rational Unified Process (RUP) and Extreme Programming (XP). We discuss the similarities and differences between each of these popular software development processes.

Appendix B discusses how the UML can be used with J2EE. In addition, this appendix elaborates on how J2EE fits into the book's overall discussions.

Appendix C provides sample code for our first UML discussion found in Section 3.6 in Chapter 3.

Development teams are confronted with a variety of challenges when developing software in today's dynamic technology landscape. With so many new technologies available, it's paramount that we use them to our benefit. We must understand the aspects of an individual technology that can provide maximum benefit, while ignoring those aspects that are less significant.

In addition, when taking advantage of these technologies, it is important that we allow them to work together in a united fashion. This allows the strengths of one technology to address the weaknesses of another, which, ultimately, contributes to the development of a more resilient, robust, and extensible software system that exhibits high degrees of quality. Alexander's "Quality Without a Name" in software development can be realized through the power of convergence.

CHAPTER 1

OO Principles and Patterns

Developing more resilient systems should be our first course of action. Reuse will follow.

When designing object-oriented systems, the challenges are numerous, and the solutions are various. How do we identify an approach that will help ensure we are creating an extensible, robust, and easily maintainable system? One way is by using design patterns. Design patterns are proven design solutions that can be tailored to fit the context of a particular design challenge. In essence, they are reusable design templates. While the notion of patterns has hit mainstream development since the seminal work published in 1995 by the Gang of Four [GOF95], the number of patterns available has become almost unmanageable. So many patterns are available today that attempting to find a pattern that can solve difficult design challenges conceivably could take longer than discovering a new solution, which if designed efficiently, is probably documented as a pattern somewhere anyway. When we can't find a pattern that solves our challenges, we can take an approach during design that will ensure we are solving our challenges correctly, given the absence of a readily available pattern. Such approaches are based on some fundamental principles of object orientation.

While these fundamental principles can provide helpful guidance when developing object-oriented software, our understanding of object orientation must come first. It is virtually impossible to apply a principle when we don't fully understand the value of that principle. Therefore, we must understand not only the principles, but also the true benefits of object orientation, as well as the goals that these benefits enable us to effectively and gracefully achieve.

1

1.0   Principles, Patterns, and the OO Paradigm

By this time, we've all been saturated with the benefits of objects. Reuse is the Holy Grail of object orientation. Unfortunately, a lot of the works discussing object orientation exist at such a theoretical level that they can be difficult to interpret and apply pragmatically, or these works exist at such a detailed level that it can be difficult to derive a concise vision of the paradigm in its entirety. Understanding concepts such as abstraction, inheritance, encapsulation, and polymorphism is wonderful, but they are just concepts and don't provide much guidance in creating more reusable and highly maintainable systems. In fact, our discussion in this book assumes a basic understanding of these terms.

We can achieve reuse, create more flexible designs, and understand the object-oriented paradigm more thoroughly by studying and applying patterns. But even patterns don't serve as a guiding set of principles that are universally applicable, and with the proliferation of patterns over the past couple of years, simply finding the most appropriate pattern can be a daunting task. This begs some interesting questions. What are the fundamental principles of the object-oriented paradigm? Is there a set of guiding principles that we can consistently and faithfully apply to help us create more robust systems? In fact there is, and we discuss the most useful principles in Section 1.1, later in this chapter.

Before we explore these principles, however, it's important to revisit the true benefit of object orientation. We've been told that reuse is the nirvana of programming, and object orientation provides it. The reason reuse has been so heavily touted is because it impacts the bottom line. When we use easily pluggable objects, which are highly reusable, we reduce the time required to develop applications. When we develop faster, we develop more cheaply as well. Certainly, one of the benefits of object orientation can be reuse; however, it may not be the most important benefit. In the December 2000 issue of *The Rational Edge*, Walker Royce cited two interesting statistics:

- For every $1 you spend on development, you will spend $2 on maintenance.
- Only about 15% of software development effort is devoted to programming. [WR00]

These statistics are astounding. The cost of maintaining a system is twice that of developing it. This being the case, we need a paradigm that facilitates system maintenance as much as, if not more than, reuse. Granted, effectively reusing objects can help in reducing system maintenance, but it doesn't necessarily guarantee it. In fact, consider the following:

Given a class R that is being reused by both classes A and B, if A requires new or modified behaviors of R, it would make sense that any changes to R would be reflected in B as well. While this is true, what happens if B does not desire this new behavior? What if this new behavior defined for R actually broke B? In this case, we have reuse, but we don't have a high degree of maintenance.

You might already be thinking of ways in which this scenario can be resolved. You might be saying that you wouldn't have done it this way in the first place, and there are certainly many ways to resolve the preceding problem. The granularity of the method contributes greatly to the likelihood of its reusability. The fact remains that each design is centered around flexibility, which brings us to Royce's second statistic cited earlier. If we are spending roughly 15 percent of our time programming, what are we spending the remaining 85 percent of our time doing? The answer is design, or at least variations of what many of us associate with a traditional design phase in the software development lifecycle. Of course, we also spend time managing requirements, planning projects, and testing. Focusing strictly on the design activity, had we designed the previously described example in a more effective manner, it is likely that our maintenance cost would have been reduced. But it's this design aspect that is so difficult. Therefore, following a set of guiding principles serves us well in creating more flexible designs.

Inheritance and Reuse

Those readers new to object orientation typically assume a close relation exists between inheritance and reuse. We want to debunk this myth immediately. Though reuse is touted as a benefit of object orientation, it is in fact a goal. Reuse cannot be taken for granted, nor is it guaranteed. In reality, achieving reuse requires a lot of effort and discipline, and we'll spend a lot of time in this book talking about this aspect of object orientation.

In addition, because inheritance is new to most developers exposed to objects for the first time, a false correlation typically is made between inheritance and reuse. While reuse can be achieved through inheritance,

(continues)

(continued)

it's not the primary benefit that inheritance provides. Inheritance can be used to achieve multiple goals and can be categorized two different ways. First, *interface inheritance* is the use of inheritance to achieve polymorphic behavior. Many of the principles that we discuss later in this chapter (see Section 1.1) take advantage of interface inheritance. Second, *implementation inheritance* is utilizing inheritance for reuse. While implementation inheritance can be beneficial, it should not be heavily relied upon as the mechanism of reuse. The ramifications of doing so can be detrimental.

Java is one of the first languages to make explicit the difference between interface and implementation inheritance. In Java, the `extends` keyword exemplifies implementation inheritance (with a small amount of interface inheritance through abstract methods), whereas the `implements` keyword illustrates interface inheritance. Therefore, stating that Java doesn't support multiple inheritance is not entirely true because Java does support multiple inheritance of interfaces.

Ultimately, the design chosen for our software system will impact the maintainability of our system. We call a design that impacts the maintainability of our system the software's *architecture*, and designing a system with a resilient architecture is of utmost importance. Because we know that requirements change, the resiliency of our architecture will impact our system's survival. However, the ability of our system to change, or grow to meet new requirements, and still survive are conflicting goals, known as the *architecture paradox* [SUB99].

What Is Design?

We associate design with some activity or phase within a traditional software development lifecycle. In this book, however, when we refer to design, we refer to the set of best practices and principles of object orientation that are continuously applied throughout all phases of the software development lifecycle. We even imply that lifecycle phases such as requirements, construction, and testing contain small slices of time where an emphasis is placed upon the practices and principles of design.

Suppose we have a system that fulfills its full set of requirements. As the requirements begin to change, the software begins to die, and its survival is challenged. In order to restore its survivability, we need to change the software. With each change, the software's architecture is compromised. As more changes are made, the software becomes harder to maintain. Because changes become so difficult to make, the costs associated with maintaining the system eventually reach a point where future maintenance efforts cannot be justified or introduce new errors. At this point, our system has lost its ability to grow, and it dies. Therefore, as depicted in Figure 1.1, as changes increase, survivability decreases.

This experience is a frustrating one, and it's common to blame others for these changing requirements. However, businesses typically drive these changes, and we shouldn't try to place the blame elsewhere. In fact, the problem is not with the changing requirements. We already know from experience that requirements change. A commonly quoted adage cites three certainties in life: death, taxes, and changing requirements. The fact that requirements change and compromise our systems' internal structures is not the fault of changing requirements, but the fault of our design. Requirements always change, and it is our job to deal with it!

Fortunately, one of the benefits of the object-oriented paradigm is that it enables us to easily add new data structures to our system without having to modify the existing system's code base. We achieve this through the power of inheritance and polymorphism, illustrated in Section 1.1.1, later in this chapter.

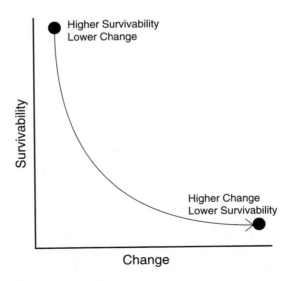

Figure 1.1   Architecture Paradox

These data structures in the object-oriented paradigm are classes. A class encapsulates behavior and data, and because we can add new classes to our system without modifying the existing code base, we can add new data and behaviors as well. Once we understand how we can realize this power when developing our applications, the only remaining trick is to apply this flexible concept to the areas within the system that are most likely to change. In this chapter, we learn how to apply this power. Throughout the remainder of this book, we examine how to identify these areas of an application requiring this flexibility.

So how do we go about designing a system that exhibits the power to make enhancements without having to actually modify the existing code base? The answer is to apply fundamental principles and patterns in a consistent, disciplined fashion. In fact, many experienced developers have an existing repertoire of proven techniques that they pull out of their bag of tricks to guide them during development. Until recently, there was not an effective way for developers to share these proven techniques with others.

Today, the software development industry abounds with patterns, of which many categories exist. Most of us have probably heard of patterns, and we will not devote our discussion here to duplicating work that has already been successfully documented. Instead, we provide an executive summary on patterns, including a few examples later in this chapter (see Section 1.3).

Patterns come in many forms. Architectural patterns focus on driving the high-level mechanisms that characterize an entire application. Analysis patterns help in solving domain-dependent obstacles. Design patterns help us solve a broad range of technical design challenges. We'll find that using patterns in conjunction with other patterns typically contributes to the achievement of the most flexible, robust, and resilient designs. Again, we'll see this firsthand as we progress throughout the book.

First, let's explore a more formal definition of a pattern:

A design pattern systematically names, motivates, and explains a general design that addresses a recurring design problem in object-oriented systems. It describes the problem, the solution, when to apply the solution, and its consequences. It also gives implementation hints and examples. The solution is a general arrangement of objects and classes that solve the problem. The solution is customized and implemented to solve the problem in a particular context. [GOF95]

Examining this definition further illustrates the potential of patterns. All patterns have a name, which enables a developer to easily refer to, and communicate with, other developers the intent of a particular pattern. Patterns help solve design challenges that continually surface. Each situation, however, is invariably different in some regards. A well-documented pattern describes the consequences of using it, as well as providing hints and examples of how to effectively utilize it. Consequently, when we use a pattern, it is unlikely that we'll implement it in the exact same manner each time.

Patterns can be thought of as algorithms for design. Certain algorithms have slight differences based on the implementation language, just as patterns vary based on the context in which they're applied. Most developers who have written sorting routines can understand the basic algorithm associated with the term *bubble sort*. Similarly, those familiar with patterns understand the structure and intent of a Strategy pattern. This naming convention is a benefit of using patterns because they enable us to communicate complex designs more effectively. Many more benefits are associated with the use of patterns, such as taking advantage of proven designs, creating more consistent designs, and providing a more concrete place to start when designing.

Patterns typically are discovered by some of the most talented object-oriented developers in the world. These patterns usually go through an intensive review and editing cycle, and thus they are proven design solutions. The review and editing cycle enables less-experienced developers to gain insights that will make their own designs as flexible as those of an experienced developer. In fact, the review and editing cycle may be the single greatest benefit associated with using patterns, because they are essentially the collective work of the most experienced designers in the object-oriented community.

Although the value of patterns is real, realizing this value also implies knowing which pattern is appropriate to use in a specific context, and how it can be applied. Because of the proliferation of patterns, it can be difficult to efficiently find a pattern that best fits a need. Principles, in comparison to patterns, exist at a higher level. The majority of patterns adhere to an underlying set of principles. In this regard, we can think of patterns as being instances of our principles. Principles are at the heart of object-oriented design. The more patterns we understand, the more design alternatives we can consider when architecting our systems. It's highly unlikely, however, that we'll ever completely understand, or even have knowledge of, all of the patterns that have been documented. By adhering to a more fundamental set of principles, it's likely that we'll encounter patterns that are new to us—patterns that may have been documented but that we aren't aware of. Or we may even discover new patterns. The point is that while patterns provide a proven starting point when designing, principles lie at the heart of what we need to accomplish when designing resilient, robust, and maintainable systems. Understanding these principles not only enhances our understanding of the object-oriented paradigm, but also helps us understand more about patterns, when to apply them, and the foundation upon which patterns are built.

1.1   Class Principles

As mentioned previously, principles lie at the heart of the object-oriented paradigm. The principles discussed in subsequent sections can help guide us during design when it might be difficult to find the most applicable pattern. We typically first look to patterns in solving our challenges. However, if we are unable to find an appropriate pattern, or are unsure if we should use a particular pattern, we should always take into consideration the principles discussed in the following sections. In fact, patterns typically are tailored slightly to fit a particular need, and these principles should be carefully considered when customizing a pattern. Many of the principles presented here first appeared in Robert Martin's *Design Principles and Design Patterns* [MARTIN00], which serves as an excellent complement to this discussion.

When applying these principles to Java, they can be broken into two categories. The first category focuses on relationships that exist between classes. These principles typically form the foundation of many design patterns. The second category of principles focuses on relationships between packages. These principles form the foundation of many architectural patterns. Keep in mind that at this point, we are primarily concerned with understanding the core concepts present within these principles. Application of these principles typically is dependent on a set of guiding heuristics, which we will continually elaborate on, and refine, as we progress throughout the book.

1.1.1   Open Closed Principle (OCP)

Classes should be open for extension but closed for modification.

The Open Closed Principle (OCP) is undoubtedly the most important of all the class category principles. In fact, each of the remaining class principles are derived from OCP. It originated from the work of Bertrand Meyer, who is recognized as an authority on the object-oriented paradigm [OOSC97]. OCP states that we should be able to add new features to our system without having to modify our set of preexisting classes. As stated previously, one of the benefits of the object-oriented paradigm is to enable us to add new data structures to our system without having to modify the existing system's code base.

Let's look at an example to see how this can be done. Consider a financial institution where we have to accommodate different types of accounts to which individuals can make deposits. Figure 1.2 shows a class diagram with accompanying descriptions of some of the elements and how we might structure a portion of our system. We discuss in detail the elements that make up various

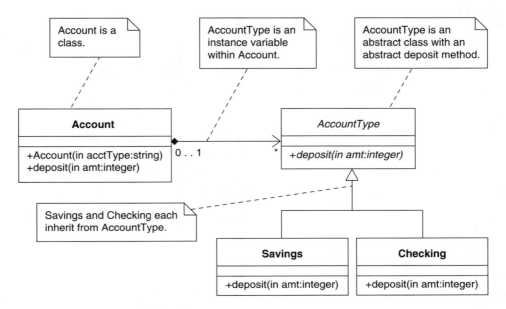

Figure 1.2   Open Closed Principle (OCP)

diagrams and the Unified Modeling Language (UML) in general in Chapter 3. For the purposes of our discussion in this chapter, we focus on how the OCP can be used to extend the system.

Our Account class has a relationship to our AccountType abstract class. In other words, our Account class is coupled at the abstract level to the Account-Type inheritance hierarchy. Because both our Savings and Checking classes inherit from the AccountType class, we know that through dynamic binding, we can substitute instances of either of these classes wherever the AccountType class is referenced. Thus, Savings and Checking can be freely substituted for AccountType within the Account class. This is the intent of an abstract class and enables us to effectively adhere to OCP by creating a contract between the Account class and the AccountType descendents. Because our Account isn't directly coupled to either of the concrete Savings or Checking classes, we can extend the AccountType class, creating a new class such as MoneyMarket, without having to modify our Account class. We have achieved OCP and now can extend our system without modify its existing code base.

Therefore, one of the tenets of OCP is to reduce the coupling between classes to the abstract level. Instead of creating relationships between two concrete classes, we create relationships between a concrete class and an abstract class, or in Java, between a concrete class and an interface. When we create an

extension of our base class, assuming we adhere to the public methods and
their respective signatures defined on the abstract class, we essentially have
achieved OCP. Let's take a look at a simplified version of the Java code for Figure 1.2, focusing on how we achieve OCP, instead of on the actual method
implementations.

```java
public class Account {
    private AccountType _act;

    public Account(String act) {
        try {
            Class c = Class.forName(act);
            this._act = (AccountType) c.newInstance();
        } catch (Exception e) {
            e.printStackTrace();
        }
    }

    public void deposit(int amt) {
        this._act.deposit(amt);
    }
}
```

Here, our Account class accepts as an argument to its constructor a String representing the class we wish to instantiate. It then uses the Class class to dynamically create an instance of the appropriate AccountType subclass. Note that we
don't explicitly refer to either the Savings or Checking class directly.

```java
public abstract class AccountType  {
    public abstract void deposit(int amt);
}
```

This is the abstract AccountType class that serves as the contract between our
Account class and AccountType descendents. The deposit method is the
contract.

```java
public class CheckingAccount extends AccountType {
    public void deposit(int amt) {
        System.out.println();
        System.out.println();
        System.out.println("Amount deposited in checking account: "
                            + amt);
        System.out.println();
        System.out.println();
    }
}
public class SavingsAccount extends AccountType {
    public void deposit(int amt)  {
        System.out.println();
        System.out.println();
```

```
            System.out.println("Amount deposited in savings account: "
                                + amt);
            System.out.println();
            System.out.println();
        }
    }
```

Each of our `AccountType` descendents satisfies the contract by providing an implementation for the `deposit` method. In the real world, the behaviors of the individual `deposit` methods would be more interesting and, given the preceding design, would be algorithmically different.

1.1.2 Liskov Substitution Principle (LSP)

Subclasses should be substitutable for their base classes.

We mentioned in our previous discussion that OCP is the most important of the class category principles. We can think of the Liskov Substitution Principle (LSP) as an extension to OCP. In order to take advantage of LSP, we must adhere to OCP because violations of LSP also are violations of OCP, but not vice versa. LSP is the work of Barbara Liskov and is derived from Bertrand Meyer's Design by Contract.[1] In its simplest form, LSP is difficult to differentiate from OCP, but a subtle difference does exist. OCP is centered around abstract coupling. LSP, while also heavily dependent on abstract coupling, is in addition heavily dependent on preconditions and postconditions, which is LSP's relation to Design by Contract, where the concept of preconditions and postconditions was formalized.

A *precondition* is a contract that must be satisfied before a method can be invoked. A *postcondition*, on the other hand, must be true upon method completion. If the precondition is not met, the method shouldn't be invoked, and if the postcondition is not met, the method shouldn't return. The relation of preconditions and postconditions has meaning embedded within an inheritance relationship that isn't supported within Java, outside of some manual assertions or nonexecutable comments. Because of this, violations of LSP can be difficult to find.

To illustrate LSP and the interrelationship of preconditions and postconditions, we need only consider how Java's exception-handling mechanism works. Consider a method on an abstract class that has the following signature:

---

[1]A concept that Bertrand Meyer built into the Eiffel programming language and discusses in *Object-Oriented Software Construction*. See [OOSC97].

```
public abstract deposit(int amt) throws InvalidAmountException
```

Assume in this situation that our `InvalidAmountException` is an exception defined by our application, is inherited from Java's base `Exception` class, and can be thrown if the amount we try to deposit is less than zero. By rule, when overriding this method in a subclass, we cannot throw an exception that exists at a higher level of abstraction than `InvalidAmountException`. Therefore, a method declaration such as the following isn't allowed:

```
public void deposit(int amt) throws Exception
```

This method declaration isn't allowed because the `Exception` class thrown in this method is the ancestor of the `InvalidAmountException` thrown previously. Again, we can't throw an exception in a method on a subclass that exists at a higher level of abstraction than the exception thrown by the base class method we are overriding. On the other hand, reversing these two method signatures would have been perfectly acceptable to the Java compiler. We can throw an exception in an overridden subclass method that is at a lower level of abstraction than the exception thrown in the ancestor. While this does not correspond directly to the concept of preconditions and postconditions, it does capture the essence. Therefore, we can state that any precondition stipulated by a subclass method can't be stronger than the base class method. Also, any postcondition stipulated by a subclass method can't be weaker than the base class method.

To adhere to LSP in Java, we must make sure that developers define preconditions and postconditions for each of the methods on an abstract class. When defining our subclasses, we must adhere to these preconditions and postconditions. If we do not define preconditions and postconditions for our methods, it becomes virtually impossible to find violations of LSP. Suffice it to say, in the majority of cases, OCP will be our guiding principle.

1.1.3   Dependency Inversion Principle (DIP)

Depend upon abstractions. Do not depend upon concretions.

The Dependency Inversion Principle (DIP) formalizes the concept of abstract coupling and clearly states that we should couple at the abstract level, not at the concrete level. In our own designs, attempting to couple at the abstract level can seem like overkill at times. Pragmatically, we should apply this principle in any situation where we're unsure whether the implementation of a class may change in the future. But in reality, we encounter situations during development where we know exactly what needs to be done. Requirements state this very clearly, and the probability of change or extension is quite low. In these situations, adherence to DIP may be more work than the benefit realized.

At this point, there exists a striking similarity between DIP and OCP. In fact, these two principles are closely related. Fundamentally, DIP tells us how we can adhere to OCP. Or, stated differently, if OCP is the desired end, DIP is the means through which we achieve that end. While this statement may seem obvious, we commonly violate DIP in a certain situation and don't even realize it.

When we create an instance of a class in Java, we typically must explicitly reference that object. Only after the instance has been created can we flexibly reference that object via its ancestors or implemented interfaces. Therefore, the moment we reference a class to create it, we have violated DIP and, subsequently, OCP. Recall that in order to adhere to OCP, we must first take advantage of DIP. There are a couple of different ways to resolve this impasse.

The first way to resolve this impasse is to dynamically load the object using the `Class` class and its `newInstance` method. However, this solution can be problematic and somewhat inflexible. Because DIP doesn't enable us to refer to the concrete class explicitly, we must use a `String` representation of the concrete class. For instance, consider the following:

```
Class c = Class.forName("SomeDescendent");
SomeAncestor sa = (SomeAncestor) c.newInstance();
```

In this example, we wish to create an instance of the class `SomeDescendent` in the first line but reference it as type `SomeAncestor` in the second line. This also was illustrated in the code samples in Section 1.1.1, earlier in this chapter. This is perfectly acceptable, as long as the `SomeDescendent` class is inherited, either directly or indirectly, from the `SomeAncestor` class. If it isn't, our application will throw an exception at runtime. Another more obvious problem occurs

Abstract Coupling

Abstract coupling is the notion that a class is not coupled to another concrete class or class that can be instantiated. Instead, the class is coupled to other base, or abstract, classes. In Java, this abstract class can be either a class with the abstract modifier or a Java interface data type. Regardless, this concept actually is the means through which LSP achieves its flexibility, the mechanism required for DIP, and the heart of OCP.

when we misspell the class of which we want an instance. Yet another, less apparent, obstacle eventually is encountered when taking this approach. Because we reference the class name as a string, there isn't any way to pass parameters into the constructor of this class. Java does provide a solution to this problem, but it quickly becomes complex, unwieldy, and error prone.

Another approach to resolving the object creation challenge is to use an object factory. Here, we create a separate class whose only responsibility is to create instances. This way, our original class, where the instance previously would have been created, stays clear of any references to concrete classes, which have been removed and placed in this factory. The only references contained within this class are to abstract, or base, classes. The factory does, however, reference the concrete classes, which is, in fact, a blatant violation of DIP. However, it's an isolated and carefully thought through violation and is therefore acceptable.

Keep in mind that we may not always need to use an object factory. Along with the flexibility of a factory comes the complexity of a more dynamic collaboration of objects. Concrete references aren't always a bad thing. If the class to which we are referring is a stable class, not likely to undergo many changes, using a factory adds unwarranted complexity to our system. If a factory is deemed necessary, the design of the factory itself should be given careful consideration. This factory pattern has many design variants, some of which are discussed later in this book (see Chapter 9).

Blatant Violation: A Good Thing?

At this point, you might be wondering how a blatant violation can be a good thing. Keep in mind that our goal should be to create a more highly maintainable system. The tools that enable us to create these types of systems are the principles discussed in this chapter. Therefore, it is important that each principle be given careful consideration and that violations of these principles are conscious design decisions. While an object factory may violate DIP, it does so at the expense of allowing another module within the application to adhere to OCP. Therefore, any changes are localized to the factory and should not impact its clients.

1.1.4 Interface Segregation Principle (ISP)

Many specific interfaces are better than a single, general interface.

Put simply, any interface we define should be highly cohesive. In Java, we know that an interface is a reference data type that can have method declarations, but no implementation. In essence, an interface is an abstract class with all abstract methods. As we define our interfaces, it becomes important that we clearly understand the role the interface plays within the context of our application. In fact, interfaces provide flexibility: They allow objects to assume the data type of the interface. Consequently, an interface is simply a role that an object plays at some point throughout its lifetime. It follows, rather logically, that when defining the operation on an interface, we should do so in a manner that doesn't accommodate multiple roles. Therefore, an interface should be responsible for allowing an object to assume a single role, assuming the class of which that object is an instance implements that interface.

While working on a project recently, an ongoing discussion took place as to how we would implement our data access mechanism. Quite a bit of time was spent designing a flexible framework that would allow uniform access to a variety of different data sources. These back-end data sources might come in the form of a relational database, a flat file, or possibly even another proprietary database. Therefore, our goal was not only to provide a common data access mechanism, but also to present data to any class acting as a data client in a consistent manner. Doing so clearly would decouple our data clients from the back-end data source, making it much easier to port our back-end data sources to different platforms without impacting our data clients. Therefore, we decided that all data clients would depend on a single Java interface, depicted in Figure 1.3, with the associated methods.

At first glance, the design depicted in Figure 1.3 seemed plausible. After further investigation, however, questions were raised as to the cohesion of the `RowSetManager` interface. What if classes implementing this interface were read-only and didn't need insert and update functionality? Also, what if the data client weren't interested in retrieving the data, but only in iterating its already retrieved internal data set? Exploring these questions a bit further, and carefully considering the Interface Segregation Principle (ISP), we found that it was meaningful to have a data structure that wasn't even dependent on a retrieve action at all. For instance, we may wish to use a data set that was cached in memory and wasn't dependent on an underlying physical data source. This led us to the design in Figure 1.4.

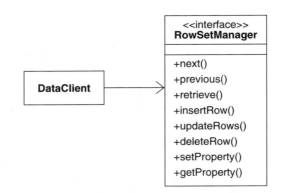

Figure 1.3   Violation of Interface Segregation Principle (ISP)

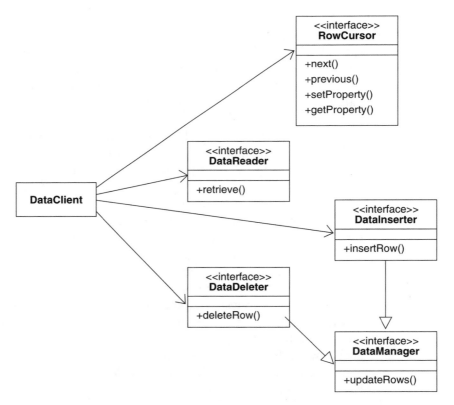

Figure 1.4   Compliance to Interface Segregation Principle (ISP)

In Figure 1.4, we see that we have segregated the responsibilities of our RowSetManager into multiple interfaces. Each interface is responsible for allowing a class to adhere to a cohesive set of responsibilities. Now our application can implement the interfaces necessary to provide the desired set of functionality. For example, we're no longer forced to provide data update behavior if our class is read-only.

1.1.5   Composite Reuse Principle (CRP)

Favor polymorphic composition of objects over inheritance.

The Composite Reuse Principle (CRP) prevents us from making one of the most catastrophic mistakes that contribute to the demise of an object-oriented system: using inheritance as the primary reuse mechanism. The first reference to this principle was in [GOF95]. For example, let's turn back to a section of our diagram in Figure 1.2. In Figure 1.5, we see the AccountType hierarchy with a few additional attributes and methods. In this example, we have added a method to the ancestor AccountType class that calculates the interest for each of our accounts. This approach seems to be a good one because both our Savings and MoneyMarket classes are interest-bearing accounts. Our Checking class is representative of an account that isn't interest bearing. Regardless, we justify this by convincing ourselves that it's better to define some default behavior on an ancestor and override it on descendents instead of duplicating the behavior across descendents. We know that we can simply define a null operation on our Checking class that doesn't actually calculate interest, and our problem is solved. While we do want to reuse our code, and we can prevent the Checking class from calculating interest, our implementation contains a tragic flaw. First, let's discuss the flaw and when it will surface. Then we'll discuss why this problem has occurred.

Let's consider a couple of new requirements. We need to support the addition of a new account type, called Stock. A Stock does calculate interest, but the algorithm for doing so is different than the default defined in our ancestor AccountType. That's easy to solve. All we have to do is override the calculateInterest in our new Stock class, just as we did in the Checking class, but instead of implementing a null operation, we can implement the appropriate algorithm. This works fine until our business realizes that the Stock class is doing extremely well, primarily because of its generous interest calculation mechanism. It's been decided that MoneyMarket should calculate interest using the same algorithm as Stock, but Savings remains the same. We have three choices in solving this problem. First, redefine the calculateInterest method on our `AccountType` to implement this new algorithm and define a new method on `Savings` that implements the older method. This option isn't ideal because it involves modifying at least two of our existing system classes, which is a blatant violation of OCP. Second, we could simply override `calculateInterest` on our `MoneyMarket` class, copy the code from our `Stock` class, and paste it in our `MoneyMarket` `calculateInterest` method. Obviously, this option isn't a very flexible solution. Our goal in reuse is not copy and paste. Third, we can define a new class called `InterestCalculator`, define a `calculateInterest` method on this class that implements our new algorithm, and then delegate the calculation of interest from our `Stock` and `MoneyMarket` classes to this new class. So, which option is best?

The third solution is the one we should have used up front. Because we realized that the calculation of interest wasn't common to all classes, we shouldn't have defined any default behavior in our ancestor class. Doing so in any situation inevitably results in the previously described outcome. Let's now resolve this problem using CRP.

In Figure 1.6, we see a depiction of our class structure utilizing CRP. In this example, we have no default behavior defined for `calculateInterest` in our

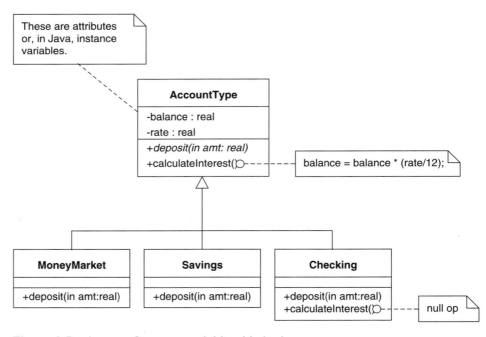

Figure 1.5   Account Structure with New Methods

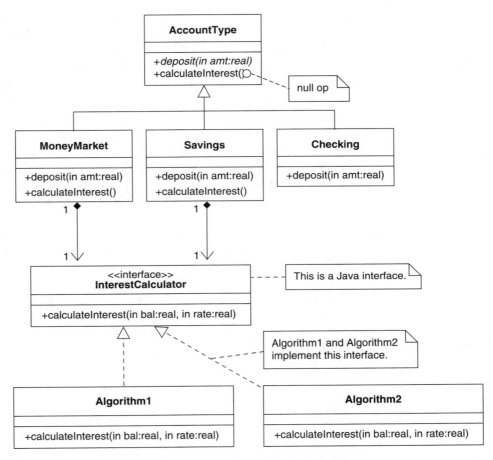

Figure 1.6 Compliance to Composite Reuse Principle (CRP)

AccountType hierarchy. Instead, in our calculateInterest methods on both our MoneyMarket and Savings classes, we defer the calculation of interest to a class that implements the InterestCalculator interface. When we add our Stock class, we now simply choose the InterestCalculator that is applicable for this new class or define a new one if it's needed. If any of our other classes need to redefine their algorithms, we can do so because we are abstractly coupled to our interface and can substitute any of the classes that implement the interface anywhere the interface is referenced. Therefore, this solution is ultimately flexible in how it enables us to calculate interest. This is an example of CRP. Each of our MoneyMarket and Savings classes are composed of our

InterestCalculator, which is the composite. Because we are abstractly coupled, we easily see we can receive polymorphic behavior. Hence, we have used polymorphic composition instead of inheritance to achieve reuse.

At this point, you might say, however, that we still have to duplicate some code across the Stock and MoneyMarket classes. While this is true, the solution still solves our initial problem, which is how to easily accommodate new interest calculation algorithms. Yet an even more flexible solution is available, and one that will enable us to be even more dynamic in how we configure our objects with an instance of InterestCalculator.

In Figure 1.7, we have moved the relationship to InterestCalculator up the inheritance hierarchy into our AccountType class. In fact, in this scenario, we are back to using inheritance for reuse, though a bit differently. Our AccountType knows that it needs to calculate interest, but it doesn't know how actually to do it. Therefore, we see a relationship from AccountType to our InterestCalculator. Because of this relationship, all accounts calculate interest. However, if one of our algorithms is a null object [PLOP98] (that is, it's an instance of a class that implements the interface and defines the methods, but the methods have no implementation), and we use the null object with the Savings class, we now can state that all of our accounts need to calculate interest. This substantiates our use of implementation inheritance. Because each account calculates it differently, we configure each account with the appropriate InterestCalculator.

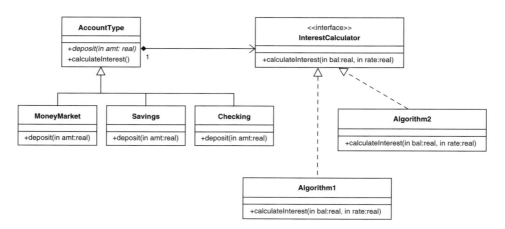

Figure 1.7   Refining CRP Compliance with Ancestral Relationship

So how did we fall into the original trap depicted in Figure 1.5? The problem lies within the inheritance relationship. Inheritance can be thought of as a generalization over a specialization relationship—that is, a class higher in the inheritance hierarchy is a more general version of those inherited from it. In other words, any ancestor class is a partial descriptor that should define some default characteristics that are applicable to any class inherited from it. Violating this convention almost always results in the situation described previously. In fact, any time we have to override default behavior defined in an ancestor class, we are saying that the ancestor class is not a more general version of all of its descendents but actually contains descriptor characteristics that make it too specialized to serve as the ancestor of the class in question. Therefore, if we choose to define default behavior on an ancestor, it should be general enough to apply to all of its descendents.

In practice, it's not uncommon to define a default behavior in an ancestor class. However, we should still accommodate CRP in our relationships. This is easy to see in Figure 1.6. We could have easily defined default behavior in our `calcuateInterest` method on the `AccountType` class. We still have the flexibility, using CRP, to alter the behaviors of any of our `AccountType` classes because of the relationship to `InterestCalculator`. In this situation, we may even choose to create a null op `InterestCalculator` class that our `Checking` class uses. This way, we even accommodate the likelihood that `Savings` accounts can someday calculate interest. We have ultimate flexibility.

1.1.6   Principle of Least Knowledge (PLK)

For an operation O on a class C, only operations on the following objects should be called: itself, its parameters, objects it creates, or its contained instance objects.

The Principle of Least Knowledge (PLK) is also known as the Law of Demeter. The basic idea is to avoid calling any methods on an object where the reference to that object is obtained by calling a method on another object. Instead, this principle recommends we call methods on the containing object, not to obtain a reference to some other object, but instead to allow the containing object to forward the request to the object we would have formerly obtained a reference to. The primary benefit is that the calling method doesn't need to understand the structural makeup of the object it's invoking methods upon. The following examples show a violation of PLK and an implementation that does not violate PLK:

```
//violation of PLK
public class Sample {
    public void lawTest(AnObject o) {
        AnotherObject ao = o.get();
        ao.doSomething();
    }
}
```

```
//adherence to PLK. Note that AnObject
//would forward the doSomething request
//on to AnotherObject, which it con-
tains.
public class Sample {
    public void lawTest(AnObject o) {
        o.doSomething();
    }
}
```

The obvious disadvantage associated with PLK is that we must create many methods that only forward method calls to the containing classes internal components. This can contribute to a large and cumbersome public interface. An alternative to PLK, or a variation on its implementation, is to obtain a reference to an object via a method call, with the restriction that any time this is done, the type of the reference obtained is always an interface data type. This is more flexible because we aren't binding ourselves directly to the concrete implementation of a complex object, but instead are dependent only on the abstractions of which the complex object is composed. In fact, this is how many classes in Java typically resolve this situation.

Consider the java.sql.ResultSet interface. After an SQL statement has been executed, Java stores the SQL results in a ResultSet object. One of our options at this point is to query this ResultSet object and obtain metainformation pertaining to this set of data. The class that contains this metainformation is the ResultSetMetaData class, and it's contained within the ResultSet class. If PLK were adhered to in this situation, we wouldn't directly obtain a reference to this ResultSetMetaData class, but instead would call methods on the ResultSet, which subsequently would forward these requests to the ResultSetMetaData class. However, this would result in an explosion of methods on the ResultSet class. Therefore, a getResultSetMetaData method on ResultSet does return a reference to ResultSetMetaData. At first, this would seem to be a blatant violation of PLK. However, ResultSetMetaData is an interface data type and, therefore, we aren't bound to any concrete implementation contained within ResultSet. Instead, we're coupled only to the abstractions of which ResultSet is composed.

This solution is a perfectly acceptable alternative to a direct implementation of PLK. The caveat is that careful consideration should be given to DIP. As long as this is done, we shouldn't have increased maintenance problems. The most important aspect is that we're bound, or coupled, to the internal structure of a class at an abstract level. Therefore, the class that is obtaining the reference to the object via the method call is taking advantage of DIP and, subsequently, OCP.

1.2 Package Principles

Throughout the course of development, it's common for development teams to spend a chunk of time designing the system. Much of this time, however, is spent creating a flexible class structure, with little time actually being devoted to the system's package structure. The relationships between packages typically aren't considered, and the allocation of classes to packages isn't carefully thought through. This carelessness is unfortunate because the relationships between packages are just as important as the relationships between the classes. The relationships between the packages of an application are referred to as the *package dependencies*, and we next examine principles that help to create a more robust dependency structure between our packages.

1.2.1 Package Dependency

It isn't uncommon to find that many developers haven't realized that relationships do exist among the packages within a Java application. The dependencies between packages often go unnoticed. Logically, however, if a class contains relationships to other classes, then packages containing those classes also must contain relationships to other packages. These package relationships can tell us a great deal about the resiliency of our system, and the principles discussed in Sections 1.2.2 through 1.2.7 enable us to more objectively measure the robustness of our package relationships.

First, let's examine what is meant by a *package dependency*. In Figure 1.8, we see a class diagram depicting two packages, A and B. Within each of these packages exist two classes. Class Client exists in package A and class Service in B. Simply stated, if class Client references in any way class Service, then it must hold true that Client has a structural relationship to class Service, which implies that any changes to the Service class may impact Client. Figure 1.8

A Subtle Relation

If class Client has a relation to class Service, then it's obvious that the packages containing these two classes also have a relationship, formally known as a *package dependency*. It's not so obvious that these class and package relationships can be considered two separate views of our system. One is a higher-level package view, the other a lower-level class view. In addition, these two views serve to validate each other. You'll find information on this subject in Chapter 10.

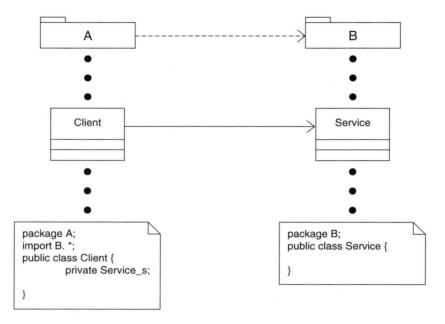

Figure 1.8   Package and Corresponding Class Relationships

illustrates how this relationship exists between packages, classes, and source code.

Let's examine this relationship from a different viewpoint. If the contents of package A are dependent on the contents of package B, then A has a dependency on B; and if the contents of B change, this impact may be noticeable in A. Therefore, the relationships between packages become more apparent, and we can conclude the following:

> *If changing the contents of a package P1 may impact the contents of another package P2, we can say that P1 has a package dependency on P2.*

Packages may contain not only classes, however, but also packages. In Java, importing the contents of a package implies we have access only to the classes within that package and don't have access to classes in any nested packages. The Unified Modeling Language (UML), however, doesn't take any formal position on nested packages. The question of how to deal with nested packages is left to the development team. We use the terms *opaque* and *transparent* to define the two options. *Opaque visibility* implies that a dependency on a package with nested packages doesn't imply access to these nested packages. *Transparent visibility*, on the other hand, does carry with it implicit dependencies.

Because the UML takes no formal position, development teams must define how they wish to deal with package dependencies. Several options are available. First, teams may take their own position and state that all package dependencies are either opaque or transparent. Any variation from this norm must be modeled explicitly. In situations such as these, we recommend selecting opaque. Adopting transparent visibility doesn't enable us to restrict access to nested packages. On the other hand, if opaque is adopted as a standard, we can always explicitly model relations to nested packages on separate diagrams. For purposes of discussion throughout this book, we assume all package dependency relationships are opaque.

An alternative approach is to create stereotypes that can be attached to the dependency relation. Consequently, visibility is determined by the stereotype attached to the dependency. Some obvious pitfalls include those relationships with no stereotype attached. Unless a default is assumed, we cannot know what the transparency is, and making any assumptions can be dangerous. In addition, because only a single stereotype can be attached to any modeling element, we may be forced to make a decision if other stereotypes are being considered for the same dependency relationship. Let's now turn our attention to the discussion of the package principles.

1.2.2 Release Reuse Equivalency Principle (REP)

The granule of reuse is the granule of release.

Whenever a client class wishes to use the services of another class, we must reference the class offering the desired services. This should be apparent from our previous discussions and is the basis upon which package relationships exist. If the class offering the service is in the same package as the client, we can reference that class using the simple name. If, however, the service class is in a different package, then any references to that class must be done using the class' fully qualified name, which includes the name of the package.

We also know that any Java class may reside in only a single package. Therefore, if a client wishes to utilize the services of a class, not only must we reference the class, but we must also explicitly make reference to the containing package. Failure to do so results in compile-time errors. Therefore, to deploy any class, we must be sure the containing package is deployed. Because the package is deployed, we can utilize the services offered by any public class within the package. Therefore, while we may presently need the services of only a single class in the containing package, the services of all classes are available to us. Consequently, our unit of release is our unit of reuse, resulting in the Release Reuse Equivalency Principle (REP). This leads us to the basis for this principle, and it should now be apparent that the packages into which classes are placed have a tremendous impact on reuse. Careful consideration must be given to the allocation of classes to packages.

1.2.3   Common Closure Principle (CCP)

Classes that change together, belong together.

The basis for the Common Closure Principle (CCP) is rather simple. Adhering to fundamental programming best practices should take place throughout the entire system. Functional cohesion emphasizes well-written methods that are more easily maintained. Class cohesion stresses the importance of creating classes that are functionally sound and don't cross responsibility boundaries. And package cohesion focuses on the classes within each package, emphasizing the overall services offered by entire packages.

During development, when a change to one class may dictate changes to another class, it's preferred that these two classes be placed in the same package. Conceptually, CCP may be easy to understand; however, applying it can be difficult because the only way that we can group classes together in this manner is when we can predictably determine the changes that might occur and the effect that those changes might have on any dependent classes. Predictions often are incorrect or aren't ever realized. Regardless, placement of classes into respective packages should be a conscious decision that is driven not only by the relationships between classes, but also by the cohesive nature of a set of classes working together.

1.2.4   Common Reuse Principle (CReP)

Classes that aren't reused together should not be grouped together.

If we need the services offered by a class, we must import the package containing the necessary classes. As we stated previously in our discussion of REP (see Section 1.2.2), when we import a package, we also may utilize the services offered by any public class within the package. In addition, changing the behavior of any class within the service package has the potential to break the client. Even if the client doesn't directly reference the modified class in the service package, other classes in the service package being used by clients may reference the modified class. This creates indirect dependencies between the client and the modified class that can be the cause of mysterious behavior. In fact, we can state the following:

> *If a class is dependent on another class in a different package, then it is, in fact, dependent on all classes in that package, albeit indirectly.*

This principle has a negative connotation. It doesn't hold true that classes that are reused together should reside together, depending on CCP. Even though classes may always be reused together, they may not always change together. In striving to adhere to CCP, separating a set of classes based on their likelihood to change together should be given careful consideration. Of course, this impacts REP because now multiple packages must be deployed to use this functionality. Experience tells us that adhering to one of these principles may impact the ability to adhere to another. Whereas REP and Common Reuse Principle (CReP) emphasize reuse, CCP emphasizes maintenance.

1.2.5   Acyclic Dependencies Principle (ADP)

> *The dependencies between packages must form no cycles.*

Cycles among dependencies of the packages composing an application should almost always be avoided. In other words, packages should form a directed acyclic graph (DAG). In Figure 1.9, we see two separate diagrams illustrating the relationships among Java packages. First, let's explore what these relationships imply; then we will explain why we want to avoid cyclic dependencies. In the diagram at the left of Figure 1.9, package A has a dependency on package B, and package B has a dependency on package A. In Java, this implies that some class in package A imports package B and uses a class in package B. Also, some class in package B imports package A and uses some class. The following code illustrates this scenario:

```
package A;
import B.*;
public class SomeAClass {
    private ClassInB b;
}
```

```
package B;
import A.*;
public class SomeBClass {
    private ClassInA a;
}
```

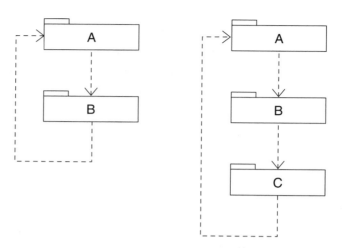

Figure 1.9   Violation of Acyclic Dependencies Principles (ADP)

The problem with this code is that, because the classes in these packages are coupled, the two packages become tightly coupled, which has a tremendous impact on REP. If some class C in a different package, call it X, uses SomeBClass in package B, it definitely implies that when package B is deployed, package A also must be deployed because SomeBClass is coupled to SomeAClass in package A. Neglecting to deploy package A with B results in runtime errors. In fact, were an application to have cyclic dependencies among the packages that compose it, REP would be so negatively impacted that all of these classes may as well exist in the same package. Obviously, we wouldn't desire this degree of coupling because CCP also would be severely compromised. Regardless, when developing Java applications, we should rarely find ourselves in a situation where we have violated the Acyclic Dependencies Principle (ADP). The consequences of doing so are dire, and we should avoid it at all costs.

If we do identify cyclic dependencies, the easiest way to resolve them is to factor out the classes that cause the dependency structure. This is exactly what we have done in Figure 1.10. Factoring out the classes that caused the cyclic dependencies has a positive impact on reuse. Now, should we decide to reuse package B in our previous example, we still need to deploy package A`, but we don't need to deploy package A. The impact of this situation is not fully realized until we take into consideration more subtle cycle dependencies, such as the indirect cyclic dependency illustrated at the right in Figure 1.9, and its subsequent resolution in the diagram at right in Figure 1.10.

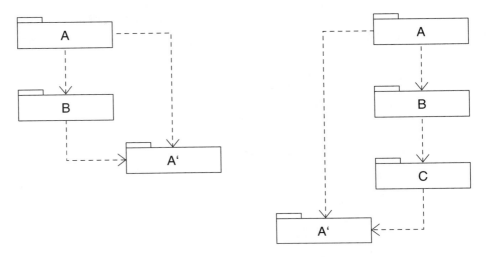

Figure 1.10   Acyclic Dependencies Principles (ADP) Compliance

1.2.6   Stable Dependencies Principle (SDP)

Depend in the direction of stability.

At first glance, the Stable Dependencies Principle (SDP) seems to be stating the obvious. However, exploring more deeply, we find the SDP contains an interesting underlying message. In the context of software development, stability often is used to describe a system that is robust, bug free, and rich in structure. In a more general sense, stability implies that an item is fixed, permanent, and unvarying. Attempting to change an item that is stable is more difficult than inflicting change on an item in a less stable state. Applying this richer meaning of stability to software implies that stable software is difficult to change. Before we revolt, however, let's point out that simply because software is stable doesn't mean that it's riddled with bugs. Stable software can certainly be robust, bug free, and rich in structure. Subsequently, the stability of our software system isn't necessarily related to its quality. Less stable software can be of high quality, yet it also can easily experience change. Stability is a characteristic indicating the ease with which a system can undergo change, and with Java, we are most concerned with the resiliency of our packages.

At this point, it's useful to ask what makes a package difficult to change. Aside from poorly written code, the degree of coupling to other packages has a dramatic impact on the ease of change. Those packages with many incoming dependencies have many other components in our application dependent on them. These more stable packages are difficult to change because of the far-reaching consequences the change may have throughout all other dependent packages. On the other hand, packages with few incoming dependencies are easier to change. Those packages with few incoming dependencies most likely will have more outgoing dependencies. A package with no incoming or outgoing dependencies is useless and isn't part of an application because it has no relationships. Therefore, packages with fewer incoming, and more outgoing dependencies, are less stable. Referring again to Figure 1.10, we can say that package A` is a more stable package, whereas package A is a less stable package, taking into consideration only the ease with which either of these packages can undergo change.

In previous sections, we've discussed that our software should be resilient and easily maintainable. Because of this, our assumptions lead us to believe that all software should be less stable, but this belief isn't always correct. Stability doesn't provide any implication as to the frequency with which the contents of a package change. Those packages having a tendency to change more often should be the packages that are less stable in nature. On the other hand, packages unlikely to experience change may be more stable, and it's in this direction that we should find the dependency relations flowing. Combining the concepts of stability, frequency of change, and dependency management, we're able to conclude the following:

• Packages likely to experience frequent change should be less stable, implying fewer incoming dependencies and more outgoing dependencies.
• Packages likely to experience infrequent change may be more stable, implying more incoming dependencies and fewer outgoing dependencies.

It should now be obvious that we naturally depend in the direction of stability because the direction of our dependency makes the packages more or less stable. Any dependency introduced, however, should be a conscious decision, and one that we know may have a dramatic impact on the stability of our application. Ideally, dependencies should be introduced only to packages that are more stable. The conscious nature of this decision is captured by our next principle, which describes the technique we employ to create more stable or less stable packages.

Up to this point, we've been carefully referring to the stability of packages as either more stable or less stable. Packages are typically not characterized as stable or unstable. Instead, stability is a metric that can be measured and is a numerical value between 0 and 1. The stability of a package can be measured using some fairly straightforward calculations. Consider the following formula:

where

$$I = \frac{Ce}{Ca + Ce}$$

I represents the degree of instability associated with the package.

Ca represents the number of external classes dependent on classes internal to this package.

Ce represents the number of internal classes dependent on classes not internal.

A package becomes more stable as I approaches 0 because this implies no outgoing dependencies. As I approaches 1, a package is less stable. Less stable packages have fewer incoming dependencies, whereas more stable packages have more incoming dependencies.

1.2.7   Stable Abstractions Principle (SAP)

Stable packages should be abstract packages.

Assuming we do wish to depend in the direction of stability, we're left with no choice but to structure packages so that the less stable packages exist atop a package hierarchy, and more stable packages exist at the bottom of our package hierarchy. The diagram in Figure 1.10 is indicative of this relationship. At this point, it's extremely important that the packages that are lower in our package hierarchy must be the most resilient packages in our system, because of the far-reaching consequences of changing them.

As we've discussed, one of the greatest benefits of object orientation is the ability to easily maintain our systems. The high degree of resiliency and maintainability is achieved through abstract coupling. By coupling concrete classes to abstract classes, we can extend these abstract classes and provide new system functions without having to modify existing system structure. Consequently, the means through which we can depend in the direction of stability, and help ensure that these more depended-upon packages exhibit a higher degree of stability, is to place abstract classes, or interfaces, in the more stable packages. We can now state the following:

- More stable packages, containing a higher number of abstract classes, or interfaces, should be heavily depended upon.

- Less stable packages, containing a higher number of concrete classes, should not be heavily depended upon.

A simple metric can help determine the degree of abstractness associated with a package. Consider the following formula:

where
$$A = \frac{Na}{Nc}$$

A is the abstractness of the package.
Na is the number of abstract classes and interfaces.
Nc is the number of overall classes and interfaces.

Values of A approaching 0 imply a package has few abstract classes. Values of A approaching 1 imply a package consists of almost entirely abstract classes and interfaces.

It is ideal if the abstractness of a package is either 1 or 0 and as far away from 0.5 as possible. A value of 0.5 implies that a package contains both abstract and concrete classes and, therefore, is neither stable nor instable. A goal of all packages should be a high degree or low degree of abstractness, depending heavily upon its role within the application.

It now should be apparent that any packages containing all abstract classes with no incoming dependencies are utterly useless. On the other hand, packages containing all concrete classes with many incoming dependencies are extremely difficult to maintain. Therefore, in terms of SDP and the Stable Abstractions Principle (SAP), we can only conclude that as abstractness (A) increases, instability (I) decreases.

1.3   Patterns

Any discussion of patterns could easily fill multiple texts. This section doesn't even attempt to define a fraction of the patterns that can be useful during development. Instead, we emphasize the common components of a pattern, as well as introduce a few common patterns that have multiple uses. As the discussion continues throughout this book, additional patterns are introduced as the need warrants. The discussion in this section serves two purposes. First, we describe the intent of the patterns, a few problems that they might help resolve, and some consequences of using the pattern. This discussion should help in understanding how patterns can be used and the context in which they might be useful. Second, and most important for this discussion, we explore the consistent nature with which the principles previously discussed resurface within these patterns.

This topic is important because, as mentioned previously, patterns may not always be available for the specific problem domain or, if available, may possibly be unknown. In these situations, a reliance upon some other fundamental principles is important.

1.3.1 Strategy

Undoubtedly, the Strategy pattern is one of the simplest patterns and is a direct implementation of OCP. The purpose of a Strategy, as stated in [GOF95], is to

> *Define a family of algorithms, encapsulate each one, and make them interchangeable.*

In fact, the `InterestCalculator` class in Figure 1.7 is a Strategy. The individual `Algorithm` classes encapsulate the various interest calculations. These are our family of algorithms, and they are made interchangeable by implementing the `InterestCalculator` interface. This is the structural aspect of the Strategy. The behavioral aspects of a Strategy are a bit more interesting and are typically discussed in the context of the consequences that result as the application of that pattern. For instance, where does the concrete Strategy instance get created? Creating it within the client class removes many of the advantages of using Strategy, which becomes more apparent when considering the coupling that exists between the client class and the concrete Strategy classes. In Figure 1.7, if the `AccountType` class actually created the `InterestCalculator` Strategy, the `AccountType` class would have to be modified each time a new `Algorithm` class was added to our system. This solution isn't ideal and, in fact, doing so violates OCP, even though Strategy attempts to achieve OCP. A better approach may be for a separate class to create the concrete Strategy. Structuring the system in this manner is common, and the end result is the incorporation of a Factory pattern into the system. The sole responsibility of the Factory pattern, introduced in Chapter 9, is to create instances of objects. At this point, it could be stated that even though a Factory is used, OCP still is violated because any new concrete Strategy classes now require a modification of the Factory. While this statement is true, careful consideration should be given to the ease with which this maintenance has been achieved versus the strict adherence to a principle. While there are many alternatives to this approach, we've found that using a Factory in this situation is not only easily understood, but easily maintainable as well. In fact, while it may be a small violation of OCP, the points within our application that refer directly to the concrete Strategy classes are so small in number (one) that we don't even consider it a violation of OCP.

Also note that when using a Strategy, we have to determine when and where to use it. Obviously, numerous places could take advantage of a Strategy. The trick is to keep OCP in mind. Does the system need to have this flexibility at this point? The intent is not to use Strategy, or any other pattern for that matter, anywhere that it could be used, but to use the appropriate pattern in the appropriate context. Should the context call for this degree of flexibility, a Strategy should be considered. Were we not familiar with the Strategy pattern, nor any other pattern that accommodated the need, reliance upon the fundamental principles would have yielded similar results. In fact, our discussion in Section 1.1.5 resulted in the derivation of the Strategy pattern, prior to ever having heard of Strategy.

1.3.2   Visitor

The Visitor pattern is not widely used, yet it serves as an excellent example illustrating the true power of the object-oriented paradigm. The discussion up to this point has focused on the fact that the object-oriented paradigm allows a system to be easily extended with new classes, without having to modify the existing system. The structured paradigm didn't accommodate this need in the same flexible manner. In fact, it already has been clearly illustrated in Figure 1.7 that a system can be extended without having to modify the existing system. What if, however, we want to add new operations to an existing set of classes? This task is a more difficult one because defining a new method on a class presents huge obstacles if the system has made any attempt whatsoever to adhere to the previously discussed principles. The problem is that most classes are reliant upon interfaces, and the operations defined on the interface serve as the contract between the client class and the service class. This is especially true with DIP, and changing the interface results in a broken contract that can be remedied only by correcting either the client or service class and conforming to the new contract. A mechanism enabling us to attach new responsibilities to a class without having to change the class on which those responsibilities operate would be extremely valuable.

In the most rudimentary sense, consider a class that has a dynamic interface. It may be extremely difficult to determine what methods should actually reside on that class. As development progresses, and new operations are discovered, the system requires constant maintenance to change the interface. In Figure 1.11, such a class is presented. The `DynamicClass`, however, has only a single generic method named `accept`. This method accepts a parameter of type `Visitor`. Consequently, the `DynamicClass` receives an instance of a concrete `Visitor` at runtime. Each of the concrete `Visitor` classes represents a method that would have normally been found on the `DynamicClass`. We can easily extend the func-

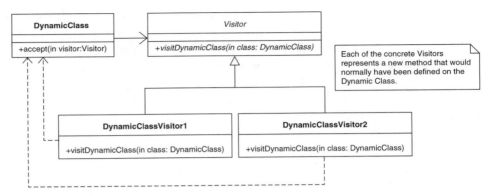

Figure 1.11 Visitor Pattern

tionality provided by DynamicClass by defining a new concrete Visitor for each method. In addition, any client of DynamicClass always will be dependent only on the generic accept method. As is now evident, it's easy to add new operations in the form of concrete Visitor classes without having to modify existing system components.

In fact, the Visitor is structurally similar to the Strategy. However, the intent as discussed is radically different. In fact, this is a major point that should be addressed in any discussion on patterns. While some patterns may appear to be structurally similar, the behavioral aspects of different patterns typically differ radically. Therefore, it becomes extremely important to understand the dynamic aspects of the challenge presented. The behavioral and structural differences in the context of a system as a whole are introduced in Chapter 4 and discussed in detail in Chapters 8 and 9.

Examining the Visitor pattern a bit further, a number of principles do surface. For instance, OCP has been adhered to; however, it comes in a different form. In this situation, it's used to support adding new methods to a class, not to support adding new data structures to a system. In addition to OCP, CRP is also used because the DynamicClass is composed of the various Visitor classes. The identification of additional principles is left as an exercise to the reader.

Up to this point, the Visitor pattern sounds fairly useful. However, as mentioned previously, the Visitor pattern isn't often used because of one major implication that it has upon our system. While the Visitor makes it easy to add new methods to the interface of a class, it makes it extremely difficult to add new classes. For instance, in Figure 1.11, consider the modifications required to the system should a new DynamicClass class be required. Creating the new DynamicClass class would be easy. It involves simply creating a new class with an `accept` method. The problem resides in the proliferation of changes that exist within our `Visitor` hierarchy. These modifications demand that a new method be added to all `Visitor` classes in the hierarchy, including the abstract `Visitor` class. Because of this, the Visitor pattern is somewhat limited in use. In fact, caution should be used any time an implementation of the Visitor pattern is considered. Interested readers should refer to [GOF95] for further reading on Visitor.

1.3.3   Layers

In Java, a class can belong to only a single package. Therefore, if classes in different packages have relationships to each other, this implies that packages have structural relationships among them as well. Stated more precisely, if a class `C1` in package `P1` has a relationship to a class `C2` in package `P2`, we can say that the package `P1` has a relationship to package `P2`. The Layers pattern focuses on the relationships that exist between packages. In layering an application, a goal is to create packages that exist at higher-level layers and are dependent on packages that exist in lower-level layers.

   For instance, a common approach to layering an application is to define a package containing all presentation, or user interface, classes; another containing domain classes, or business objects; and another containing an application kernel, which may consist of database access classes. Each of these packages exists at different layers, and the relationships between the classes contained within each package are driven by the relationships allowed between the individual layers. The caveat of layering our application is that no package existing at a lower-level layer can be dependent on any package existing at a higher-level layer. This is important and is the defining characteristic of a layered application. In fact, this pattern is an implementation of ADP. However, while layering an application may seem obvious, successfully doing so can be tedious. For now, we defer any in-depth discussion on layering to Chapter 10, where we discuss architectural modeling and its various consequences. Our purpose has been served in this chapter by illustrating that the Layers pattern is supportive of the aforementioned ADP.

1.4   Conclusion

The object-oriented paradigm goes beyond the fundamental concepts and terms associated with it. Of course, while understanding core terms such as *polymorphism*, *encapsulation*, and *inheritance* is important, understanding the essence of the paradigm and pragmatically applying fundamental concepts is vital. In this chapter, we introduced a set of principles that will serve as a guide throughout the various phases of the software lifecycle, and the remainder of this book, helping to ensure our designs are more resilient, robust, and maintainable.

Whereas principles provide a reliable foundation for our design efforts, patterns can raise the level of abstraction, providing a more concrete starting point, and allowing our designs to grow more quickly. Many benefits are associated with taking advantage of design patterns. Because of this popularity, however, a proliferation of patterns has saturated the marketplace, making it difficult to separate the more useful patterns from those less so. In such situations, emphasizing the principles can help produce a more reliable and desired outcome. Regardless, both principles and patterns will be given the majority of our attention as we move through our chapters.

CHAPTER 2

Introduction to the UML

Why should I use the UML? What can it contribute to my software development effort?

To effectively utilize any technology, we must understand what it can positively contribute to the software development effort. Therefore, before adopting the Unified Modeling Language (UML), we should answer the following questions:

Why should I use the UML?

What can it contribute to my software development effort?

We begin by formally introducing the UML and defining its intended role in software development, as stated by the UML's original creators. Then we take a brief tour through the history of the UML. To finish, we explore some of the challenges encountered during software development today, and how the UML can help reduce these challenges to manageable tasks.

2.0 The UML Defined

The Unified Modeling Language User Guide states the following:

The UML is a language for

- Visualizing
- Specifying
- Constructing
- Documenting

the artifacts of a software-intensive system. [BOOCH99]

Visual Programming

Don't let this analogy to Java confuse you. The UML is not a visual programming language. The UML enables us to create an expression of our application in the form of a model. We can't express many implementation-specific details in the UML. The UML does map nicely to Java, and this mapping is discussed in Chapter 3. Helping you to model, and ultimately design, more effectively is a goal of this book.

Exploring this definition further enables us to realize the true intent of the UML. As stated previously, the UML is a language. As such, it has an associated set of rules that must be adhered to if we are to create well-formed, precise models, just as Java has a set of syntax rules that must be adhered to in order to create compilable applications. Because it's only a language, and not a methodology, the UML doesn't dictate how we use the models we create nor the order in which we create them. This misconception was one of the greatest ones associated with the UML early in its life. The UML is not a software process.

To further differentiate the UML from a software process, let's consider an analogy. Because Java is a language, the only stipulation to create an application that will compile is to create an application structure that is syntactically correct. On the other hand, Java doesn't dictate how we relate the internal elements of our system, nor does it impose any design restrictions. Therefore, when we create a Java application, we not only must write code that is syntactically correct, but we also must design the application. As discussed in Chapter 1, various principles and patterns can help guide us in creating a more resilient architecture, which is similar to the UML. The only stipulation the UML imposes upon

A History Lesson?

History of any sort is extremely important, and the software industry is no exception. It's important to understand the value of a standardized modeling language, as well as the historical impact other languages have had on the UML. If we ignore this aspect of the UML, we are doomed to repeat the same mistakes in the UML that were made with other modeling languages.

us is to create diagrams that are syntactically correct. How we organize our diagrams and what artifacts to produce is the role of a software process. Different processes will guide us through the creation of a different set of artifacts, which is a major advantage of the UML. Because it's process independent, we can integrate the most desirable pieces into our existing software process.

In Table 2.1, we provide descriptions for the previously listed bulleted points (from *The Unified Modeling Language User Guide*).

Table 2.1   Characteristics of the UML

Term	Description
Visualizing	We're all familiar with the developer who spends time at work struggling with a complex challenge, only to doodle out a solution on a napkin at that evening's happy hour. In fact, most of us have probably done something similar. There's something special about creating a visual representation. It makes it easier to understand and work through the problem. The visual and formal nature of the UML takes this doodling a few steps further. Because the UML is a formal language, with its own set of rules, it enables other developers familiar with the language to more easily interpret our drawings.
Specifying	We must communicate our software system using some common, precise, and unambiguous communication mechanism. Again, the formal nature of the UML facilitates this specification quite nicely.
Constructing	We already know that the UML is a formal language with its own set of syntactical rules. Because of this formality, we can create tools that interpret our models. Obviously, because these tools can interpret our models, they can map the elements to a programming language, such as Java. Many tools do support this forward-engineering concept. In fact, this is one of *(continues)*

Table 2.1   Characteristics of the UML *(continued)*

Term	Description
	the advantages of using a formal modeling tool. It enforces the syntactical rules of the UML.
Documenting	The models we create are just one of the artifacts produced throughout the development lifecycle. Using the UML in a consistent fashion produces a set of documentation that can serve as a blueprint of our system.

2.1   Origin

The history of the UML is rich, and while we won't go into detail, it's important to understand its deep roots. The UML's original designers, Grady Booch, Ivar Jacobson, and James Rumbaugh, realized the software industry was saturated with a variety of object-oriented modeling languages and methodologies. Instead of creating another new language, they decided to incorporate the best of the existing languages and methodologies. In October 1995, version 0.8 of the Unified Method was released. After some minor revision, including a change in its name, version 0.9 of the Unified Modeling Language was introduced in June 1996. About this time, the software industry began to take interest in the unification effort, and after some additional revisions, version 1.0 of the UML was submitted to the Object Management Group (OMG) for industry standardization in January 1997. At this point, a Revision Task Force was formed by OMG to serve as the UML's governing body. On November 14, 1997, UML 1.1 was adopted by OMG as the industry standard modeling language. Since that time, the UML has gone through some minor revisions, mostly pertaining to use cases, and in June 1999, UML 1.3 was adopted, which is the version of the UML described in this book.

In Figure 2.1, we see some of the languages and methods that contributed to the UML.

A complete definition of the UML is contained within the "OMG Unified Modeling Language Specification" and can be found on the OMG Web site at www.omg.org. This specification is a robust set of documentation, including but not limited to, the following:

- **UML Summary:** A brief history and introduction to the UML
- **UML Semantics:** The various semantics and rules that compose the UML and contribute to the creation of well-formed models

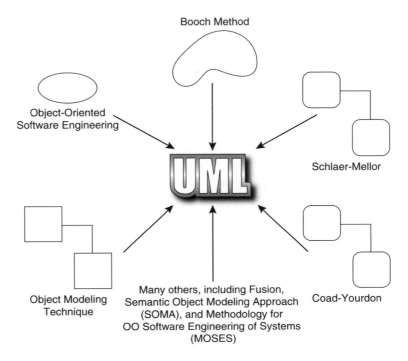

Figure 2.1 Foundations of the UML

- **UML Notation Guide:** Expression of the graphic syntax composing the UML
- **UML Extensions:** Standard UML extension for the unified process and business modeling

While this specification is a complete set of documentation and provides insight to the thought and careful planning that went toward the creation of the UML, it's not exciting reading. It's meant primarily for tools vendors, and a book such as this one provides a more valuable explanation of how the UML can be used most effectively.

2.2 Role of Modeling

To really understand why we would want to adopt any technology, it's first important to understand what problem the technology is trying to solve. Realistically, it does no good to adopt a new technology if it doesn't solve some problem or overcome some challenge. Adopting the UML is no different.

2.2.1   The Challenge

A number of challenges are associated with software development. However, none presents more obstacles than that of changing requirements. In Chapter 1, we learned that it costs twice as much to maintain a system as it costs to develop it, and that during development, only 15 percent of our time is actually devoted to programming. These statistics are proof that a system is never really complete until it has been removed from production and is no longer functioning. Until that point, time and money are spent adding new features, fixing bugs, and even improving its internal structure. This entire maintenance effort is typically the result of growing and changing requirements. If requirements were static, once these requirements were realized in a functioning system, the system would be complete and require no more maintenance, ultimately incurring no additional cost. So the real challenge in software development is dealing with these changing requirements. Therefore, we need a technology that helps us deal effectively with changing requirements.

Before we explore how we can more effectively manage a dynamic set of requirements, let's first review why changing requirements are so frustrating to deal with. In Chapter 1, we briefly discussed the architecture paradox. This paradox recognizes that a system has the competing goals of survivability and evolvability. In order for a system to survive, it must meet requirements, but as requirements change, the system must evolve. Failure to evolve to these changes means the system loses its survivability. Therefore, our system's archi-

Maintenance versus Reuse

The object-oriented paradigm carries with it the promise of reuse. However, reuse may not be the true benefit of object orientation. If the main obstacle in software development is accommodating changing requirements, we should be in search of a technology that allows our systems to adapt more flexibly to change. Fortunately, object orientation carries with it this benefit at least as much as, if not more than, the benefit of reuse. In Chapter 1, we briefly discussed this issue. We offer a gentle reminder here because of the emphasis that we'll place on architecting resilient systems that are easier to maintain versus attempting to architect systems that realize a high degree of reuse, at least initially. Stressing resiliency will continue to be a key aspect of our discussions as we progress through the remainder of this book.

tecture directly impacts the ability of a system to evolve gracefully. This is the same conclusion reached in Chapter 1, and it now becomes clear that the following holds true:

> *The cost to maintain a system is directly related to the resiliency of the system's architecture.*

Therefore, the challenge in developing software is to develop software that is well architected.

2.2.2   Complexity of Architecture

Developing software is an inherently complex process. In *The Mythical Man-Month*, Frederick Brooks cites two complexities associated with software development. He categorizes them as *essential complexities* and *accidental complexities* [BROOKS95]. Essential complexities are those difficulties that are inherent in the nature of software, whereas accidental complexities are difficulties that attend the production of software but can be eliminated.

There have been many attempts to eliminate accidental complexity. Examples of accidental complexity include a mismatch of tools or paradigms, a lack of formal methodologies or models, and awkward programming languages. Years ago, we wrote software using assembly language, which was a time-consuming process. Programming languages have evolved since then, and today we are able to focus more on our problem domain and spend less time struggling with various technical issues such as performance and hardware constraints. With each of these advances, certain accidental complexities are reduced. These advances, however, introduce new accidental complexities, such as those associated with mapping an object-oriented system to a relational database for persistent storage, known as the *object/relational impedance mismatch*.

The more interesting of these complexities, essential complexity, cannot be eliminated and is inherent in the nature of software. It's fairly common to see comparisons between software engineering and other engineering disciplines. The electronics industry has a set of canned components that can be used in many different types of electronics, which carries with it obvious advantages. Why do we not have similar components in the software industry? Only recently has this concept of component-based development been gaining steam. The problem is that certain properties of software development aren't found in many other engineering disciplines. First, software is invisible. Obvious contradictions aren't easily caught because software has no geometric representation as electronic components do. No dictating physics are associated with software. When designing an electric circuit, or building a skyscraper, mathematical limitations are placed on what we can do. Software typically doesn't have this same set of restraints. Because of its invisibility, software often is seen as infinitely changeable. It would be absurd to consider changing the structure of a 100-story high-rise once it's 90 percent complete. This doesn't always hold true with software. Therefore, we need to create software systems that are infinitely malleable. Put simply, people and businesses change, and demand that the software do so as well. Therefore, the fashioning of these complex, yet malleable, structures in a programming language can be a difficult and challenging task. This task is the complex essence of software engineering, and when we're able to reduce this essential complexity, we'll have taken a small step forward.

2.2.3   The Remedy

Because we can't eliminate essential complexity, we can hope only to reduce it. The UML, and visual modeling, is a tool that can be used to help reduce essential complexity. By creating visual representations of our software system, it's easier to identify contradictions that may have been previously overlooked. Thus, visual modeling enables us to create systems that are flexible enough to achieve a higher degree of resiliency. While it isn't necessarily true that we wouldn't be able to create a flexible design without modeling, creating a visual representation of a system can help all individuals involved to more fully understand that system. Consequently, each of these individuals will see a common system with little ambiguity. This common perspective helps increase communication among our team members and also helps each team member more fully understand the system. If we better understand something, we can work with it more effectively.

Though we may never be able to accommodate every single change scenario, working toward this goal gives our system the extra degree of flexibility that it might need to survive longer and grow into the future. In addition to visual modeling, associated principles, patterns, and other proven best practices just might give us what we need to turn adequate designs into great designs.

2.3   Benefits

At this point, we should have a much clearer understanding of what the UML is and what it is not. We've also probably begun to formulate our own theories as to why we would want to model, and what some of the benefits of doing so are. In this section, we discuss the obvious, and the not-so-obvious, benefits of the UML.

Modeling as an Activity

While we often discuss modeling as if it were an activity, we must keep in mind that we shouldn't treat modeling as a formal stage in the software development lifecycle. Nor should we be led to believe at any point in time that creating a model adds value to our system. The only value that can be added to our system comes in the form of source code that is error free and functionally correct. In fact, while we use the term *modeling*, we model primarily to produce higher-quality designs. However, modeling does contribute to the creation of a successful system by helping us manage complexity and solve difficult challenges. Consequently, modeling is an omnipresent activity performed throughout all stages of the software development lifecycle. We model because it helps us analyze problems and design more effective solutions that can be communicated effectively.

One of the greatest benefits of using the UML is that it facilitates a common, precise, unambiguous, and unified communication mechanism. While other modeling languages may claim to provide the first of these three benefits, only the UML can lay claim to unification. It's the industry standard modeling language. For those of us who continue to take advantage of the benefits provided from other traditional languages, a transition to the UML provides the added benefit of unification.

Modeling also enables us to create simplified representations of our systems. By modeling at different levels of abstraction, we can communicate a different intent by creating different models. We have to be cautious here. If we model at too high a level of abstraction, our model loses the value of its original intent. Regardless, the ability to communicate bits and pieces of the overall system contributes to a more manageable understanding of our system. We'll continue to explore this concept as we progress throughout this book.

As we've seen, developing software is an inherently complex process. Just like the developer who doodles on a napkin to gain further insight into the problem at hand, modeling serves as an excellent problem-solving mechanism. Reaching resolution on our most complex problems in visual form prior to coding contributes to a more resilient system. Similar to problem solving, modeling can help us validate our theories. When confronted with a problem, it's highly likely that we will consider multiple solutions. Modeling can validate that we've chosen the solution that is most viable considering the context of the problem.

While we discuss the UML throughout this book in the context of developing Java applications, the UML is language independent. In Chapter 3, we define the mappings from the UML to Java. Mappings such as these exist for any other object-oriented programming language.

2.4   Conclusion

Modeling has taken a strong foothold in software development and is undoubtedly here to stay. The UML was created to provide the software development community with a standard, unified modeling language. The UML has a rich history and was created by some of the most well-respected methodologists in the software industry.

While modeling is not the silver bullet for software development, it has numerous benefits, which include enhanced communication, validation of our design theories, and helping to simplify an inherently difficult process. By taking advantage of these benefits, we can produce systems that will survive as the demands of our users and business change. In some regards, all projects utilize a certain degree of modeling. The choice to use a formal language such as the UML should be given serious consideration. The result can be a much more resilient design, which can reduce the cost associated with the maintenance effort.

CHAPTER 3

Fundamental UML

To effectively use UML, we must understand how we represent diagrams in code.

Before attempting to understand how the UML can be used on a software project, we first must understand some of the fundamental elements that compose the UML. By understanding these fundamental elements, we gain insight into the building blocks of the UML at all levels. In this chapter, we begin our studies of many of the most commonly used elements within the UML and how these elements map to the Java language.

This type of discussion often is centered around the UML metamodel. This metamodel describes many of the entities and the relationships between these entities that compose the UML. While this discussion is important, the metamodel becomes truly important for those individuals responsible for developing modeling tools. For the majority of corporations, focusing on the metamodel to gain a deeper understanding of the UML may not be the best use of their time. Our discussion in this chapter takes a different approach. We'll emphasize how the UML is built from the ground up, emphasizing the most often used elements.

3.0 Models and Views

The UML is more than a set of disjointed diagrams. Instead of examining the UML from a diagram-centric perspective, let's turn our attention to an illustration of the UML from three different perspectives. Figure 3.1 depicts three divisions within the UML. Further insight into these divisions enables us to realize

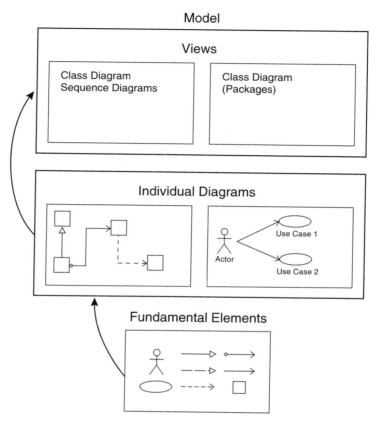

Figure 3.1   UML Perspectives

one of the greatest benefits of modeling, which is creating different views of our software system.

3.0.1   Fundamental Elements

At the lowest level in Figure 3.1 exist the fundamental elements. These basic building blocks are the elements of which diagrams are composed. By themselves, these elements contribute little to the specification of a software system. However, understanding the intent of each element enables us to create precise diagrams because each of the elements has a very unambiguous meaning. These lower-level elements are described in detail in Section 3.2, later in this chapter. Keep in mind that once we understand the characteristics of an element, these characteristics apply wherever that element is used.

3.0.2 Diagrams

Above the fundamental elements is the perspective on the UML that many of us are familiar with. The individual diagrams contribute more to the specification of a software system than a single building block. In essence, we can think of a diagram as the composition of many of the fundamental elements. For the majority of us, diagrams play the most important role in contributing to the specification of our software system. These diagrams are the mechanism that developers use to communicate and solve problems in the complex aspects of the system. For instance, class diagrams, which describe the structural relationships that exist among the classes within our system, can guide developers in understanding our software system's class structure.

As we begin to incorporate the UML into our environment, it's typical to begin by using the individual diagrams to communicate our software structure and solve problems in the challenging design scenarios. For developers, the most common diagram is the class diagram. Each of the other diagrams, however, plays an important role as well. Because of the specific nature of each diagram, it can be quite effective to use diagrams in conjunction with one another to help us more fully understand our system.

3.0.3 Views

As we become more proficient in modeling, we begin to realize that using a combination of diagrams to communicate is most effective. For instance, a class diagram is valuable in communicating the structural relationships that exist

---

Models and Views

A *model* is a self-contained representation of a system. Given a model, a user need not have any other information from other models to interpret the system. A *view* can be thought of as any artifact that helps to simplify the representation of our system. A view is a slice through a model, whereas a model is a complete view of a system. In this regard, a view is a subset of a model, and in fact, a model is a view, albeit a complete one. A view focuses on communicating the system from a particular perspective. Views almost always omit elements of a model not relevant to the given situation. In this regard, views describe the architecturally significant elements of a model from a particular perspective. The differences

(continues)

(continued)

between a model and a view are subtle. Our intent in this discussion is to help the reader understand one of the primary advantages in modeling—that is, to create different representations of the system from different perspectives to aid in communication, while maintaining consistency throughout.

between the individual classes within our application. However, a class diagram says nothing about the ordering of messages sent between the objects within our application. By combining a class diagram with a diagram whose intent is to communicate our system's dynamics, the ability to communicate our system's overall intent becomes more powerful.

The combination of a class diagram with a diagram whose intent is to communicate our system's dynamics is a *view*. A view is a depiction of our system from a particular perspective. By combining diagrams to form complete views into the system, we have the innate ability to represent the system from many different perspectives. In Philippe Kruchten's article, "Architectural Blueprints—The 4+1 View Model of Software Architecture," he describes five distinct views from which individuals associated with the software development process actually see the system [KRUCHTEN95]. Figure 3.2 shows these views, and Table 3.1 describes them. As we model our applications, we can create complete models, each containing multiple views. While each of these views represents the system from a different perspective, each represents it from a perspective that is significant to different individuals associated with the development initiative.

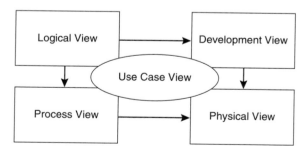

Figure 3.2   The 4+1 View Model of Software Architecture

Adapted from Kruchten, Philippe, "The 4+1 View Model of Software Architecture," *IEEE Software*, November 1995.

Table 3.1 View Descriptions

View	Description
Use case	This view documents the system from the customer's perspective. Terminology used in this view should be domain specific. Depending on the technical nature of our audience, we should avoid obscure technical terms. Diagrams most common in this view are the use case diagrams and, less common, activity diagrams. Organizations transitioning to the UML may wish to work only with use case diagrams early and experiment with activity diagrams over time.
Design	This view documents the system from designer's and architect's perspective. Diagrams most common in this view are class and interaction diagrams (either sequence or collaboration), as well as package diagrams illustrating the package structure of our Java application.
Development	This view documents the components that the system is composed of. This view typically contains component diagrams. Except for the most complex Java applications, this view is optional.
Process	This view documents the processes and threads that compose our application. These processes and threads typically are captured on class diagrams using an active class. Because of the advanced nature of active classes, coupled with the volume of use, active classes are beyond the scope of this discussion. For information, refer to [BOOCH99].
Physical	This view documents the system topology. Deployment diagrams that compose this view illustrate the physical nodes and devices that make up the application, as well as the connections that exist between them.

These different views are extremely important because end users, developers, and project stakeholders most likely have different agendas, and each looks at the system quite differently. While each of these perspectives might be different, they represent the same system and should be consistent in the information they convey. In addition, our views can be used to validate each other. The specification contained within one view is consistent with the specification within another. Because of this consistency, we can trace the specification in one view through the realization of that specification in another. The result is an excellent way to ensure that when requirements in our use case view change, they can be traced through the other views, enabling us to make the appropriate changes. This concept of traceability is further discussed in Chapter 4.

The views in Figure 3.2 may not be the only views from which we look at the system. We might consider creating a view that is responsible for representing the architecturally significant elements within an application. In fact, a view's intent is to model architecturally significant elements that are relevant to the perspective the view represents. In some situations, we may be interested in representing the architecturally significant elements of our system fulfilling a set of security requirements. In this case, we might create a security view. Architectural modeling is discussed in detail in Chapter 10. The point is that whenever we need to communicate about the system from a particular perspective, we can create a view into the system from that perspective, which is consistent with all other views we have created.

3.1   Core Diagrams

As we've seen, we can combine diagrams that form models and that can serve as views into our system. This capability is illustrated at a higher level in Figure 3.3. If an advantage in modeling is to combine diagrams to form views into our system, then it only makes sense that each diagram has a different focus on what it communicates.

Examining the intent of these diagrams, we see that each falls into one of two categories. Behavioral diagrams depict the dynamic aspects of our system. They are most useful for specifying the collaborations among elements that satisfy the behavior of our system's requirements. Structural diagrams depict the static aspect of our system. These diagrams are most useful for illustrating the relationships that exist among physical elements within our system, such as classes.

Of these diagrams, the three most commonly used are use case, sequence, and class diagrams. These three typically are used on all software development projects taking advantage of the UML. While still important, the remaining diagrams have a more specialized focus, which isn't to say that these remaining dia-

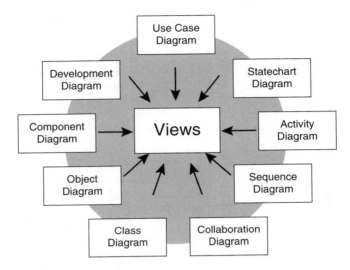

Figure 3.3 Diagrams Composing the UML

grams don't serve an important purpose. They definitely do—usually in cases where a specific, complex portion of our system must be communicated or more fully understood. Our discussion of using the UML with Java begins with a focus on these three diagrams.

3.1.1 Behavioral Diagrams

Behavioral diagrams communicate the aspects of the system that contribute to satisfying the system's requirements, typically captured in the form of use cases. Table 3.2 describes the five diagrams that fall into this category. Of these diagrams, the most commonly used are use case, sequence, and collaboration diagrams. While still useful, activity and state diagrams typically are used on an as-needed basis. Activity diagrams visually represent behaviors captured by use cases. State diagrams, on the other hand, are used to illustrate complex transitions in behavior for a single class.

Use case diagrams are centered around the business processes that our application must support. Most simply, use case diagrams enable us to structure our entire application around the core processes that it must support. Doing so enables us to use these use cases to drive the remainder of the modeling and development effort.

Sequence and collaboration diagrams are forms of interaction diagrams, which model the interactions among a set of objects. Interaction diagrams are

Table 3.2 Behavioral Diagrams

Diagram	Description
Use case	Shows a set of actors and use cases, and the relationships between them. Use case diagrams contribute to effective model organization, as well as modeling the core behaviors of a system.
Activity	Models the flow of activity between processes. These diagrams are most useful in detailing use case behavior. An activity diagram doesn't show collaboration among objects.
State	Illustrates internal state-related behavior of an object. Transitions between states help identify, and validate, complex behavior. A class can have at most a single state diagram.
Sequence	Semantically equivalent to a collaboration diagram, a sequence diagram is a type of interaction diagram that describes time ordering of messages sent between objects.
Collaboration	A type of interaction diagram that describes the organizational layout of the objects that send and receive messages. Semantically equivalent to a sequence diagram.

used often, primarily because they capture the messages sent between objects, which is of utmost importance to architects, designers, and developers.

Both sequence and collaboration diagrams fall into the interaction diagrams category because these diagrams are semantically equivalent—that is, they specify the same behaviors. The difference is the vantage point from which they express them. Collaboration diagrams focus on the spatial layout of the object interactions. They're useful in identifying structure among the classes, because the format of a collaboration diagram is similar in layout to that of a class diagram. Sequence diagrams, on the other hand, are focused on communicating the time ordering of messages sent among the objects. Because of their similar nature, it's quite common for a development team to standardize on the usage of either a sequence or collaboration diagram but not on both.

3.1.2   Structural Diagrams

Diagrams in this category are focused on specifying the static aspects of our system. Table 3.3 describes the structural diagrams. Of these four diagrams, the class diagram is most often used. In fact, when transitioning to the UML, most organizations tend to use class diagrams first because they are excellent mechanisms for communication among developers, as well as tools that can be used for problem solving.

There are two forms of class diagrams. The first is the most commonly understood and consists of the classes that compose our system and of the structure among these classes. Unfortunately, the second is not often used but is of equal importance and can be most effective in helping developers understand our system from a high level. A type of class diagram, called a *package diagram*, often represents the Java packages and the dependencies between them that our application consists of. An example of a package diagram is provided in Figure 3.6.

The remaining structural diagrams, while still useful, have niches in modeling that are focused on certain types of applications. Without undermining the

Table 3.3   Structural Diagrams

Diagram	Description
Class	Illustrates a set of classes, packages, and relationships detailing a particular aspect of a system. This diagram is likely the most common one used in modeling.
Object	Provides a snapshot of the system illustrating the static relationships that exist between objects.
Component	Addresses the static relationships existing between the deployable software components. Examples of components may be .exe, .dll, .ocx, jar files, and/or Enterprise JavaBeans.
Deployment	Describes the physical topology of a system. Typically includes various processing nodes, realized in the form of a device (for example, a printer or modem) or a processor (for example, a server).

importance of these diagrams, suffice it to say that use of these diagrams should be dictated by the complexity of our system. Component diagrams might be used to show the software components within our application. Components aren't equivalent to classes. A component might be composed of multiple classes. Deployment diagrams, which illustrate the physical topology of our system, are most useful when we have a complex configuration environment. If our application is to be deployed to multiple servers, across locations, a deployment diagram might be useful. Object diagrams depict the structural relationship that exists among the objects within our running application at a given point in time. When we think of the runtime version of our system, we typically think of behavior. Many people have found that object diagrams are most useful in fleshing out the instance relationships among objects, which in turn can help verify our class diagrams. Beyond this, object diagrams are not often used.

3.2   Fundamental Elements

Our discussion on the fundamental elements is in two sections. Section 3.2.1 discusses the structural elements that represent abstractions in our system. Structural elements typically are elements that encapsulate the system's set of behaviors. In Section 3.2.2, we discuss the relationships that define how the structural elements relate to each other. Throughout our discussions of these elements, we provide mappings to the Java language.

3.2.1   Structural Elements

We have broken our discussion of structural elements into two sections. In Section 3.2.2, we discuss Java-independent entities, which are elements that don't have a Java language mapping. Then, in Section 3.2.3, we turn our attention to the Java-dependent entities, which are elements that have a straightforward Java mapping. The UML includes other structural elements that are beyond the scope of our discussion.

In our discussion of the structural elements, we use a template. At the top left is the name of the element. In the top center of the template is a graphic representing the element as it appears on a diagram. On the top right is the diagram(s) on which this element most often appears. Syntactically, placing these elements on diagrams not documented here might be correct. However, because we're using a simple approach, our discussion is focused on the diagram on which this element appears most often. In some cases, elements appear on more than one diagram, and in these special cases, the documentation reflects that. The top right section of the template is broken down into the following categories:

- **Specific diagram:** This element can appear on any of the diagrams mentioned at the beginning of this chapter. Replace *specific* with the diagram name.
- **Structural diagram:** This element can appear on any of the structural diagrams, as categorized at the beginning of this chapter.
- **Behavioral diagram:** This element can appear on any of the behavioral diagrams, as categorized at the beginning of this chapter.
- **Combinatorial:** Any combination of the preceding can be used.

Following the top section of each element is a description of that element. In Section 3.2.3, a table with two columns is included. The left column shows a Java code snippet. The right column shows the UML representation of this code.

3.2.2   Java-Independent Entities

Actor   **Use Case Diagram**

An actor represents a role that a user of the system plays. An actor always is external to the system under development. An actor need not always be a person. An actor might be another external system, such as a legacy mainframe from which we are obtaining data, or possibly a device, which we must obtain data from, such as a keypad on an ATM machine.

Use Case   **Use Case Diagram**

A use case represents a sequence of actions that a software system guarantees to carry out on behalf of an actor. When defining use cases, the level of granularity becomes important. The level of granularity varies among systems. The one constant is that a use case should always provide a result of an observable value to an actor. Primary business processes typically are good candidates for use cases. This way, these individual use cases can drive the development effort, which is focused on core business processes. This enables us to trace our results throughout the development lifecycle. A use case should be focused on the system from a customer's perspective.

Collaboration   Use Case Diagram

A collaboration is somewhat beyond the scope of our discussion in this book. However, because we use examples in later chapters, it should be introduced for completeness. Collaborations most often are used to bring structure to our design model. They enable us to create sequence and class diagrams that work in conjunction with each other, to provide an object-oriented view into the requirements that our system satisfies. A collaboration typically has a one-to-one mapping to a use case. This way, while use cases represent requirements from a customer's vantage point in the use case view, a collaboration models these same set of requirements from a developer's perspective.

Object   Interaction and Object Diagrams

An object is an instance of a class. It is represented by a rectangle. An object can be named in three different ways. First, and probably most common, we can specify the class that this object is an instance of. This is done by specifying the class name in the object rectangle. The class name is preceded by a semicolon and underlined. Second, we can specify only the object name, neglecting the class name, which is done by omitting the class name and semicolon and simply typing the object name and underlining it. In this naming scenario, we don't know the class that this object is an instance of. The third way to represent an object is to combine the two previously mentioned approaches.

An object can also be thought of as a physical entity, whereas a class is a conceptual entity. At first glance, it may seem odd that an object doesn't have a Java language mapping. In fact, it does. An object in the UML maps directly to an object in Java. However, when developers create Java applications, they are creating Java classes, not Java objects. Developers never write their code inside a Java object. Thinking about this a little differently, we think of objects as existing at runtime and classes as existing at design time. Developers create their code and map the UML elements to Java at design time, not runtime. Therefore, while a UML object maps directly to an object in Java, no Java language mapping represents a UML object.

3.2.3 Java-Dependent Entities

Class

Class Name
Attributes
Operations

Class Diagram

A class is a blueprint for an object. A class has three compartments. The first represents the name of the class as defined in Java. The second represents the attributes. Attributes correspond to instance variables within the class. An attribute defined in this second compartment is the same as a composition relationship. The third compartment represents methods on the class. Attributes and operations can be preceded with a visibility adornment. A plus sign (+) indicates public visibility, and a minus sign (−) denotes private visibility. A pound sign (#) denotes protected visibility. Omission of this visibility adornment denotes package-level visibility. When an attribute or operation is underlined, it indicates that it's static. An operation may also list the parameters it accepts, as well as the return type, as follows:

Java	**UML**
``` public class Employee { private int empID; public double calcSalary() { ... } } ```	Employee -empID:int +calcSalary():double

Package

Class Diagram

A general purpose grouping mechanism, packages can contain any other type of element. A package in the UML translates directly into a package in Java. In Java, a package can contain other packages, classes, or both. When modeling, we typically have packages that are logical, implying they serve only to organize our model. We also have packages that are physical, implying these packages translate directly into Java packages in our system. A package has a name that uniquely identifies it.

Java	UML

`package BusinessObjects;`
 	
`public class Employee {`
 	
`}`	

Interface ⭕ **Class Diagram**

An interface is a collection of operations that specify a service of a class. An interface translates directly to an interface type in Java. An interface can be represented either by the previously shown icon or by a regular class with a stereotype attachment of <<interface>>. An interface typically is shown on a class diagram as having realization relationships with other classes.

Java	UML

`public interface CollegePerson {`
`    public Schedule getSchedule();`
 	
`}`
	⭕
	CollegePerson
	—————
	getSchedule()

3.2.4   Java-Dependent Relationships

The following examples illustrate the relationships in isolation based on the intent. Though syntactically correct, these samples could be further refined to include additional semantic meaning within the domain with which they are associated.

Each of the following relationships appear on diagrams in the structural category, most likely class diagrams. Though some, such as association, also appear on use case diagrams, their discussion is beyond the scope of this book.

Dependency **Structural Diagram**

A "using" relationship between entities that implies a change in specification of one entity may affect the entities that are dependent upon it. More concretely, a dependency translates to any type of reference to a class or object that doesn't exist at the instance scope, including a local variable, reference to an object obtained via a method call, as in the following example, or reference to a class' static method, where an instance of that class does not exist. A dependency also is used to represent the relationship between packages. Because a package contains classes, we can illustrate that various packages have relationships between them based upon the relationships among the classes within those packages.

Java	UML

``
public class Employee {
    public void
calcSalary(Calculator c) {
        ...
    }
}
``
	Employee - - - - -> Calculator

Association $\longrightarrow$ Structural & Use Case Diagrams

A structural relationship between entities specifying that objects are connected. The arrow is optional and specifies navigability. No arrow implies bidirectional navigability, resulting in tighter coupling. An instance of an association is a link, which is used on interaction diagrams to model messages sent between objects. In Java, an association translates to an instance scope variable, as in the following example. Additional adornments also can be attached to an association. Multiplicity adornments imply relationships between the instances. In the following example, an Employee can have 0 or more TimeCard objects. However, a TimeCard belongs to a single Employee (that is, Employees do not share TimeCards).

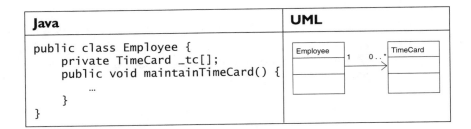

Java	UML

``
public class Employee {
    private TimeCard _tc[];
    public void maintainTimeCard() {
        ...
    }
}
``
	Employee 1 0..* TimeCard

Aggregation Class Diagram

A form of association representing a whole/part relationship between two classes, an aggregiation implies that the whole is at a conceptually higher level than the part, whereas an association implies both classes are at the same conceptual level. An aggregation translates to an instance scope variable in Java. The difference between an association and an aggregation is entirely conceptual and is focused strictly on semantics. An aggregation also implies that no cycles are in the instance graph. In other words, an aggregation must be a unidirectional relationship. The different in Java between an association and aggregation is not noticeable. As stated previously, it's purely a matter of semantics. If you are unsure as to when to use an association or an aggregation, use an association. An aggregation need not be used often.

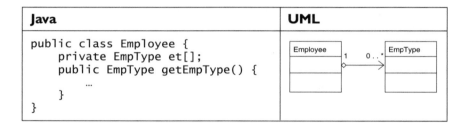

Composition Class Diagram

A special form of aggregation, which implies lifetime responsibility of the part within the whole, composition is also nonshared. Therefore, while the part doesn't necessarily need to be destroyed when the whole is destroyed, the whole is responsible for either keeping alive or destroying the part. The part cannot be shared with other wholes. The whole, however, can transfer ownership to another object, which then assumes lifetime responsibility. The *UML Semantics* documentation states the following:

> *Composite aggregation is a strong form of aggregation which requires that a part instance be included in at most one composite at a time and that the composite object has sole responsibility for the disposition of its parts. [SEM01]*

The relationship below between `Employee` and `TimeCard` might better be represented as a composition versus an association, as in the previous discussion.

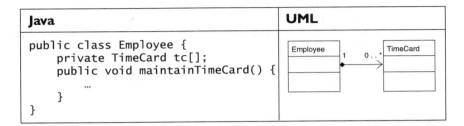

Java	UML
| ```java
public class Employee {
    private TimeCard tc[];
    public void maintainTimeCard() {
        ...
    }
}
``` | Employee 1 0..* TimeCard |

Generalization   Class and Use Case Diagrams

Illustrating a relationship between a more general element and a more specific element, a generalization is the UML element to model inheritance. In Java, a generalization directly translates into use of the `extends` keyword. A generalization also can be used to model relationships between actors and use cases.

Java	UML
| ```java
public abstract class Employee {

}
public class Professor extends
Employee {

}
``` | Employee ◁ Professor |

Realization   Class Diagram

A relationship that specifies a contract between two entities, in which one entity defines a contract that another entity guarantees to carry out. When modeling Java applications, a realization translates directly into the use of the `implements` keyword. A realization also can be used to obtain traceability between use cases, which define the behavior of the system, to the set of classes that guarantee to realize this behavior. This set of classes that realize a use case are typically structured around a collaboration, formally known as a *use case realization*.

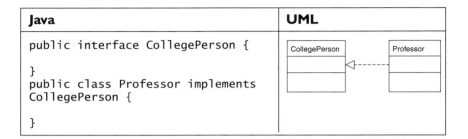

Java	UML
| ```java
public interface CollegePerson {

}
public class Professor implements
CollegePerson {

}
``` | |

3.3   Annotations

The only true annotational item in the UML is a note. Annotations simply provide further explanation on various aspects of UML elements and diagrams.

Notes   **Any Diagram**

Notes in the UML are one of the least structured elements. They simply represent a comment about your model. Notes can be, though need not be, attached to any of the other elements and can be placed on any diagram. Attaching a note to another element is done via a simple dotted line. If the note is not attached to anything, we can omit the dotted line. The closest thing that notes translate to in Java is a comment. However, it isn't likely that we would copy the text from a note and place it in our Java code. Notes provide comments regarding our diagrams; comments describe code in detail.

Java	UML
| ```java
/** Here is an example of a Java
comment. Typically, this text
will not be exactly the same as
the text contained within the
note.
*/
``` | Here is an example of a note in UML. Notice the dotted line denoting attachment. |

3.4   Extensibility Mechanisms

The extensibility mechanisms don't necessarily have direct mappings to Java. However, they're still a critical element of the UML. These mechanisms are commonly used across diagrams, and understanding their intent is important.

We can create our own mechanisms, which enables us to customize the UML for our development environment. We should use caution in creating our own mechanisms. The UML is a robust language. Before defining our own extension mechanisms, we should be sure the mechanism does not already exist within the language.

Stereotype

A stereotype is used to create a new fundamental element within the UML with its own set of special properties, semantics, and notation. UML profiles can be created that define a set of stereotypes for language-specific features. For instance, Sun is currently working on a UML profile that defines a mapping between the UML and Enterprise JavaBeans (EJB).

Tagged Values

Tagged values enable us to extend the UML by creating properties that can be attached to other fundamental elements. For instance, a tagged value may be used to specify the author and version of a particular component. Tagged values also can be associated with stereotypes, at which point attachment of the stereotype to an element implies the tagged value.

Constraint

Constraints enable us to modify or add various rules to the UML. Essentially, constraints enable us to add new semantics. For example, across a set of associations, we may use a constraint to specify that only a single instance is manifest at any point in time.

3.5   Introduction to Diagrams

These sample diagrams provide illustrations of how we interpret various relationships on individual diagrams. We also discuss how these different diagrams can be used in conjunction with each other to further enhance communication. Our example here depicts the Java event-handling mechanism used within the Abstract Windowing Toolkit (AWT). When developing Java applications, it's quite common to use a pattern similar to that of AWT to handle events within our application. In fact, this event-handling mechanism within Java is an implementation of the observer [G0F95] and command design pattern [G0F95].

3.5.1   Sequence Diagram

The rectangles at the top of our sequence diagram in Figure 3.4 denote objects. Objects have the same rectangular iconic representation as classes. There are three primary ways to name objects. The first, seen at the far left in Figure 3.4, is to provide an object name. When using this form, we don't necessarily know the name of the class that this object is an instance of. This representation, not seen in Figure 3.4, is commonly used to represent the fact that any object, regardless of its type, can invoke the flow of events that this sequence diagram is modeling. The second, represented by the remaining objects, denotes that an object is an instance of a specific class. This form is illustrated by preceding the name of the class with a colon. The third way of naming an object is to use a combination of the previously described two approaches. This way is not shown on Figure 3.4. Of the three ways to name objects on sequence diagrams, the second is most common. In each instance, the object's name is underlined.

A directed arrow represents messages on sequence diagrams. Associated with this directed arrow is typically a method name denoting the method that is

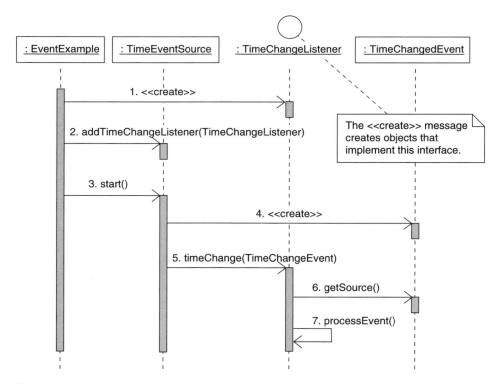

Figure 3.4   Sequence Diagram for Event-Handling Simulation

triggered as the result of the object's communication. In Figure 3.4, which simulates Java's AWT event-handling mechanism, my `EventExample` object sends a method to the `TimeEventSource` object. This message results in the `addTimeChangeListener()` method being triggered. The ordering of the messages sent between objects is always read top to bottom and typically is read left to right, although reading left to right is not a requirement. Be sure to notice the notes used in Figure 3.4 to enhance understanding.

Let's walk through the sequence diagram in further detail. The numbers that follow correspond to the numbers in Figure 3.4.

1. Some `EventExample`, which can be any object in our system, begins our event simulation by creating a `TimeChangeListener` object. Obviously, we can't have a true instance of an interface, and we certainly won't. However, it's important to communicate that the `TimeEventSource` isn't coupled to the implementation of the `TimeChangeListener` but to the listener itself. That is clearly communicated in Figure 3.4.

2. The `EventExample` object now registers the `TimeChangeListener` with the `TimeEventSource` object.

3. `EventExample` calls start on the `TimeEventSource`, which begins sending events to the listeners that have been registered with it.

4. The `TimeEventSource` creates a `TimeChangeEvent` object. This `TimeChage Event` object encapsulates information regarding this event.

5. The `TimeEventSource` loops through each of its listeners, calling the `timeChange` method on each.

6. Optionally, the `TimeChangeListener` can obtain a reference to the object that caused the event notification. This reference is returned a generic reference to `java.lang.Object`.

7. `TimeChangeListener` calls its `processEvent()` method to handle processing the event.

In Figure 3.4, notice that we have attached a note to the `TimeChangeListener` interface specifying that we will actually create a class that implements this interface. This note allows for a great deal of flexibility in our diagram, because the entire message sequence holds true regardless of what class we use in place of `TimeChangeListener`. We also may wish to use a note to specify that when the `TimeEventSource` object notifies its listeners of a time change; it may notify multiple listeners, resulting in a loop. The point is that developers who need to interpret this diagram, and use it to construct code, must have the information provided in the notes to effectively construct code. Notes are a great aid in helping us understand more fully the details associated with this sequence of events. Notes appear on most diagrams and should be used often.

We typically have many sequence diagrams for a single class diagram because any society of classes most likely interacts in many different ways. The intent of a sequence diagram is to model one way in which the society interacts. Therefore, to represent multiple interactions, we have many sequence diagrams.

Sequence diagrams, when used in conjunction with class diagrams, are an extremely effective communication mechanism because we can use a class diagram to illustrate the relationships between the classes. The sequence diagram then can be used to show the messages sent among the instances of these classes, as well as the order in which they are sent, which ultimately contribute to the relationships on a class diagram. When an object sends a message to another object, that essentially implies that the two classes have a relationship that must be shown on a class diagram.

3.5.2   Class Diagram

The class diagram in Figure 3.5 is a structural representation of the Java AWT event simulation. Note each of the relationships that appear on this diagram. First, our `EventExample` class has relationships to `TimeEventSource` and `TimePrinter`, which corresponds to the messages an `EventExample` object must send to instances of these classes. On our sequence diagram in Figure 3.4, however, we didn't see a `TimePrinter` object. In fact, the sequence diagram did contain a `TimePrinter`, but it was in the form of the `TimeChangeListener` interface, which the note on the diagram in Figure 3.4 didn't clarify. As we can see in Figure 3.5, the `TimePrinter` implements the `TimeChangeListener` interface. Also, notice the structural inheritance relationships depicted on this diagram that weren't apparent in Figure 3.4.

When interpreting the diagrams, it often is easiest to place the class diagram and sequence diagram side by side. Begin reading the sequence diagram, and as the messages are sent between the objects, trace these messages back to the relationships on the class diagram. Doing so should be helpful in understanding why the relationships on the class diagram exist. After having read each of the sequence diagrams, if you find a relationship on a class diagram that can't be mapped to a method call, you should question the validity of the relationship.

3.5.3   Package Diagram

Package diagrams are really a form of a class diagram. The difference is that a package diagram shows the relationships between our individual packages. We can think of a package diagram as a higher-level view into our system. This

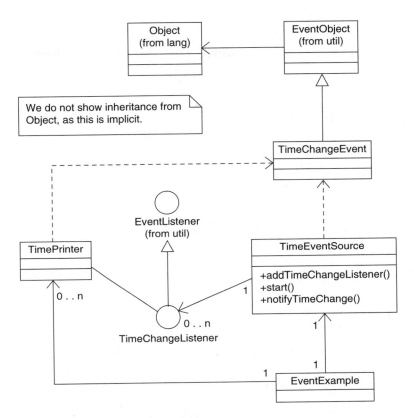

Figure 3.5 Class Diagram for Event-Handling Simulation

becomes important when understanding the system's architecture. The dependency relationships illustrated in Figure 3.6 provide an indication of the direction of the structural relationships among the classes within the various packages. Notice that the eventhandling package is dependent on the util package, which implies that classes within eventhandling can import classes within util but not vice versa. This distinction is an important one because our package dependencies must be consistent with the relationships expressed on the corresponding class diagrams.

Package diagrams, when combined with class diagrams, are an extremely effective mechanism to communicate a system's architecture. A diagram such as the one in Figure 3.6 provides a high-level glimpse into a system's overall structure. Based on this high-level view, developers can make assumptions regarding the relationships between individual classes, which becomes especially helpful as new developers join the project and need to be quickly brought up to speed—

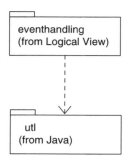

Figure 3.6   Package Diagram for Event-Handling Simulation

or when developers need to maintain a system they may have previously worked on but haven't interacted with in some time. Either way, this form of "architectural modeling" is beneficial. The code for this example can be found in Appendix C.

3.6   Conclusion

As we've seen, many of the elements that compose the UML have a precise mapping to the Java programming language, which is consistent with the claims that the UML is a precise and unambiguous communication mechanism. As individuals associated with software development, we must interpret each of these elements in a fashion that is faithful to this claim. Different interpretations of these elements can result in miscommunication, which is one of the challenges the UML attempts to resolve.

Though the UML is precise and unambiguous, we also must make sure that we don't derive more meaning than our diagrams actually convey. The UML is not a visual programming language but a modeling language. As such, the intent is not to model at the same level of detail at which code exists. For instance, an association has a multiplicity adornment associated with it at each end. If at one end the muliplicity is 0..*, we must interpret this as an optional collection. Therefore, we must accommodate for the potential of a null object reference in our code. The way in which we accommodate this is typically left up to the implementor. It may be implemented as an array, a vector, or a custom collection class. The diagram typically doesn't state how to implement something, communicating instead only that we must accommodate that need.

CHAPTER 4

The UML and Software Process

The goal is to develop better software, not necessarily to develop software better.
Emphasize principles, not process. Doing so enables us to improve process by adjusting principles.

The role of software process (which we define in section 4.0) in any software development effort is extremely important. While the UML is not coupled to any software process, nor is it a process itself, the true value of the UML is fully realized when utilized with a process. Unfortunately, the software industry isn't as standardized on the issue of software process as it is on the issue of which modeling language to use. Today, the industry abounds with software processes, each of which falls into a few specific categories. Our intent in this chapter isn't to present a favorite process nor to create a new process. Instead, from the existing set of widely recognized software processes, we cull the best practices associated with software development that can contribute to a successful project.

In fact, were we to carefully evaluate some of the more common processes today, we would find that within each process exists a common thread of best practices. These best practices have been compiled over the course of many years by some of the industry's best methodologists. Therefore, even if we aren't interested in adopting a formal software process, we should be interested in understanding how we can take advantage of the best practices that help us develop better software. In this chapter, we explore these best practices and how the UML can be used with them. Appendix A discusses two popular processes: the Rational Unified Process (UP) and Extreme Programming (XP).

Formal Process

Many formal processes focus on the production of documentation. While this documentation serves in maintaining the system, it's extremely important to remember that the goal of our software development effort is not to produce excessive amounts of documentation, but to produce an executable system that meets users' requirements. Documentation should be produced only if it contributes to the successful production of an application that fulfills user requirements. Regardless of what any process calls for, our goal in software development must be to develop better software, not to follow each step of a formal process that promises to help us develop software better. Remember that the intent is not to model but to analyze problems and design effective solutions.

4.0   Process Defined

Though we refuse to focus explicitly on any existing process, it's important that we understand what a software process is. First, any software process should have a universal goal. This goal must be to translate a set of user requirements into an executable system fulfilling those requirements. At first, this goal may seem obvious; however, examining many processes reveals that the intent of some may be to produce documentation. While documentation serves an important role, it isn't the primary work we wish to produce when developing software. We must remind ourselves that the only documentation that we should consider producing is that which contributes to a more successful piece of software.

Second, we want to define the term *software process* in an easily understood manner: A software process defines who does what and when they do it throughout the course of a software development effort. Unfortunately, this definition is oversimplified. In addition, the set of steps composing a process should be repeatable. If a process isn't repeatable, it's difficult to ensure that each of the systems we develop achieve a consistent rate of success. A process also must be customizable. Because no two development efforts are the same, as we reuse processes on new development efforts, we must apply the best of what works on the present development project, discarding anything that doesn't contribute to success. In fact, most processes recommend this approach. While many discussions on software processes present the process in a structured and rigid manner, it isn't by intent. They're presented in this manner to help us understand the process basics. At each point in the process, different organizations will need to apply the process somewhat differently. In this sense, a formal process is simply a template that can be applied to a software development effort and customized as needed.

As stated previously, the goal of any process must be the creation of a system that fulfills user requirements. As such, processes define roles that individuals must fulfill to create tangible items that contribute to a system's success. Therefore, throughout the course of this book, we use the term *worker* when referencing a role that an individual is playing when developing software. We use the term *artifact* in reference to a tangible item that is produced by a worker. Finally, an *activity* represents the actions performed by a worker to produce an artifact. These activities contain the best practices that, when carried out by workers, contribute to the creation of a more successful software system.

4.1   Best Practices

While our primary emphasis is to discuss how we can take advantage of the UML to develop better software, a number of other contributing factors, with the UML being only a single aspect, are pertinent. A tool such as the UML serves us well only when used in conjunction with these other aspects. Therefore, while our emphasis may steer toward the UML, we do so in a fashion that carefully considers many other best practices of object-oriented design and

Terminology

Though at times our terminology may resemble that used within other common software processes, it's purely coincidental. While our discussion in this chapter is focused on best practices, it in no way promotes one process over another. In this sense, we are process independent throughout our discussions. We feel that different development teams demand different software processes, based on team dynamics and organizational culture, but that all software processes should promote a common set of best practices.

software development. Using each of these best practices in conjunction with the UML yields a more resilient system, and we intend to consider each of these practices as our discussions progress, emphasizing the UML.

Our best practices, discussed in this section, emphasize those practices that contribute most to the timeframe between the gathering of requirements and the representation of these requirements in code. While certainly other best practices exist that encompass other stages of the full software lifecycle, they're beyond the scope of our discussion.

4.1.1   Behavioral Driven

So far in this book, we've stressed that the success of our system is directly related to how well it fulfills user requirements. Requirements, from the user's perspective, represent the behavior of the system. Our users typically don't care how the application is internally structured. An elegant internal architecture doesn't help much if it doesn't meet user requirements or at least adapt gracefully to these requirements. Therefore, our entire development effort must emphasize the realization of these requirements within our software application.

Ironically, this approach is a bit different from how developers, architects, or designers typically look at the software system. Before these workers can begin designing or coding a system's behavior, a structural skeleton must first be in place. This structural skeleton is our system's architecture. In this regard, these workers typically work in the reverse order from the order in which most other workers involved in software development work. Users, analysts, testers, and others typically view a system from a behavioral aspect. Consequently, because users and analysts work together to establish the system's requirements, it only makes sense that these requirements are documented in a behavioral fashion. Therefore, before a developer, designer, or architect can truly begin designing the system, he or she must first determine a structure for the system that accommodates the required behavior. We've described a subliminal transformation that takes place. Because the system is structured around the concept of classes, packages, and their relationships, a developer must first translate the behavioral requirements into a set of objects that collaborate. Based on these collaborations, structural relationships among the classes will be discovered, and this determines the system's structure.

Whether the previously described transformation takes place explicitly or implicitly, it does take place. In fact, this transformation takes place as we progress throughout the various stages of the software lifecycle. Therefore, each stage produces a set of artifacts that serve as inputs into the next stage. In Section 4.2, we introduce techniques that can be used to make this transformation more precise. In Chapter 8, when we discuss behavioral modeling, we explore more fully how this transformation can be performed.

4.1.2   Architecture Centric

A heavy emphasis must be placed on the architecture of our software systems. We've briefly explored the impact that architecture has on our software. Whether the process is centered on the development of components or a robust set of classes, architecture plays a key role. In Chapter 1, we discussed the impact that the desire for a system to evolve has upon the architectural stability of our software system. Because of this impact, our system's architecture plays a key role in how well our system can adapt to change. Therefore, we must emphasize our system's most significant elements throughout all stages of the development lifecycle. In Chapters 7, 8, and 9, we emphasize the many design decisions we face during development and their resulting impact on our software's architecture. In addition, Chapter 10 is devoted exclusively to the exploration of ways to model our system's architectural mechanisms.

4.1.3   Iterative

In debating iterative development, some individuals associate iterative development with hacking, which is not the case. Iterative development focuses on growing the system in small, incremental, and planned steps. At the beginning of each iteration, a well-established set of goals must be established. If not, we should question the value of the iteration. At the end of each iteration, these goals should be realized. If not, we need to accommodate the goals in subsequent iterations. Iterative development requires continuous planning to help mitigate risk. Continuous planning makes iterative development different from the traditional waterfall model. When developing iteratively, we don't attempt to identify up front all requirements the system must eventually support. Instead, shorter cycles enable us to almost continuously identify requirements and design effective solutions. These two approaches to software development are discussed more thoroughly in Section 4.2.

Unlike other best practices, such as refactoring (discussed in Section 4.1.4), iterative development is a management best practice, not a developer best practice. Project management and project stakeholders typically determine the time period spent on a single iteration. While an iteration should produce a set of artifacts, these artifacts don't necessarily have to be external but may be internal to the development team. Regardless, the importance of iterative development can't be underestimated. Iterations enable us to continuously emphasize our other best practices.

4.1.4   Refactoring

As we develop software, the most emphasis typically is placed on providing support for requirements within the system. Throughout the course of implementing requirements, it isn't uncommon to encounter areas within our application that are inflexible. This should be expected because it's only natural that the internal structure should be compromised as we add more code to a system. Refactoring is the process of improving our software's internal structure. In the first notable work on refactoring, Martin Fowler provides the following definition:

> *Refactoring is the process of changing a software system in such a way that it does not alter the external behavior of the code, yet improves its internal structure. [FOWLER99]*

This definition makes an extremely important distinction. Refactoring implies that the modifications we make to a software system are to improve the structure, not to provide features enhancement. This distinction is subtle but critical. These two maintenance activities should be kept separated by crisp boundaries. Not separating them will complicate our testing efforts: We won't know whether the errors we encounter are the result of a change based on the evolution of requirements or due to an enhancement of our code structure.

This point emphasizes another extremely valuable practice when refactoring. Whenever we change the structure of our code, whether it be to accommodate a requirements change or to improve our system's architecture, a chance always exists that the change may introduce a bug. Because of this possibility, it's important that we create programmatic tests that can be used to validate that any change made to our code structure hasn't introduced any new uncertainties. If the tests run correctly, we can assure ourselves of their accuracy.

Refactoring is an extremely valuable tool. Yet some development teams view refactoring as overhead and discourage its application, which is a critical mistake. Consider the importance that architecture plays within our development effort. If we truly believe that the architectural resiliency of our application impacts the ease with which we perform the maintenance activity, then we should make sure that refactoring takes place to ensure that our system's skeletal structure evolves as the system grows, to accommodate further growth in the future. Assuming we have test cases that can validate any changes, it should ease any trepidation we have pertaining to refactoring. In fact, refactoring is just one technique we can employ to ensure we maintain our architecture-centric views throughout development, because of refactoring's emphasis on improving our application's design.

4.1.5   Visual Modeling

In Chapter 2, we discussed the importance of the UML in the software development effort. We explained its advantages by visualizing our software systems and using it as a communication and problem-solving tool throughout the entire development lifecycle. When we are unsure of the approach we wish to take when solving a complex design problem, it's advantageous to spend some time elaborating the design in visual form first, and using the precise and unambiguous nature of the UML to obtain feedback from peers and mentors. Doing so contributes to a more resilient, effective, and flexible design. Like refactoring, the UML is a way to maintain our architecture-centric views throughout development.

4.1.6   Simple Prototypes

Even the most experienced designers lack the ability to create perfect software on their first attempt. Therefore, creating simple, throwaway prototypes early and often contributes to a more resilient, robust, and flexible final product. At first, this effort may seem wasteful, but considering that our first attempt at design never exactly reflects the final product, creating these simple prototypes is justified. Consider the following stated by some very well-respected technologists:

- In the *Mythical Man-Month*, Frederick Brooks states that we should "plan to throw one away; you will, anyhow." [BROOKS95]

Modeling and Refactoring

Modeling and refactoring are two complementary, not competing, techniques that can be used to help emphasize architecture. Refactoring is typically performed after the code is written and involves rewriting a portion of the code, resulting in an easier to understand, more flexible structure. Modeling, on the other hand, emphasizes establishing architecture prior to writing code, with the intent of specifying early a clear, concise architecture. In this regard, modeling can be thought of as an active approach to architecture, and refactoring as an emergent approach. When used in conjunction, we maintain our architectural focus throughout the development lifecycle.

- In *Patterns for Evolving Frameworks*, Don Roberts and Ralph Johnson state that "People develop abstractions by generalizing from concrete examples. Every attempt to determine the correct abstractions on paper without actually developing a running system is doomed to failure. No one is that smart." [PLOP98]

Seeing your design work, and proving its effectiveness, even at a high level, provides a great deal of comfort. Our prototypes often can evolve into our first attempt at the system, other times not, which largely depends on how "right" our initial design was. Either way, the purpose of the prototype is well served. Keep in mind, too, that these prototypes need not always be related to the user interface; in fact, many times, they won't be. Instead, they serve as validation of our initial design and can be thought of as tests that confirm that our design actually works as intended.

4.2   Development Lifecycle and the UML

Much has been written comparing and contrasting the pros and cons of conventional waterfall versus modern iterative lifecycle models. We see no room for debate on this issue at all because we are firm believers that an iterative approach is used regardless. Because of the impossibility of performing each step of the development lifecycle once and only once, expecting to produce a system that is flexible, resilient, and robust, we simply assume that each of the previous steps of that lifecycle have to be revisited in the future.

One of the primary differences between the waterfall and iterative lifecycle model is planning and risk mitigation. The iterative lifecycle plans to iterate through the development and refinement of requirements many times because it's understood that requirements change. Through planning, we can change scope, adjust resources, or modify the time we have to develop, subsequently mitigating risk. Because all requirements aren't fixed initially, we accommodate risk by making continual adjustments throughout the project lifecycle.

In contrast, a waterfall lifecycle attempts to capture all requirements initially, before moving onto the next phase of the development lifecycle. In addition, because our requirements are organized around business processes, which we call *use cases*, it's much easier to identify the higher-priority use cases and focus on developing the functionality for them first. The likelihood also is high that individual use cases can be developed simultaneously.

Open for debate, however, is the length of time spent on each activity throughout the lifecycle. While some feel that more time spent early on design results in a more stable code base, others feel that because of the unpredictable nature of software, spending more time on design early is wasteful. We don't

Mitigating Risk

Risk mitigation is critical. Performing all steps of software development lifecycle for each iteration enables us to identify areas of risk earlier, which is one of the primary advantages of the iterative lifecycle model over the waterfall model. The waterfall model emphasizes risk later in the process. While not intentional, risk mitigation is much more difficult. As obstacles are encountered during a waterfall project, it's much easier to put off dealing with the obstacle until later, instead focusing on the simpler aspects of the system first. Dealing with these obstacles later in the project reduces the likelihood that any contingency plans can be implemented.

intend to discuss which way is best; instead, we feel it is largely dependent on the nature of the project. Projects with large teams or more mission-critical, high-risk projects are apt to spend more time analyzing and designing to help mitigate risk. The amount of time spent planning often is dictated by project stakeholders and isn't open for discussion. In contrast, projects with small teams, or less critical projects, may take a more relaxed approach. Regardless of the intensity of our process, we feel strongly that utilizing the best practices contributes to developing a more successful software system. In fact, placing more emphasis on the best practices over any particular process yields the advantage of being able to improve the process by adjusting the principles, which is the focus of our discussion in this chapter. In Appendix A, we also discuss process, emphasizing the Rational Unified Process (RUP), and Extreme Programming (XP).

In Figure 4.1, we see the traditional stages of the software development lifecycle. While, at first, it may appear that a single iteration is simply an instance of a more traditional waterfall approach, this assumption isn't always incorrect. In fact, it's more appropriate to consider the amount of time devoted to each stage of the process throughout the development effort. A typical scenario is indicated by the percentages associated with each stage. While no uniformly, global percentages apply, these values serve to represent the amount of time spent within each stage, which can vary tremendously based on the project. As we progress through our discussions, we focus on two primary aspects of the software lifecycle. First, we discuss the previously described best practices and how they are applied to build better software. This discussion includes how the best practices should be applied at different stages of the development lifecycle. Second, we focus on the dynamics that take place when executing an iteration, instead of attempting to perform the various activities of each iteration linearly.

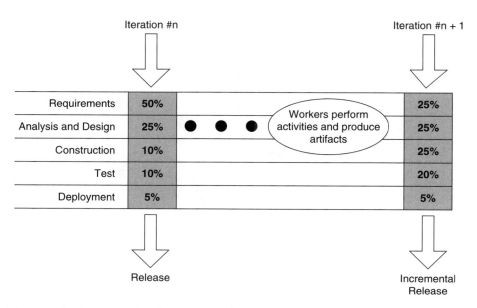

Figure 4.1   Iterative Lifecycle

Regardless of what iteration we're currently developing, it's important to execute each stage of the process. Neglecting to execute any step of the process results in a situation where an important artifact may not have been generated or a potential issue not identified. For instance, in an early iteration, we may spend 65 percent of our time analyzing requirements. Though we may not be ready to begin coding the fully realized application, we may wish to develop small prototypes that help us more fully understand the requirements in a technical manner. This process is advantageous to all workers involved. On many projects, those gathering requirements aren't the same individuals responsible for coding. Therefore, by enabling the architects, designers, and developers to participate earlier in the project, they gain further insight into the domain-specific software requirements, and how these requirements can be represented technically. This is the first step in identifying the architectural mechanisms that might be utilized within our system to ensure the application is resilient, flexible, and robust.

As we progress through our discussions of the various artifacts produced within each stage, many unanswered questions undoubtedly will surface. In the first five chapters, we emphasize the artifacts produced and how they're related. The remaining chapters explore best practices associated with the creation of these various artifacts, especially as the practices relate to object-oriented design in Java. Because of this, much of what we talk about takes place between the creation of our use cases and the construction of our code—the critical time within the life of a system where the most significant decisions pertaining to the software's architecture are made. Therefore, a discussion of the test and deployment stages, while we acknowledge are important stages, is largely omitted from this text.

4.2.1   Requirements

Our top priority during requirements is to establish agreement with users who are identifying the primary functions the system must support. This process is required because we can't design our system until we understand what that system must do. In earlier iterations, more time is spent analyzing requirements, which is reflected by the percentage values in Figure 4.1. These requirements drive not only the current iteration, but also future iterations, resulting in an application development effort that emphasizes behavior.

During the requirements-gathering process, it's important that workers, most likely analysts, produce artifacts that capture the specifications of the system. The primary artifact produced during requirements is the use case model. This model captures the essence of the system from a user's perspective. In this sense, the use case model is analogous to the use case view presented in Chapter 3. The use case model typically is composed of the following set of elements:

- **Glossary:** A glossary may be produced that defines the significant terms used on the project.
- **Activity diagrams:** Activity diagrams are discussed in Chapter 3.
- **Use case diagrams:** Also discussed in Chapter 3, use case diagrams contain a set of related use cases, each of which captures a primary business process in a behavioral fashion. Use case diagrams clearly illustrate which actors initiate and participate in which use cases. Use case diagrams also are excellent at showing the crisp boundaries of the system.
- **Use cases:** Each use case identifies a primary business process that provides a result of observable value to an actor.
- **Actors:** An actor represents a role played by a user of the system. Actors are always external to the system.
- **Relationships:** Relationships appear on use case diagrams and illustrate the relationships between actors and the use cases they can initiate. Other, less frequently used, relationships exist as well.
- **Use case specifications:** A use case specification is associated with each use case and is a more detailed description of the requirements

associated with the business process represented by the use case. This specification typically contains information that includes a high-level introduction to the use case and a description of the use case's many different sequence of actions. The use case specification is explored in Chapter 6.

- **Packages:** As noted in Chapter 3, packages are grouping mechanisms that enable us to structure our system in a manner that makes it easier to understand. Packages in the use case model typically are used to differentiate the significant processes our application supports.
- **User interface prototype:** Graphical prototypes representing the flow of the application, and how it will look to users, can help tremendously in working with users to flesh out requirements. In this sense, a user interface prototype can serve two purposes. The first is to provide developers the foundation upon which to base the user interface. The second is that users think more in terms of what they want the system to do when they actually can see what the system might look like.

Of course, these elements are only a sampling of some of the artifacts that might be produced as the result of the requirements stage. In fact, depending on the development process, these artifacts may vary. It's common, and actually highly recommended, that development teams produce the artifacts that are most useful in the context instead of producing a set of artifacts specified by a process. As we move from requirements to analysis and design, it's important that we capture the essence, from the user's perspective, of what the system should do.

In Figure 4.2, we see a sampling of the composition of a use case model. The use case diagram in the figure illustrates an oversimplified diagram representing an online banking system. A bank customer actor can view account information online, as well as transfer funds between accounts. In this system, each of these

Use Case Model Structure

The way in which we organize our use cases is important. Effective organization means that it will be easier to find business processes and associated behavior. However, even more important is satisfying user requirements in the allotted time frame. Don't spend a lot of time trying to find the best solution the first time. Instead, find something that works and continue to refine and improve that system throughout the development effort.

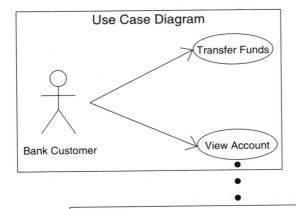

Figure 4.2   Requirements Artifacts and Model Structure

use cases is treated as two separate business processes, both of which can be initiated by any bank customer.

Beneath the use case diagram in Figure 4.2, we see the use case specification for the View Account use case. This specification describes the purpose of the use case, as well as providing descriptions for the most significant variants of the View Account business process. Attached to each use case is a specification describing it. This description serves as a valuable source of information about the main events of a use case. In Figure 4.2, the primary flow represents the path through the use case that would be indicative of the desired outcome for a bank customer. Ultimately, however, numerous other events can cause the system to stray from this primary flow. Thus, we can state that a single use case has multiple flows of events. For instance, what should our system do when the bank customer specifies an invalid login? These variations of the primary flow are typically called *alternate flows*. In the simplified case shown in Figure 4.2, we didn't specify any alternate flows, but a discussion on this topic is in Chapter 6. In this chapter, we are most concerned with how our use case model is structured.

4.2.2   Analysis and Design

During the analysis and design stage, we must transform the specified requirements into a set of collaborating objects that fulfill those requirements. The stability and thoroughness of the requirements gathered have a tremendous impact on our ability to do so successfully. If the requirements are fairly stable, and not likely to undergo changes soon, we should have a much easier time designing our system. If, on the other hand, requirements are extremely dynamic and generally instable, designing a system will be extremely difficult, if not impossible. We typically find that we are somewhere in the middle. In such cases, we must identify those areas most likely to change and turn back to our analysts and users, asking for more information, or if that isn't possible, we should spend additional time designing these more dynamic areas of the system.

At this point, our requirements have been identified, and it's time to begin identifying the set of artifacts that will represent our application from a more technical perspective. Again, in Chapter 6, we discuss how to do this part of the process. In this chapter, we discuss what we want to produce. Given the set of requirements, it's time to realize these requirements in the form of a design model, which contains the following important artifacts:

- **Architecture document:** During development, the internal structure of our system should be driven by a guiding set of principles that serve as the technical vision upon which our system is built. The architecturally

Analysis versus Design

The line between analysis and design in an object-oriented system is not a fine one. If such a line existed, analysis would emphasize the conceptual model and design, the specification model. However, it's not recommended that we create separate analysis and design models because they involve too much overhead. Instead, we recommend that the analysis model grow into the design model. In fact, due to the nature of object-oriented design and encapsulation, we'll find it's common for a portion of the system to be designed in detail, whereas another portion of the system is barely designed at all. This is the power of abstraction and is manifest in the various interfaces that exist across the seams in our system.

significant elements should be captured and made available to enforce restrictions placed upon our software's infrastructure, and to aid developers in understanding the software's infrastructure. The architecture document captures the most architecturally significant elements across all models created. In this regard, the architecture document contains the significant use cases, classes, packages, and any other artifact that characterizes the architectural theme of an application.

- **Interaction diagrams:** As mentioned in Chapter 3, interaction diagrams illustrate the behavior of a portion of the system via a set of collaborating objects.
- **Class diagrams:** Also mentioned in Chapter 3, a class diagram illustrates the structural relationships among classes. Class diagrams are useful for showing the coupling that exists between classes, including relationships involving usage, inheritance, and interface realization.
- **Package diagrams:** While not a formal diagram in the UML, a package diagram is one of the most useful. Package diagrams enable us to represent our system's high-level dependency structure. In this sense, a package diagram is the specification of our software system at a much higher level of abstraction. The importance of package diagrams, and how to use them effectively, is discussed in Chapter 10, when we discuss architectural modeling.
- **Packages:** The design model contains two types of packages. First are those packages that enable us to differentiate various views of the design model, such as use case realizations, process models, and implementation models. Second are those packages that map directly to our Java source code and application package structure. They are represented in code during construction.
- **Data models:** Business applications take a data-centric view of the world. Therefore, most business applications focus on supplying data to a user and applying various behavioral business rules to that data. In this regard, generating a data model is critical. The creation of a data model is performed during analysis and design based on the requirements set forth during requirements gathering.
- **Process models:** A process model illustrates the processes and threads that compose an application. Similar to how we trace use cases to the classes that realize these use cases, we trace these classes to the processes and threads in which they run. The process model and process view discussed in Chapter 3 are synonymous. We do not discuss process models in this book.
- **Implementation models:** An implementation model shows the components that compose our application. In Java, a component may consist

of multiple classes. For example, an Enterprise JavaBeans (EJB) component may be composed of many different classes that provide the EJB
with its functionality. The implementation model traces the components to the classes that provide the components with their functionality. The implementation model and development view discussed in
Chapter 3 are synonymous. Components are briefly discussed in
Section 10.5.

Again, the intent of the analysis and design stage is to produce a set of artifacts that serve as useful inputs into the construction stage. Our system is fully
and exactly realized at the construction stage. We should produce analysis and
design artifacts only if they serve as useful inputs to construction. Needlessly
producing artifacts that serve only as documentation and provide no value during construction should be seriously questioned.

In Figure 4.3, we again see our View Account use case, though in a somewhat different context. In this figure, our use case is attached via a generalization relationship to a collaboration element. In Chapter 3, we introduced the
collaboration element and stated that while a use case represents requirements
from a customer's vantage point in the use case view, a collaboration models
these same set of requirements from a developer's perspective. The primary benefit of using a collaboration is to achieve traceability. *Traceability* is the ability
to trace elements in one view into elements in another view. In Figure 4.3, our
collaboration is named "View Account Realization" because it's going to serve
as the set of elements that are responsible for representing the View Account use
case from a developer's perspective.

Similar in nature to how a use case has an associated use case specification,
a collaboration has an associated set of interaction and class diagrams, called a
use case realization. For each flow of events associated with a use case, an asso-

System of Transformations

We mentioned previously that transformations take place when we
develop software and represent behavioral requirements with an object-
oriented structure. These behavioral transformations are our use case realizations, and they can be an extremely effective way to work through
complex requirements. As we mentioned in Section 4.2.1, and we'll continue to stress throughout this book, these techniques are useful, but they
aren't applicable in all situations. Some use cases may be simple enough
that we express their realizations directly in code.

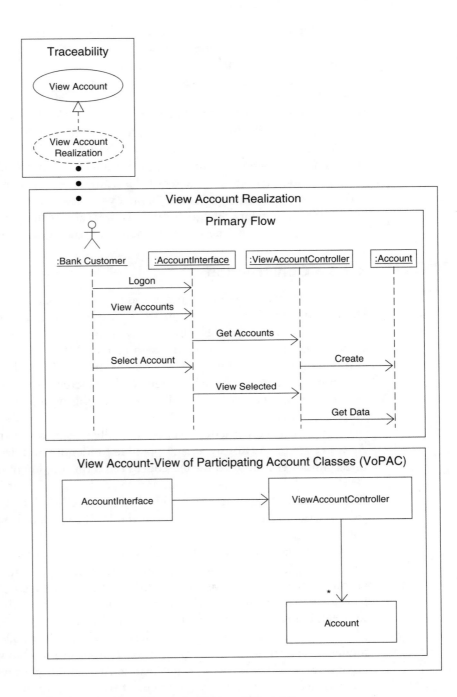

Figure 4.3 Analysis and Design Artifacts and Model Structure

ciated interaction diagram is created, specifying the objects working together to realize that use case. Because a message can be sent to an object only if the two classes have a structural relationship, upon identifying the set of behaviors realizing a use case, we can analyze our interaction diagrams, identifying the structural relationships. This results in a class diagram, which we'll call the "View of Participating Classes (VOPC)" because it is the set of classes that participate in the realization of the use case to which they are attached.

At this point, we should clearly see the traceability that has been established. Were the View Account use case to undergo a requirements change, there should be no question as to the set of classes that have to be modified to accommodate that requirements change. In fact, we're assured of this because we can trace the requirements change through the traceability diagram, into the collaboration and corresponding set of interaction diagrams that realize that use case.

4.2.3   Construction

At this point, we are ready to begin coding our application. The design model should have established at least an architectural vision that will serve as a guide throughout development. Playing an important role at this point are the ambiguities that might surface when translating our UML diagrams into source code. If different developers interpret different elements differently in code, identical diagrams could result in inconsistent code structures. In Chapter 3, we presented the mappings from the UML to Java. At this point, we should apply these mappings diligently.

As we begin construction, we undoubtedly will encounter many unknowns. As we've stated previously, it isn't possible to identify and design for all of the uncertainties encountered during code. Nor is this the intent of the UML. The UML is not a visual programming language, and as such, it isn't possible nor desirable to represent every single Java entity in a UML diagram. If we could do so, we wouldn't need to design using the UML; we could immediately begin construction.

Our previously produced models should serve as guides through the construction stage. They should communicate precisely what the architectural vision of our system is, as established during the analysis and design stage. Developers should understand the constraints imposed by the architecture, as well as the mechanisms to which the architecture adheres.

As we begin to translate our models to code and our code strays from our model, it is important that we make a conscious decision as to why. Quite possibly it's because the design was not flexible enough. Or perhaps it's because we don't understand completely the intent of the design. In both cases, we should

Expendable Diagrams

Some diagrams aren't intended to survive the life of our system. UML diagrams serve two purposes: communication and problem solving. If a diagram risks becoming outdated because it specifies the system at a lower level, it doesn't mean that it was created wastefully. Perhaps it was created to help the original designer overcome a complex design challenge. If, however, a diagram is created for other reasons, its existence should be questioned. On the other hand, if we are forward- and reverse-engineering our code, more detailed diagrams don't run the risk of becoming outdated because we can always reverse-engineer our code to reveal the most current diagrams.

seriously consider analyzing the problem again and consider an alternative, possibly more flexible, solution. It can have a dramatic impact on our system.

We also must decide which UML diagrams will live as our system grows and which are deemed expendable. No one has ever said that because we create a diagram, we must maintain that diagram. If the intent of a diagram is to solve a problem, quite possibly, it has served its purpose. If, however, the intent of our diagram is to serve as an ongoing communication mechanism, it's more important that the diagram be synchronized with our system. Assuming we aren't using an automated tool to keep synchronized, the level of detail represented in these persistent diagrams can be a cause for concern. We must be cautious and avoid falling prey to extreme model maintenance.

The diagrams we choose to grow with our system should be those requiring the least amount of effort to maintain. These diagrams typically communicate higher-level abstractions and usually aren't representative of a detailed aspect of our system. It's more common for these diagrams to capture the essence of what the system, or a significant segment of the system, does. It can be difficult to convince ourselves that discarding diagrams is acceptable. Consider that once a system is built, diagrams serve only as the system's specification. Of course, the problem with technical specifications is that we can trust them only if we are sure they're accurate. If we aren't able to trust a diagram, it's of no value because we must eventually analyze the code to find our answer anyway.

The code we would write as the result of our View Account realization follows. Note the instance variables defined as the result of the associative relationships depicted on the class diagram in Figure 4.3. Of particular interest is the declaration of the accounts `Vector` in the `ViewAccountController` class, which is derived as a result of the many multiplicity indicators on that class diagram. The code that follows is the direct result of applying the UML to Java language mappings introduced in Chapter 3:

```
public class AccountInterface {
    private ViewAccountController _controller;

    public void Logon() { … }
    public void ViewAccount { … }
    public void SelectAccount { … }
}
public class ViewAccountController {
    private java.util.Vector accounts;

    public void GetAcounts() { … }
    public void ViewSelected() { … }
}
public class Account {
    public Object GetData() { … }
}
```

4.2.4   Testing

While one of the most important stages within the software lifecycle, testing is too often the most ignored. Testing is the point at which we validate that our system adheres to the set of requirements set forth by the users or project stake-holders. Many different types of testing are performed to validate a software system, including unit testing, integration testing, system testing, functional testing, performance testing, and load testing. In this section, we emphasize the testing performed by developers.

At the most fundamental level, we should be testing constantly. After each small change or feature enhancement, we should test to make sure that the latest addition to the system hasn't broken it. While testing is beyond the scope of our discussion, it should be performed continuously. A test model may be produced that reflects the various test scenarios the system must pass to reach deployment.

4.2.5   Deployment

Once we've built and tested our application, we're ready to deploy our application to a production environment. In terms of the UML, this stage typically involves creating a deployment diagram. Deployment diagrams illustrate the physical topology of a system, usually by showing the devices and processors, along with the accompanying connection, that make up the physical infrastructure of the application. Deployment diagrams fall within the physical view of our system, which is beyond the scope of discussion in this book, not because of complexity, but simply because we emphasize best practices of design. We do encourage studying additional material, such as *The Unified Modeling Language User Guide* [BOOCH99], to obtain a deeper understanding of the benefits associated with deployment diagrams.

4.3 The Full Lifecycle

Figure 4.4 illustrates the full lifecycle of traceable artifacts, with the aspects of interest to us illustrated in an expanded form. In the top left corner exists a use case. This use case documents a business process and is contained in the use case view. To the direct right of the use case, traced along the realization relationship, we see a collaboration signifying the realization for this use case. Expanded beneath this realization is a set of interaction diagrams and a class diagram illustrating the UML diagrams that comprise the realization. The center section containing the various packages indicates that the classes contained within the realizations must be allocated to their respective packages before we can begin coding. In this regard, our realizations serve as a "work area" where we transform the use cases to a behavioral collaboration of objects. However, because each use case can be transformed independently, at some point, we must bring all of our use case realizations together in the form of our completed system. This stage is a great opportunity to begin identifying potential reuse areas within the application, and we expand on this discussion in Chapter 6.

At the bottom left in Figure 4.4, we see three additional packages. Each of these packages indicates a different view of our system. While we won't elaborate on these packages, it's important to note that the packages representing our application in the center section should be traced to the processes and threads, components, and physical machines within each of the views at the bottom left.

4.4 Conclusion

In this chapter, we presented the important role that software process plays in producing more reliable, architecturally resilient, and functionally correct software. The best practices presented in this chapter serve as a guide throughout all stages of the software development lifecycle. Pragmatically, instead of religiously, applying these best practices in the production of various artifacts will contribute to the successful creation of a software system that fully and accurately meets user expectations.

Any and all artifacts that don't directly contribute to the development of software that meets our users' needs should be seriously questioned. In this

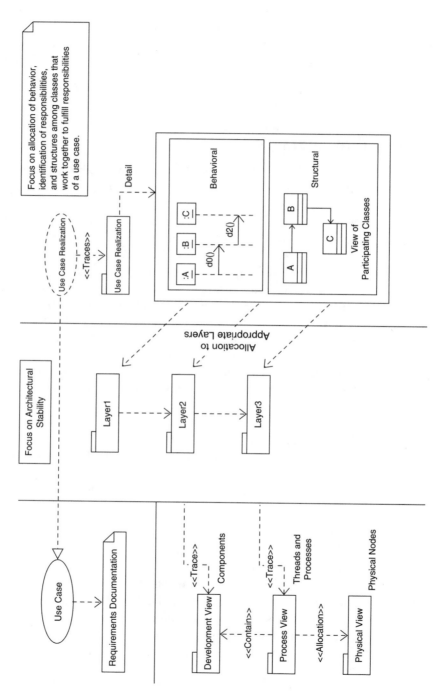

Figure 4.4   Lifecycle Traceability Map

chapter, we've presented a number of artifacts that we might consider productive and that can contribute to a more complete software specification. Each of these artifacts is closely related, and when built on top of each other, the true power of the UML is fully realized.

We should be cautious when producing detailed, low-level diagrams because they risk becoming outdated as our internal code structure changes. Instead, higher-level, architecturally significant diagrams should be created that communicate our architecture and solve complex architectural challenges. In general, our golden rule should be to *produce any artifact only if it contributes positively to the development of better software.*

CHAPTER 5

Modeling Strategies

The way that we incorporate the UML into our development efforts contributes significantly to its successful adoption and, more importantly, to the success of our systems.

Technologies can be broken out into two categories: those that are critical to the development of software, and those that are helpful but not required. Programming languages, such as Java, fall into the first category. Without these primary technologies, we can't produce the source code that, when compiled, serves as the executable system. Many other technologies are supplementary technologies that contribute to the successful development of software but are not required for the production of an executable system. In fact, many of the best practices, including the UML and refactoring (the latter is discussed in Chapter 4), fall into this second category. Because many of these technologies are viewed as supplementary, it's easy to succumb to project pressures and revert to "hackerish" ways, failing to take advantage of the benefits of using these supplements. In fact, at these critical points in the life of our system, we most need these value-added complements.

Consequently, the way that we adopt the UML and integrate it into our development environment typically determines the success of using it. Many factors, many of which are not technical, impact this decision. The culture of our development team and the traditional approach to developing software can have a dramatic impact on our integration strategy. In this chapter, we examine some of the components that impact our development team's adoption of the UML. This adoption, or transitional, period is driven by an integration strategy.

5.0   Integration Goals

When integrating the UML into our environment, we must consider the benefits we wish to realize from its use. Ironically, some organizations often attempt to utilize a technology without having a clear vision of the benefits they wish to gain from it. In this section, we discuss the different ways that we can use the UML in our development efforts, which we call our *integration goal*. In Section 5.1, we discuss the *integration factors* that impact our goals when adopting an overall UML *integration strategy*.

Figure 5.1 illustrates two aspects that impact our integration efforts. A development approach defines the degree to which our development team will use a common UML vision to specify a system, whereas a tool approach represents the software tools our team will use. A development approach and tool approach combine to form the goals of our overall integration strategy. These two approaches, shown in Figure 5.1, represent boundary conditions, and many variants of each can be applied. A successful adoption typically is dictated by, among other things, organizational and team dynamics, which is the emphasis of our discussion on integration factors in the next section.

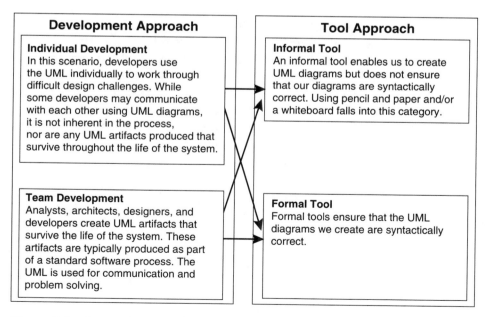

Figure 5.1   Aspects Impacting Integration

5.0.1   Development Approach

The development approach defines the degree to which our team will adopt the UML. While individual development and team development represent the two extremes, it's also possible to adopt variations of each of these extremes. In this section, we discuss some of the issues and benefits of each development approach.

5.0.1.1   Individual Development

The individual development approach may be the simplest approach to integration, yet it most likely offers the least return. It's unlikely that any formal integration strategy will be needed, and the individual development approach typically is a grassroots effort that is driven by team members interested in the UML and the advantages of modeling. Other team members, not interested, may react negatively to their fellow team members spending project time learning the UML. It's not uncommon for friction to exist as "time spent on design" may not be the "way things are done around here." In fact, project stakeholders and management may not realize that this effort is actually under way.

It's also likely that other best practices aren't currently being taken advantage of, and a formal, repeatable software process may not be in place. The result may be software systems that are difficult to extend and grow as requirements change. The difficulty often can be traced back to inflexible software architectures resulting from failure to actively establish an architectural vision.

On the other hand, teams that come together and decide that they want to take advantage of what the UML offers can benefit from this approach. Allowing team members to familiarize themselves with various best practices on an individual basis helps after a formal integration strategy is devised, because at that point, many people have a feeling for how to best use the various technologies. Individuals have probably explored different ways to apply these best practices and have written a list of modeling idioms that, when shared with other team members, contributes positively to a more formal integration strategy. Unfortunately, teams such as this are somewhat rare because all team members must be individually driven to excel with technology, as well as to admit when mistakes are made and learn from them.

Possibly the greatest advantage when using the individual development approach is the low cost or negligible resource overhead. Little investment need be made in training, and if the project is a grassroots effort, it's doubtful that a great amount was spent on a formal modeling tool. Therefore, it isn't necessary that individuals adhere to strict UML syntax because any diagram created typically will be used only to solve an immediate challenge. Keep in mind, however, that these inconsistencies create unwanted ambiguities in our diagrams that may result in communication challenges, and team members eventually may question the value of the UML.

Diagrams may be drawn using an informal drawing tool, or possibly not an electronic tool at all, instead opting for a whiteboard or pencil and paper. While a useful approach for problem solving, these types of diagrams usually exist without any traceability benefits realized by using repeatable processes. Instead of producing models that live and grow with the system, individual diagrams usually are produced in a vacuum, making it difficult for artifacts to survive their immediate need.

Because we're typically working individually to solve problems, one of the most notable disadvantages of this approach is that little cohesion may exist among team members in establishing a common architectural vision. This lack of cohesion results in architectural instability, and team members typically don't have a concise and consistent vision of our system's structure or behavior. Based on this single, though major, disadvantage, we recommend that any integration strategy eventually should emphasize a team development concept.

5.0.1.2   Team Development

A team development approach offers more reward than an individual approach to development. Any team approach should heavily emphasize the value of establishing an architectural vision and many other best practices. While the entire team might not contribute to the creation of the various architectural mechanisms, they certainly will use some common models to communicate the architecture and grow the system into the future.

In addition to the architectural advantages associated with the team approach, full lifecycle traceability probably can be achieved. Because all members on our team are taking advantage of the UML, the artifacts produced are traceable through each of our individual views. The simple fact that a team approach can help bring resilient architectures and lifecycle traceability to our application should be proof enough that this goal is the one we should be striving to achieve.

The challenge, however, is that all team members must understand not just the UML, but also the software process used to create our individual UML diagrams. Therefore, a team development approach typically involves a radical shift away from more traditional development methodologies to newer methodologies. The methodology used is truly the key to success when integrating the

UML on a team basis, and adopting a methodology is neither easy nor quick. Therefore, this approach requires planning and a great deal of patience. Team members should be made aware of the goals of the effort, so that each can work toward achieving the common vision. Therefore, we must consider team and lifecycle dynamics if we wish to utilize the UML throughout our team.

5.0.2   Tool Approach

The tool approach defines what, if any, supporting tools will be used to complement our development approach. The chosen tool approach must be consistent with our overall integration strategy. Less formal tools in an environment promoting a more ceremonial approach to software development may not enable our team to realize the highest degree of benefit. The converse is also true. In this section, we explore some of the advantages and disadvantages associated with using an informal versus a formal modeling tool.

5.0.2.1   *Informal Tool*

A less formal tool can provide different levels of support for the UML. Some multipurpose tools enable us to create visual diagrams but don't support the UML syntax. UML artifacts using just pencil and paper also are considered informal tools. Therefore, for our discussion in this section, we don't necessarily require that the tool be an electronic tool. Instead, the important considerations are how well the tool supports our development process, as well as how appropriately the tool supports model organization.

Using a less formal tool to create our UML artifacts typically implies that the tool doesn't provide inherent support for the UML syntax, the effect of which may be ambiguous communication among the team members. Thus, attempting to take advantage of the UML using an informal tool in a team development effort can be problematic. In addition to communication difficulties, it may be difficult to create a robust representation of our system because a tool that doesn't provide inherent UML support most likely doesn't adequately support our development process.

Because of the difficult challenges in using an informal tool in a team development effort, it's difficult to achieve a high degree of full lifecycle traceability. This difficulty may be related to the tools' lack of full lifecycle support, or it may be because the tool simply doesn't support the creation of a robust model, making it difficult to navigate the model. Therefore, a less formal tool, or a tool that doesn't map well to our development process, can be frustrating to work with.

Processes and Tools

If our development team also is considering the adoption of a formal software development process, it's important that the tools we use support the development process. The goal of any tool must be to add value to the development effort. If we continually find that a tool isn't complementary to our development efforts, we must seriously question the tool's value and thus the use of that tool. Just as any software application has requirements that our system must support, our development process has requirements that must be supported by our tools.

A less-formal tool, however, does offer some advantages. Most notably, it may be a cost-effective approach. If we can't effectively evaluate the likelihood that an integration strategy will be successful, a less-formal tool can reduce the cost of any attempt at integration. Careful consideration should be given to a phased approach, where we begin our integration efforts with an informal tool, continuously evaluating our progress. After we become comfortable with our progress, we then might begin an evaluation of tools until we find a tool that most closely supports our integration goals.

Another benefit of using an informal tool is that our development team can still actively problem-solve difficult design challenges. Whether this effort is an individual one or is made by a team, any active approach will result in a development effort that emphasizes architectural resiliency.

5.0.2.2   Formal Tool

A formal tool offers a number of advantages over that of an informal tool. However, before choosing a tool that provides support for the UML, we must carefully consider how we wish to use that tool and how well it supports our development process. We classify a formal tool as one that not only provides support for the UML syntax, but also supports effective model organization. Therefore, any formal tool should provide some degree of traceability between lifecycle artifacts. In the context of analysis and design, this implies that the tool must support traceability from the incoming artifacts, typically the requirements artifacts, through the output artifacts, which may consist of a process model, implementation model, and deployment model.

If we have decided to use a formal tool, management probably is aware of the UML integration effort. Therefore, it's vital that an integration strategy be created. If an integration strategy isn't present, we should seriously consider defining one. The lack of an integration strategy can result in frustration on the part of the development team, who might be struggling to understand the advantages of the tool, as well as how to most effectively utilize the tool. Using a formal tool on an individual basis over the long term may not provide the return on investment we should expect from purchasing such a tool. However, using a formal tool individually on a short-term basis can enable the development team to learn and understand the tool and how it can be used most effectively. This knowledge can bring great rewards, with reduced risk, in enabling team members to gain experience and insight into some modeling practices that can be learned only through experience. Regardless, this effort should be a short-term approach, and a formal integration strategy should clearly define a transition to a team development strategy. If an integration strategy hasn't been developed, it isn't uncommon to find team members, and management, questioning the value, and often the quality, of the tool simply because the true benefits haven't been fully realized.

Because of this requirement, this formal tool classification implies that the tool must support our software development process. Therefore, a formal tool most likely will be more costly than a less formal tool. The cost may be incurred due to the purchase price of the tool, the training required to learn the tool, or the time spent understanding how to most effectively use the tool. A classic mistake when adopting a formal tool is ignoring the need for formal training and mentoring in understanding the tool. If we don't allocate time and finances to the necessary training and mentoring that will be required by our development team, the likelihood of a successful tool integration effort is dramatically

Technology and Tools

Regardless of the claims of many tool vendors, support for round-trip engineering using the UML is not without its difficulties. The use of a tool's feature must be given careful consideration as to the invasive nature of that feature and the obstacles it may present. Any amount of time spent trying to understand a tool or work around a tool's bugs only detracts from the creation of software. Simply because a tool offers a feature doesn't mean we should use it. Therefore, we must assure ourselves that the use of a tool's feature brings more value to the development of software than if we weren't to use that feature at all.

reduced. We must be cautious not to divert so much effort to understanding the tool that we neglect the creation of the executable system, which is one of the greatest risks when adopting a formal tool.

On the other hand, a formal tool can offer some great advantages in the productivity of our team. While this productivity enhancement may not be realized during the initial phases of the development effort, it should be realized on subsequent upgrades or enhancements to the system. Because a formal tool should offer lifecycle traceability, it's much easier to trace changes in requirements to the classes that provide the implementation for those requirements. This can greatly facilitate system maintenance. In addition, it's more likely that the models we create will live and grow with the software system throughout the life of the system. Consequently, as new team members enter the project, it's much easier and faster for them to come up to speed on the software system's structure and behavior.

Most formal tools also offer some degree of forward- and reverse-engineering. While this characteristic offers some tremendous advantages, we must be cautious not to attempt utilizing every feature that a tool offers. The ease and efficiency with which our tool can generate code should be seriously evaluated. Any engineering of code must be more accurate and cost effective than the manual translation of our model into code. Remember that the UML isn't a visual programming language but a modeling language used to specify our software system. We shouldn't expect our UML models to generate all the code for us. Again, just because a tool offers a feature doesn't mean we should use it, nor does it imply that everyone else is using it. Our tools must add, not detract, value.

5.1   Integration Factors

In the previous section, we discussed the various approaches to integration we can take when adopting the UML as well as other best practices. In this section, we discuss those factors that must be carefully considered when creating our integration strategy. In an ideal situation, our teams use the UML in a team environment using a formal tool. This, however, may not always be possible. A number of considerations impact the time, cost, and effort required, which in turn will affect our development team's ability to realize this ideal scenario. In this section, we discuss some of these integration factors. Keep in mind that embodied within each of these integration factors are the best practices discussed in Chapter 4.

5.1.1 Development Culture

Of all the integration factors, the development culture may have the most dramatic impact on a successful integration strategy. The way that we currently develop software should determine our strategy. If our culture traditionally has accepted and promoted newer technologies, then an integration strategy most likely will be widely accepted. If, however, management and development team members are reluctant to try newer, progressive technologies, any adoption efforts may be compromised before they get under way.

In addition, we must carefully evaluate who is driving the integration effort. If it's driven by management, full lifecycle adoption probably will succeed. If the integration effort is a grassroots effort driven by the development team, others may view the effort as wasteful and as not contributing to the development of better software. At this point, any attempt at integration is difficult.

From this perspective, the most important aspects that must be considered are the goals of the adoption efforts. The value of the UML and other best practices must be carefully evaluated, and the benefits realized by using these technologies must be understood by all involved in the adoption effort. If any doubt exists at any level, these doubts must be expressed and discussed. Therefore, it's vital to establish an open communication channel and encourage feedback. In this book, we tend to stress the technological factors present in our integration efforts. However, the political and bureaucratic aspects of our development organization impacts any integration strategy.

5.1.2 Software Process

Our existing software process, or lack thereof, has a substantial effect on the degree to which we wish to utilize the UML on our software development projects. Some of the greatest advantages in using the UML, such as full lifecycle traceability and architectural stability, are directly impacted by the software process currently in use. If we're currently realizing the advantages of a repeatable software process, it undoubtedly will be much easier to take advantage of what the UML has to offer. On the other hand, if we lack an existing software process, attempting to use the UML throughout the entire lifecycle will be more difficult.

One of the most effective ways to objectively evaluate our existing software process is to examine the Capability Maturity Model (CMM—see the sidebar "The Capability Maturity Model (CMM)" in this chapter). If we are at level 3 or above, we may be ready to consider integrating the UML into our existing

The Capability Maturity Model (CMM)

The CMM describes some practices that help software development teams focus on improving the maturity of their existing software development processes. The CMM defines the following five levels of process maturity that can be used to evaluate our current processes and help us plan evolution to a higher level of maturity:

- **Level 1—Initial:** Existing software processes are often chaotic and not repeatable. Success is heavily dependent on a few heroic contributions by team members.
- **Level 2—Repeatable:** Basic practices are in place to track cost, function, and schedule. Team members can repeat these practices across projects.
- **Level 3—Defined:** Management and engineering activities are well understood and part of a well-defined software process. All projects use a version of the well-defined process.
- **Level 4—Managed:** In addition to adhering to a well-defined process, detailed measures of the software process are collected.
- **Level 5—Optimizing:** Quantitative measurements of the process are examined, and continuous process improvement is enabled.

software lifecycle. On the other hand, if we are at level 2 or below, our integration strategy also must take into consideration the adoption of a repeatable software process, prior to any attempt at utilizing the UML throughout the development lifecycle in a team environment.

Considering that we are at level 2 or below, our first order of business must be to consider whether we wish to define an integration strategy that emphasizes utilizing the UML or emphasizes the adoption of a repeatable software process. Attempting to do both simultaneously can have a detrimental impact on our strategy's success. Burdening a development team with too many new technologies simultaneously most likely will result in resistance from the development team.

5.1.3   Object-Oriented Experience

One of the advantages of the UML is that it enables us to actively establish an architectural vision prior to embarking on the construction stages of the software development effort. It does so by enabling us to communicate unambiguously many architectural options among the team members, as well as to use the powerful modeling language to problem-solve difficult design challenges. Therefore, the experience of our team in creating a flexible set of object-oriented architectural mechanisms directly impacts the resiliency of our system's architecture. Obviously, the UML guarantees us nothing if we don't have the experience necessary to use it in the most effective manner.

A team well versed in object-oriented techniques doesn't have to undergo the tremendous learning curve associated with the object-oriented paradigm. On the other hand, teams lacking a solid fundamental understanding of object-orientation may not have as much success in establishing an architectural vision that takes advantage of the benefits of object orientation. In this situation, it's less likely that the UML will contribute as positively to the specification of a robust system. Therefore, the team's experience with object orientation must be considered in the integration strategy. Time must be allotted to the training and mentoring necessary to help individuals understand the true value that object orientation provides.

5.1.4   Technological Aspects

It's common to find software development organizations that are interested in adopting the UML also to be undergoing a transition to other object-oriented tools, technologies, and languages. Development efforts that are considering the use of Java should carefully consider the experience of programmers with Java experience. The UML most likely provides the most benefit in an environment with a well-defined process, in-depth experience with object orientation, and knowledge of the implementation language. An integration strategy that doesn't take this aspect into consideration is facing an uphill battle. In fact, when we attempt to adopt a new technology, we also must take into consideration the supplementary technologies that must be understood to realize the advantages associated with the technology we are adopting.

5.1.5   Modeling Strategies

Different from the tool approach, the modeling strategy defines the level of detail at which we plan to create our individual diagrams and models. Because of the precise nature of the UML, it's possible to create models that exactly reflect the structure and behavior of our software system. Such models include the ability to define all classes present in our system and each of those class' public, protected, private, and implementation-level methods, as well as the individual method signatures. However, the dynamic nature of software can have a dramatic impact on our ability to maintain models that accurately represent our software system.

In [Fowler97], three distinct types of models are discussed. A conceptual model captures the essence of the concepts most relevant to the domain. A specification model begins to incorporate software elements not necessarily relevant to the domain but required for a flexible system, and the implementation model is an exact representation of the classes composing the system in its entirety. Discussions on each of these types of models follow.

5.1.5.1   Conceptual Model

The conceptual model captures only those elements that are relevant to the domain for which we are building the software system. Modeling at the conceptual level typically implies that our models aren't impacted by the implementation language that will be used. Its primary purpose is to help us understand more fully the domain aspects of the system. While some elements in a conceptual model may map to the chosen implementation environment, doing so isn't required, nor is it recommended to take the implementation language into consideration.

While a conceptual model has certain advantages, it may lack the precision required by developers to fully understand our system's architecture. The representation of our software system in code always has constructs that have no corresponding entity in the business domain. Proof of this fact can be found in the various collection classes in Java, such as `Vector`. For the majority of business domains, it's doubtful that a business entity exists that is equivalent to a `Vector`. Therefore, while a conceptual model helps the development team understand the domain, it doesn't necessarily help problem-solve the difficult design challenges inherent in all software development efforts.

5.1.5.2   Specification Model

The specification model is interested in capturing the essence of our software system, which typically consists of interfaces and classes that form the architectural skeleton of our system. The software system also may include the responsibilities associated with certain interfaces and classes. However, the intent of the specification model isn't to capture the detailed aspects of our software system. We are interested in capturing only those elements that contribute most to the system's description. A typical specification model includes navigability relationships on class diagrams and may include the multiplicity adornments associated with various associations. Formal method signatures typically aren't present on specification models. The majority of the models in this book are specification models.

5.1.5.3   *Implementation Model*

The implementation model exactly represents the software system under construction. Unfortunately, this approach typically is the one that many development teams new to the UML attempt to take. These teams usually become very frustrated and find that they spend as much time maintaining the model as they do writing code. This situation stems from the fact that code is very dynamic. As developers refactor their code to create new classes and methods to increase the structural resiliency of the application, the implementation model quickly becomes out of synch with the system. A model that isn't consistent with the software system is a useless model. It no longer communicates the system's structure and behavior, nor does it serve as an appropriate problem-solving medium because it doesn't reflect our current system's state. It is not uncommon for models at this level to be thrown away or no longer used as the system grows. The larger our system grows, the more work is involved in maintaining the model. Ultimately, the model requires as much maintenance as our system.

Implementation models may be most advantageous when using a tool that provides forward- and reverse-engineering capabilities. Assuming we're utilizing these features, maintaining a model at this level of detail becomes less of a burden. However, as discussed previously, the benefits realized by forward- and reverse-engineering may be outweighed by the cost and time required to use the feature appropriately. It isn't recommended that an implementation model be maintained manually. If we're interested in this level of detail, we should simply take a look at the code.

5.2   Integration Strategy

In previous sections, we've discussed the most important characteristics to consider in developing an integration strategy. Our strategy must be carefully considered and be a well-planned scheme with well-defined goals. Figure 5.2 illustrates the two primary components of our integration goals. In devising the strategy, the integration factors are an evaluation of our existing software development processes and methods, whereas the integration approach represents our ideal development processes and methods of the future. Therefore, our integration strategy must carefully consider the benefits we wish to realize from our integration and must define a clear path of execution with well-defined goals that enable our software development team to realize these benefits.

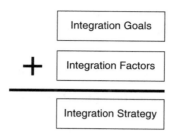

Figure 5.2   Integration Strategy Combining Integration Goals and Integration Factors

The most effective integration strategies are those that are treated as separate projects, apart from the software development project. Continuously evaluating the progress, and making appropriate modifications to the strategy, most likely results in a more satisfying experience. Breaking down the integration strategy into various phases, emphasizing the adoption of various best practices, typically helps to more effectively mitigate the risk of failure, which is in accord with the CMM.

Because of the various permutations associated with the multiple inputs to our integration strategy, it's virtually impossible to adequately define in just a few short paragraphs an integration strategy that's suitable for all organizations. Therefore, our discussion in this section presents general considerations that must be given serious thought regardless of our organization's existing methods. However, it should be clear from the previous discussion that the goal of any integration strategy is the use of a formal tool in a team development environment. We provide this caveat: It's doubtful that many teams can achieve this high level of integration in a short period of time. This isn't necessarily a reflection on the team itself, but more likely a reflection on the current state of the technologies the team is using. The time period required to successfully integrate a team development approach is largely dependent on the integration considerations.

Figure 5.3 illustrates the cost and complexity associated with any UML integration strategy. Individual developers using an informal tool is the most inexpensive option, yet it also offers the least amount of benefit. A team environment using a formal tool offers many of the advantages we've discussed, yet it also is most expensive. Striving to achieve either extreme on the benefit continuum may be unrealistic. Instead, our goal should be to reach a point on the continuum where we're utilizing the software development best practices in a manner most appropriate for our software development team.

If many of the integration factors are present, it's likely that we have a well-defined and repeatable software process, individuals who are well versed in

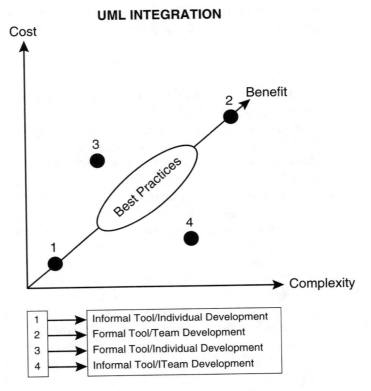

Figure 5.3 UML Integration Graph

object-oriented principles, and a solid understanding of many of our implementation tools. In this scenario, it's likely that the only aspect missing is a clear modeling strategy. In fact, at this point, UML adoption may be the next logical step in the improvement lifecycle of our existing methods. Suffice it to say, however, that in an environment such as this, the time period required to adopt the UML will be much shorter than if any of the other integration factors aren't present. However, these types of environments are also quite rare. With the exponential growth of many technologies, especially Java, mastering one aspect typically leads only to the need to master another.

Assuming that an organization is typical, it's likely that our development team lacks more than just a single integration factor. Therefore, when adopting the UML, it's important that these considerations be given careful thought as to how our environment will provide the team with the necessary information. This learning experience traditionally comes from training. While formal training can provide a solid foundation, it is highly likely that it won't suffice as the only means through which our development team learns these new technologies. It's typically more effective to utilize many of the new technologies on pilot projects. If our organization doesn't have the luxury of enabling our team to learn and experiment on a pilot project, we should consider first applying the newer technologies to a lower risk portion of a system, possibly isolating our first attempt to a subsystem. Also, we should consider utilizing the services of an experienced mentor. While the purpose of any integration strategy is to help develop better software, which should help minimize risk, risk is inherent in the integration strategy itself. A series of small wins not only enables our development team to gain experience with new technologies, but also to build confidence.

Because we can't control the existing integration factors, we must devise a strategy that takes this factor into account. We can control, however, our integration goals and the time and cost associated with the overall effort. Therefore, the integration goals we're striving to achieve should consider the benefits we wish to realize from our integration. Only then can we effectively adopt an approach that supports our efforts. For instance, if we know we're using Java as the implementation language but aren't considering forward- and reverse-engineering of our code, using specification models will be most useful.

Keep in mind that an approach to use the UML on an individual basis may not resolve the true challenge in software development. Only a team-based approach can help us create more resilient systems and manage change more effectively. All team members must be able to unambiguously understand the system in the same manner but from potentially different perspectives. The UML helps us do that, and therefore, an approach emphasizing team dynamics provides the most benefit, given that we can accommodate the various integration considerations discussed earlier. If not, an individual approach may be all we're capable of at the present time. Even so, the benefits of emphasizing architectural resiliency still can be realized by developers, and that quite possibly may be an advantage in comparison to our previous methods.

When devising an integration strategy, give careful consideration to the following questions:

- How well do we understand the tools we use?
- How well do we understand our implementation language?
- How well defined is our software development process?
- What benefits do we wish to derive from using the UML and other best practices?
- How well do our tools support our desired development process?
- How supportive is our team of adopting these new ideas?

5.3   Conclusion

Our integration strategy is heavily dependent on the current state of software development within our organization. The various integration factors provide an indication of this state. Our strategy must carefully consider these factors, and we must devise a strategy that enables us to achieve our integration goals. It's imperative that any integration strategy be realistic in the plan it sets forth. Placing unrealistic expectations on our development team only results in frustration and conflict. Evaluating the integration strategy and making adjustments should be done as necessary. Treating the integration strategy as a project in itself can bring awareness of its goals. Communicating the benefits of the strategy helps all development team members understand more fully the important role the strategy plays in developing better software.

The integration strategy should consider the best practices we're interested in taking advantage of. A phased integration strategy most likely will offer the greatest chances for success. Keep in mind that any technology that isn't helping us create better software should not be used. Don't adopt a technology because it's the latest industry trend. Instead, it should be adopted because we understand its value.

CHAPTER 6

Requirements Modeling

*Prior to establishing our system's structure, we must understand our
system's behavior. The behavior always dictates the structural flexibility required.*

As we've seen, developing successful software means we manage the entire software development process. Applying best practices diligently throughout the life of our software system helps us to more easily manage risk, accommodate growth, and maintain the survivability of our system. In this chapter and the remaining chapters, we turn our attention to applying the concepts we've discussed in previous chapters. Throughout our discussion, we keep three important points in mind—first, the value of applying, and adhering to, our object-oriented principles; second, the value that the UML can provide to more effectively communicate and specify our software systems and problem-solve difficult design challenges; and third, the important role that software process and the fundamental best practices play throughout the development lifecycle.

As we begin our journey on a new development effort, we first must understand our system's requirements. Regardless of the software process we use, we must understand the initial set of requirements the code must satisfy before we can write one line of code. These requirements are the users' and project stakeholders' demands, and they're stated in terms these individuals understand. Granted, these requirements may evolve throughout the life of our system, but the adaptive approach to development and the traceability that we've established will enable us to accommodate change. In addition, because users care very little about our system's structure, the requirements represent the behavior of our system.

Developers, on the other hand, typically emphasize the structural aspects of the system first. Before developers can begin to define the behavior of the

Information Overload

As we continue to discuss OO, the UML, Java, and software process, and introduce material that may seem new and confusing, our confidence in what we do must not be shaken because of a new technology that we may not fully understand. Our past should serve as a useful guide in helping us determine what we should and shouldn't do throughout the course of software development. The tools presented in this book serve to help us improve what we should be doing and remind us of what we shouldn't. While technology at times may be intimidating, we must continually remind ourselves that most new technologies aren't revolutionary but are evolutionary. Our present knowledge typically continues to hold true, and we simply are enhancing our existing skills.

system, they must have a structure in place that can support the behavior. Therefore, the developer's job is to create a structure that accommodates the behavior, implying that a developer must translate behavioral requirements into a static system structure, which is the purpose of analysis and design.

In this chapter, we discuss how we can effectively establish and structure our requirements specifications so that developers can more easily translate these requirements into a system that accurately supports those requirements. Because our focus in this text is to acquire skill in designing applications, detailed examination of our requirements isn't provided. Instead, we emphasize how requirements can be expressed most effectively, leaving the discussion on how to best elicit requirements to other texts.

6.0   Notation

When identifying requirements, we must bring structure to the overall set of requirements the system must satisfy, which is one of the goals of a use case model. Our first order of discussion in this section is to understand the fundamental elements and diagrams within the UML that are most commonly used in establishing requirements.

6.0.1   Actor

As discussed in Chapter 3, actors are depicted as stick figures and represent an external entity that interacts with a system. Actors are always external to the system under development, which implies they mark the boundary conditions of our system. An actor should be given a name that makes sense within the context of the use case with which they interact. Because of this, actors typically are identified by the role they play when participating with a use case. As seen in Figure 6.1, we've chosen to name our actor "Employee" instead of "Person" because we want to explicitly indicate that only employees can perform certain system functions.

While we most often think of actors as human users of a system, any external entity that a use case communicates with may be represented as an actor. Actors typically come in three varieties:

- Users
- External systems
- External devices

6.0.2 Use Case

Also introduced in Chapter 3, a use case (see Figure 6.2) represents a sequence of actions that a software system guarantees to carry out on behalf of an actor. Stated differently, a use case represents some business process that provides a result of observable value to an actor. Regardless of which definition we prefer, it's important to remember that use cases don't represent a single feature or business rule. Instead, features and rules are part of individual use cases, which our model structure should be representative of. This mistake is made often when identifying system use cases.

Another common mistake made when identifying use cases is spending too much time determining the granularity at which we represent business

Employee

Figure 6.1   Actor

Run Payroll

Figure 6.2   Use Case

processes. In earlier iterations, use cases should be defined at a high level. In later iterations, and if needed, these higher-level use cases can be broken down into finer-grained use cases. We must not forget that projects are made late one day at a time, and each day we spend mulling over what is and isn't a use case is time that could have been spent better elsewhere. Use cases enable us to prioritize our development tasks, identify high-risk business processes, and organize our development around the system's required behavior. If we find we're struggling with use case structure, instead of use case behavior, we should move on. It's likely that later activities will flesh out any major deficiencies, at which point we can correct them.

In fact, this fleshing out is the very nature of the requirements identification process. In the iterative development lifecycle, not all requirements are identified immediately. Instead, requirements are constantly being discovered, and as needed, the use cases impacted by these new requirements reflect recent discoveries.

When naming individual use cases, it's important to provide names that are meaningful. A typical naming convention for a use case is the *verb-noun* format. The name should be short; only a couple of words, and should be indicative of the business process that the use case represents. The name should tell us what the system does, not how it does it. For example, a possible use case name for an automated teller machine might be "Withdraw Funds."

6.0.3   Relationships

Associations enable us to show the relationship between the fundamental elements on a use case diagram. Associations enable us to illustrate actors and how they interact with use cases. This interaction may consist of an actor initiating a use case, which may happen when an actor elects to perform a system function, or a use case requesting the services from an external system, such as requesting data from a legacy database.

Dependencies can be used to show the relationship that may exist between two use cases. For instance, one use case might require that another use case be performed in order to complete a certain process. Or possibly many use cases have a common set of preconditions. In either case, we may elect to represent the situation as separate use cases, which is an advanced modeling technique and one not highly recommended for those just beginning with the concepts. We provide examples of dependencies on use case diagrams in Section 6.0.5 where we discuss the include and extend UML stereotypes.

Generalizations represent a special relationship between actors where one actor (the *descendant*) can participate in all of the use cases of another (the *ancestor*). Generalizations are used on use case diagrams to help simplify the overall layout. Beyond this fuction, they provide no other benefit.

6.0.4 Use Case Diagrams

Use case diagrams serve as the mechanism through which we show actors and use cases and how they interact. Figure 6.3 illustrates a simple use case diagram for a payroll system. It includes five actors and six use cases. We clearly see the use cases that the various actors can participate in. Examining more deeply the Run Payroll use case, we notice that it can be initiated by the System Clock, HR Representative, or HR Administrator. We also see that it communicates with an external Bank System. According to the definition of an actor, we can deduce that this Bank System must be an existing application that we will communicate with, which is important because it clearly defines our system's boundaries.

6.0.5 Stereotypes

Recall from Chapter 3 that stereotypes enable us to extend the UML by adding our own fundamental elements. The UML defines a set of standard stereotypes that also can be used. Two common stereotypes are *include* and *extend*, both used on use case diagrams, and both serving as extensions to the standard UML vocabulary (and each is discussed in the sections that follow). Each stereotype is attached to the *dependency relation*. In a dependency relationship, one element has a semantic relation to another, and changes to one use case may impact all dependent use cases.

6.0.5.1 Include

The include stereotype indicates that a source use case incorporates the behavior of a target use case. In Figure 6.3, we see that all use cases have an include relation to the Login use case, which indicates that when performing any of the other use cases, an actor must also participate in the Login use case. An dependency stereotyped as include implies mandatory inclusion of behavior. The include stereotype is useful when use cases are reused entirely by other use cases. It provides a way to clearly illustrate, and is an excellent medium for specifying business process reuse. However, specifying this type of relationship on a use case diagram is an advanced modeling technique and should be applied judiciously. If we question the applicability of an include relationship, it should be omitted. Little time should be devoted exclusively to identifying these types of relations.

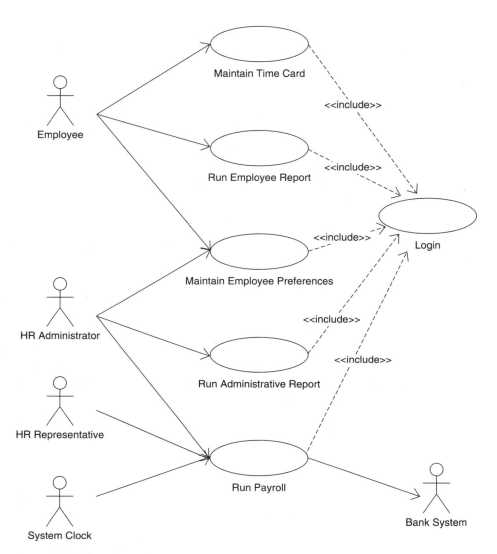

Figure 6.3 Use Case Diagram for a Payroll System

6.0.5.2 Extend

As with include, the extend stereotype is also applied to the dependency relation on a use case diagram. Extend implies that the source use case may incorporate the behavior of a target use case. Unlike the include relation, extend typically is used to specify optional use case behavior. As with use case modeling in general, the challenge in applying the extend stereotype is one of granularity. All use

Include versus Extend

While include and extend can be useful modeling techniques to add value to a use case diagram, they also can be a tar pit. It's easy to get lost in an argument over whether a dependency should be an include or extend relation. If you find yourself lost in such an argument, stop! Leave the relation as a simple dependency and move on. Later, if you reach consensus, reflect on the relation at that time. It's likely, however, that you'll regard the argument as a silly digression and one that had no positive impact on your system. We have more important decisions to make than whether a relation is an include or extend relation.

cases possess optional behavior. When using the extend relation, we must make sure that the behavior is not only optional, but also modeled as a separate use case—that is, the behavior is significant enough to an actor. We should exercise caution when using extend in the same manner as include.

6.1   Requirements Modeling

During the requirements-gathering activities, the use case model is grown. While the formality of our use case model can't be exactly defined, we can discuss those practices and artifacts that make the model well suited as an input artifact to analysis and design. The artifacts composing our use case model vary from one project to the next and from one organization to the other. Therefore, our intent in this section is to discuss some of the more useful modeling techniques when gathering our system requirements. The depth to which we specify our use case model is determined by the factors discussed in the previous chapter.

We also use this section as an opportunity to introduce a sample system that we use during our discussion of designing our system. While we present these requirements to illustrate some common modeling techniques, we should also remember that the requirements discussed here aren't meant to be exhaustive but are meant to serve as a basis for our discussion of design.

6.1.1   Problem Statement

A problem statement can be effective means for establishing the basis for the system. A problem statement typically is produced by project stakeholders, who may not be the same individuals we work with to gather system requirements. Because of this, a problem statement usually describes the purpose of the system. The problem statement introduced in the sidebar "Payroll System Problem Statement" serves as the basis upon which the remainder of our discussion on the use case model shall be based.

Payroll System Problem Statement

Our task is the creation of a new payroll system. The old system is outdated and no longer adequately manages the payroll process and the entry of employee time card information. Therefore, manual intervention is required to process the payroll. In addition to the preexisting category of salaried employee, which the current payroll process does support, our organization now accommodates two new types of employees: those employees working on commission, and those employees working on an hourly basis. The current payroll process doesn't support these two new employee types, which are described in detail later in this problem statement.

In addition to accommodating all employee types, as well as ensuring that our system can accommodate newly created categories of employees in the future, the system must also allow each of these employees to enter his or her time information via a corporate intranet using a standard Web browser. Because employees can manage only their individual time card information, a user ID and password is required of each employee prior to gaining access to this section of the corporate intranet. The payroll process can process only "signed" time cards, which are those time cards that the employee has identified as accurate.

Overall, the system will store information about the approximately 2,000 company employees. This data will be stored in the Oracle payroll database. The payroll process must run on the fifteenth and last day of each month at 12:00 a.m. All paychecks must be accurately calculated and deposited into one or more bank accounts of the employees' choosing. Employees also should be able to change personal information, such as names, addresses, and passwords. Eventually, the system must enable employees to maintain their direct deposit information via the system as well. However, this feature is beyond the scope of the initial release.

A human resources representative must be able to initiate the payroll process on demand based on a selected list of employees. When doing so, the system should cycle through the list of selected employees, running

(continues)

(continued)

payroll only for those employees. This process typically will be done by a human resources representative during normal business hours.

As stated earlier, our system must be able to track information and calculate salaries for the following three types of employees:

1. **Salaried:** These employees are paid a flat salary. However, they're still required to submit time cards that include the dates worked and the number of hours worked on those dates.

2. **Hourly:** These employees are paid based on their hourly rate. Employees working more than a standard 40-hour work week are paid 1.5 times their hourly rate.

3. **Commission:** These employees are paid a commission based on their total sales. The commission rates for commissioned employees is 10, 20, or 25 percent. In addition to the percentage rate, these employees also may receive a base salary.

The system also must allow employees to query the system. Standard queries will include the ability to view number of hours worked for a selected pay period and remaining and used vacation time.

All employee information is maintained by a human resources administrator. The administrator must be able to initiate a payroll process in a fashion similar to that of the human resources representative. In addition, the administrator also will be able to add new employees, remove employees, and change personal information about employees, including an employee's category type and an employee's password. The administrator will have additional reporting capabilities beyond that of an employee, which include various administrative reports yet to be identified.

6.1.2 Use Case Diagrams

Figure 6.3 depicts the use case diagram for our payroll system. It provides an example of what we can expect after an iteration early in the development effort. Note how this diagram enables us to very effectively communicate the primary business processes that the system must support, as well as the actors that partake in the processes. In addition, it also depicts the system boundaries.

We were cautious not to overanalyze and create a detailed set of use cases. It would have been easy for us to spend additional time and effort breaking these high-level use cases into finer-grained business processes. These use cases suffice early in the development effort because they enable us to effectively organize and plan future development. In future iterations, and as we progress through each use case, we may decide to further break a use case into one that's a bit finer grained. We'll base this decision entirely on the risk and complexity, and we'll do so only if it enables us to more effectively manage our development.

While it isn't considered an error if we break these use cases into finer-grained processes when first creating them, it isn't advantageous to create use cases that don't represent business processes providing a result of observable value to an actor. In an extreme situation, we might decide that a user entering his or her password should be represented as a use case named "Enter Password." We can identify behavior that surrounds this feature. We must validate the length of a password, validate that the correct password was entered, and possibly encrypt the password. However, the value that an actor receives by solely entering his or her password is certainly questionable, and in this situation, we should exercise caution.

Keep in mind, however, that the granularity of a use case is domain dependent. In our payroll system, Enter Password does not qualify as a full-fledged business process. If we're working on a security system, however, Enter Password might be considered a valid use case.

Also note that in our problem statement, we mention the need to access a payroll database. Although use cases must pull information from the database, this database doesn't appear as an actor on our use case diagram. Were it meaningful, we would show this external data store as an actor. In this situation, we decided that showing it as an actor wasn't a significant aspect of our system. Determining our actors is a difficult task, and the inclusion of an actor on a use case diagram varies across contexts given the priority of the situation.

While use cases may be the most popular artifact within the requirements model, they may not be the most useful. Although use cases enable us to organize our system's requirements, they don't effectively specify a system's behavior.

6.1.3   Use Case Specifications

If we could peer inside any use case, we would find a sequence of events constituting the business process represented by that use case. Use case specifications document the behavior of the business process specified by a particular use case. Looking inside the use case also would reveal that a single sequence is the desired outcome of that process. We call the entire sequence of events a use case's *flows of events*, and the desired outcome is typically called the *primary flow*. While the primary flow is usually the flow of events that is the desired sequence, it is also the highest volume flow. Of course, there are numerous other paths of execution through a particular use case, and we must consider the behaviors of these paths as well. We refer to a single path through a use case as a *scenario* or an *instance* of a use case.

Figure 6.4 illustrates the flows of events for a use case. We see the primary flow represented as a straight path through a use case. Branching from this primary flow are a number of alternate flows. These alternate flows represent exceptional conditions that cause the system to deviate from the expected behavior. For instance, the intent of our Login use case in Figure 6.3 might be to request a user ID and password from an actor before allowing access to the remainder of the system's functions. However, if the actor enters an invalid password, the system doesn't allow access to those functions. While the primary flow is to allow access to the system, an alternate flow in this situation is to prompt the user for the correct password.

Many alternate flows of events exist for a use case. For many of these alternate flows, it's possible to gracefully recover and continue on the normal execution path. If a user were to enter his or her correct password on a subsequent attempt, the system allows the user access to its function. However, some alternate flows are not recoverable—for example, when the user enters his or her password incorrectly three times as part of the same login. At this point, our system may interpret it as a potential security breach and terminate execution. This, too, is represented in Figure 6.4 by the exceptional flows ending in a double bar.

Scenarios and Flows of Events

A *scenario* is also known as an *instance* of a use case. All of the scenarios for a use case constitute a use case's flows of events. While not formally part of the UML specification, these terms are at the heart of requirements modeling. Use cases simply serve to organize our requirements model. The specification of the scenarios are the requirements.

In addition, the definition of the term *scenario* should serve as an indication of the simple elegance of specifying requirements in this fashion. A scenario is an instance of a use case, just as a class is an instance of an object. While subtle, this consistency is intentional and will aid us tremendously as we begin using the requirements to design our system.

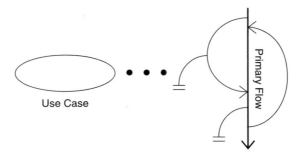

Figure 6.4   Use Case Flows of Events

Many business processes can include an infinite number of flows of events. Our intent in describing system requirements isn't to capture in the use case specification a description of each possible scenario. Instead, we focus on describing the most likely scenarios. In early iterations of a project, describing approximately ten scenarios typically suffices. When more than ten scenarios are described, we run the risk of being caught up in overanalyzing. When we specify less than ten scenarios, we may not have enough useful information to serve us during analysis and design. When dealing with more complex or more simple use cases, we may have more or less than ten scenarios. The best course of action usually is the one we feel most comfortable with. Figures 6.5 and 6.6 show sample use case specifications for the Run Payroll and Maintain Time Card use cases, respectively. These specifications are used throughout the remaining chapters in our discussion of designing applications.

6.1.4   Additional Elements

It's not uncommon to find other diagrams—most commonly, activity and sequence diagrams—included in the use case model. Refer to Chapter 4 for other elements commonly found in the use case model.

Activity diagrams also may be useful for specifying the behavior of a use case. Developers, however, don't have much need for activity diagrams, nor should developers rely on them. While activity diagrams are excellent at portraying business process flows, they don't show object collaborations,[1] which typically are most useful to developers. Some activity diagrams also advocate the creation of system sequence diagrams illustrating the boundary between a

---

[1]An object collaboration is a society of objects that talk to each other and use the services of other objects in that society to achieve some common goal.

Run Payroll Use Case Specification

Description
This use case processes payroll for each employee who has signed a time card for the pay period. Payroll is run on the fifteenth and last day of each month, or when initiated manually by a human resources representative.

Flow of Events
Primary Flow: Run Payroll Batch
1. The system retrieves a list of employees with signed time cards for the pay period.
2. The system calculates pay for each employee, based on the time card information or based on the commission rate for a commissioned employee.
3. The system generates a pay stub and prints it.
4. The system creates a bank transaction.
5. The bank transaction is sent to the bank system for processing and subsequent deposit in the employee's specified account.
6. When all employees have been processed, the system shuts down.

Alternate Flow 1: Run Payroll HR
1. The human resources representative selects one or more employees from a list of employees.
2. The system validates that the selected employees have signed time cards.
3. The human resources representative selects Run Payroll.
4. The primary flow is initiated.

Alternate Flow 2: Unsigned Time Cards
1. When running payroll, the system encounters employees with time cards that have not been signed.
2. The system generates an email to the employee notifying him or her that the time card is unsigned.

Alternate Flow 3: Database Connection Failure
1. When retrieving a list of employees, the system cannot communicate with the payroll database.
2. The system attempts three subsequent communications.
3. The system pages the appropriate on-call database administrator.

Figure 6.5 Run Payroll Use Case Specification

use case and the system. We discuss sequence diagrams in Chapter 7, but we don't advocate the creation of system sequence diagrams as described by many formal processes.

6.2 Conclusion

Each business process can be captured and represented as a use case. When identifying use cases, it's important that we create them at an appropriate level of granularity. Specification at too fine a level leads to an overly complex use case model. Use cases should represent those business processes that provide

Maintain Time Card Use Case Specification

Description
This use case enables employees to enter and update time card information. Time card information can be modified only by an employee before the time card has been electronically signed by the employee. Once the time card has been signed, it no longer can be modified by an employee.

Flow of Events
Primary Flow: Maintain Time Card
1. The employee identifies himself or herself to the system.
2. The employee chooses to maintain his or her time card from a list of options.
3. The system retrieves the employee s time card for the current pay period. If a time card does not currently exist, the system creates a new time card with start and end dates for the present pay period. The end date is the fifteenth or last day of the month, with the start date being the first or sixteenth, respectively. The employee cannot modify these dates.
4. The employee enters the number of hours worked for each day.
5. The employee saves the time card.
6. The system saves the information to the payroll database.

Alternate Flow 1: Sign Time Card
1. The employee is performing the steps in the primary flow to enter time card information.
2. The employee may choose to sign the time card. This action can be performed at any time while entering time card information.
3. The system validates that the employee has entered a valid number of hours for each day.
4. The system marks the time card as read-only and ready for payroll processing.

Alternate Flow 2: Invalid Work Hours
1. The employee is performing the steps in the primary flow to enter time card information.
2. The employee chooses to sign the time card.
3. The number of hours worked for one or more days exceeds the allowed limit of 24 or is less than the minimum of 0.
4. The system informs the employee of the inaccuracy.

Figure 6.6   Maintain Timecard Use Case Specification

some result of observable value to a project stakeholder. Each use case, however, consists of many flows of events. Each flow of events represents an actor's interaction with a use case, called a *scenario*. A scenario is typically composed of the individual features and rules that make up an application.

Most systems seem as if they are composed of a virtually unlimited number of requirements. Our use case model serves to capture requirements in a format that helps us easily understand and find what we are looking for. Perhaps even more important, our use case model is organized and structured in a format that helps us manage changing requirements, which are a trait of all systems. The goal of our use case model is to capture the exact amount of artifacts to serve as valuable input to the next stages of the software development lifecycle. If we find that some artifacts are not used in later stages, the production of these artifacts should be questioned in the future. As we'll see in the upcoming chapters, traceability among our individual models is extremely important, and each artifact should trace to some element in another model.

CHAPTER 7

Problem Analysis

Establishing an architectural vision for our system is critical to ensuring the system's integrity.

We've established some high-level requirements that our system must fulfill. Of course, many questions still remain to be answered, which is natural during an iterative lifecycle. At this point, it's time to analyze the problem and produce a set of high-level artifacts that can be used as we progress to more detailed analysis and design activities. Without doing so, we easily can become entrenched in the specificities of the design activity and lose sight that our work must become part of the greater whole. To a certain extent, use cases can be developed independent of each other. When use case are developed this way, we should make sure we have a common starting point.

In this chapter, we discuss the establishment of this common ground. And, as we'll see throughout the discussion in the chapters to come, we also make sure that we explicitly relate an individual's work to the greater whole of the system.

It's also important that each of the artifacts produced during the requirements-gathering process begins to prove its worth. We'll use these requirements and transform them into the analysis and design model. If we find that we use only half of the requirements that were captured as part of this iteration, we must question why. Thus, in this chapter, we begin the analysis and design of our application.

7.0   Notation

In this section, we review many of the fundamental elements first introduced in Chapter 3. Because the majority of our discussion at this point is focused on class diagrams, we examine some of the fundamental structural elements and their Java language mappings.

7.0.1 Class

A *class* is a blueprint for an object. A class has three compartments. The first represents the name of the class as defined in Java. The second represents the attributes, which correspond to instance variables within the class. An attribute defined in this second compartment is the same as a composition relationship. The third compartment, Operations, represents methods of the class. Attributes and operations can be preceded with a visibility adornment. A plus sign (+) indicates public visibility, a minus sign (–) denotes private visibility, and a pound sign (#) denotes protected visibility. Omission of this visibility adornment denotes package-level visibility. If an attribute or operation is underlined, it indicates that the attribute or operation is static. An operation also may list the parameters it accepts, as well as the return type, as follows:

Java	UML
```public class Employee { private int empID; public double calcSalary() { ... } }```	Employee -empID:int +calcSalary():double

7.0.2   Association   ⟶

An *association* is a structural relationship between entities specifying that objects are connected. The arrow is optional and specifies navigability. No arrow implies bidirectional navigability, resulting in tighter coupling. An instance of an association is a link, which is used on interaction diagrams to model messages sent between objects. In Java, an association translates to an instance scope variable, as in the following example. Additional adornments can also be attached to an association. Multiplicity adornments imply relationships between the instances. In the following example, an `Employee` can have zero or more `TimeCard` objects. However, a `TimeCard` belongs to a single `Employee` (that is, `Employee` instances do not share `TimeCard`s).

Java	UML
```public class Employee { private TimeCard _tc[]; public void maintainTimeCard() { … } }```	Employee 1 0..* TimeCard

7.0.3 Package

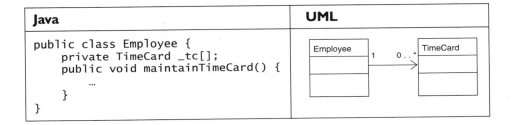

A *package* is a general purpose grouping mechanism. Packages can contain any other type of element. A package in the UML translates directly into a package in Java. In Java, a package can contain other packages, other classes, or both. When modeling, we typically include packages that are logical, implying they serve only to organize our model. We also include packages that are physical, implying these packages translate directly into Java packages in our system. A package has a name that uniquely identifies it. The following example illustrates the Java code snippet representing a UML package:

Java	UML
```package BusinessObjects; public class Employee { }```	BusinessObjects

7.0.4   Dependency   - - - - - ->

A *dependency* indicates a "using" relationship between entities, which implies that a change in the specification of one entity may affect the entities that are dependent upon it. In Chapter 3, we stated that a dependency typically translates to any type of reference to a class or object that doesn't exist at the instance scope. We also mentioned that a dependency can be used to represent the relationship between packages. This type of relationship was discussed in Chapter 1. Because a package contains classes, we can illustrate that various packages have relationships based upon the relationships among the classes within those packages. The following shows how we use the dependency relationship in this chapter:

Java	UML
/**No Java code can be written that represents the dependency relationship between packages. Instead, the dependency relationships convey the valid relationships that can exist between the classes contained in each package. In the diagram at the right, classes in the service package may import classes in the entity package but not vice versa.*/	Service ⟍ Entity

7.0.5   Stereotype   <<stereotypename>>

A *stereotype* is used to create a new fundamental element within the UML with its own set of special properties, semantics, and notation. UML profiles can be created that define a set of stereotypes for language-specific features. For instance, Sun is currently working on a UML profile that defines a mapping between the UML and Enterprise JavaBeans (EJB).

7.0.6   Collaboration

A *collaboration* is somewhat beyond the scope of our discussion; however, because we use examples of collaborations in later chapters, we need to introduce them here for completeness. Collaborations most often are used to bring structure to our design model. They enable us to create sequence and class diagrams that work in conjunction with each other to provide an object-oriented view into the requirements that our system satisfies. A collaboration typically has a one-to-one mapping to a use case. Thus, while use cases represent requirements from a customer's vantage point in the use case view, a collaboration models these same set of requirements from a developer's perspective.

7.0.7   Realization   ◁-------

A *realization* is a relationship that specifies a contract between two entities, in which one entity defines a contract that another entity guarantees to carry out. When used to represent the relationship between classes, a realization translates directly into the use of the `implements` keyword. In other contexts, however, we can use a realization to achieve a trace relationship from individual use cases and the set of classes that guarantee to fulfill the use case behavior. This set of classes that realize a use case are typically structured around a collaboration, formally known as a *use case realization*.

7.1   Identifying Initial Concepts

Recall from Chapter 4 that the purpose of analysis and design is to transform the behavior of our system into a set of objects that collaborate and, ultimately, fulfill the requirements. We call the process of representing the behavior of our system as a set of collaborating objects *behavioral modeling*, which is the subject of Chapter 8. Before we can actually begin allocating behavior to our objects, first we must have some objects in place. While behavioral modeling is an activity that emphasizes the allocation of behavior to the classes that should exhibit that behavior, it doesn't imply we work only with behavioral diagrams. The time period separating problem analysis, behavioral modeling, and structural modeling can be measured in minutes, hours, and days, not weeks and months. Consequently, prior to modeling our system's behavior, we must establish some structure to which that behavior can be allocated.

In identifying key concepts, we identify a set of candidate classes. Our intent in identifying these candidate classes is to produce entities that exist at the conceptual level. Therefore, the concepts that we introduce in this section should be domain-dependent entities. At this point, identifying various responsibilities of our initial concepts isn't important. We'll treat allocation of responsibilities as a separate activity, one that is performed a bit later. In addition, we don't care at this point whether any of our initial concepts have relationships to each other. Identifying relationships also is an activity performed later in the process. If we

Separation of Activities

The time period separating each of the core activities associated with the software development lifecycle is typically very brief, including coding and testing. By treating each of these activities as separate, it enables us to focus on one aspect of the problem. By performing each of the activities virtually simultaneously, it enables us to continually verify and grow our system.

find we're spending time associating responsibilities with our classes, or creating relationships between classes, we've overstepped the bounds of our present activity. In such case, we need to step back and reconsider the present activity, or change focus and apply the principles of another activity. What and when we do something is not as important as ensuring that when we do something, we do it consciously and give careful consideration to possible ramifications.

We can identify our initial concepts in several ways, and they aren't entirely scientific. One of the most common ways is to examine the problem statement, searching for nouns. For example, the following sentence, which is taken from the problem statement introduced in Chapter 6, enables us to identify some potential classes with our system:

> *Because employees can manage only their individual time card information, a user ID and password is required of each employee prior to gaining access to this section of the corporate intranet.*

This problem statement contains the nouns *employee* and *time card*. The statement also contains the nouns *user ID* and *password*. Shouldn't we consider these last two nouns as potential classes within our system? The answer to this question is entirely dependent on the domain. If our problem statement referred to these two nouns in terms of their doing something, it's likely that *user ID* and *password* would be classes in our system. This is because if they need to do something, they have behavior. Any noun with its own behavior or attributes should be represented as a concept. For instance, an *employee manages* his or her time card, which implies that employees have behavior. Thus, we should consider *employee* as an initial concept. Examining the complete problem statement, in addition to other artifacts within the requirements model, yields the initial concepts represented as classes in Figure 7.1.

Quite a few other techniques can be used to identify our initial concepts. Relying on domain experience also is useful. Regardless of technique, this activ-

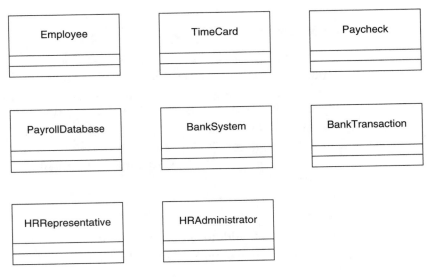

Figure 7.1   Payroll System Initial Concepts

ity shouldn't require much time. In most cases, a few minutes produces a set of quality initial concepts. The intent isn't to identify all classes within our system at one time, which is impossible. Instead, we establish a common starting point for all individuals. New classes will be introduced as necessary.

7.2   Software Specification

Our initial concepts represent the classes that are present within our domain. They represent our first attempt, in early iterations, at identifying our business objects. As we progress with developing our system, these initial classes may change slightly, or they might morph into entirely different classes. This process ultimately is dictated by the behavior our system must realize. As we begin to think in more detail about how our system will provide use case functionality, we quickly realize that our system is composed of other classes beyond just our domain classes. User interface classes must be present for those portions of the system that accommodate user interaction. More detailed design classes must be present to allow for other system-level functions to take place. Therefore, in addition to identifying our initial concepts, we also must accommodate these additional classes, though initially only at a higher level of abstraction.

In this section, we discuss the techniques that we can use to identify a more robust set of classes that compose our system. We then will use these classes in

Robustness Analysis

In Jacobson's Object-Oriented Software Engineering (OOSE), boundary, entity, and control classes are created during robustness analysis [RUP00]. However, in OOSE, robustness analysis also includes the use of stereotypes for our three different types of classes, which is perfectly acceptable. In this book, we don't use the various stereotypes simply because we need to remove the stereotypes as we move more toward the design activities, because these category of classes often are divided into multiple, more cohesive, classes.

our discussion of additional techniques that we can employ as we move from the conceptual model to the specification model.

7.2.1   Boundary

Boundary classes represent those entities that are responsible for allowing some external medium to communicate with our system. As you might guess, this external medium is represented as an actor on our use case diagram. When an actor initiates a use case or when a use case communicates with an actor, a boundary class is at work. Hence, boundary classes bridge external system elements with internal elements.

The most obvious and intuitive form of boundary class is a GUI component. The only way a human actor can interact with our system is through a visual element presented onscreen. However, boundary classes also take other forms. The use case diagram in Figure 6.3 in Chapter 6 identified a bank system as an actor. As we discussed, this bank system is an external system. In this situation, a boundary class can be used to encapsulate all communications with this external bank system. In fact, as we progress through more detailed design, it's likely that a single class won't suffice, and the creation of a more robust mechanism might be desirable. The portion of the system that must communicate with the external bank system is an excellent subsystem candidate. Subsystems are discussed in Chapter 11.

Boundary classes play an important role in our system's design. If at first glance we consider the creation of a boundary class to bridge communication between actors and use cases to be overkill, we need to ask ourselves where else this functionality would reside. We should be able to clearly realize that placing the functionality that communicates with our external bank system in one of our business classes isn't sufficient. At this point, we're left with few other

A New Concept

While the terminology of a boundary class might seem new, the object-oriented paradigm does advocate the use of boundary classes, though in different terms. Many of us realize the importance of separating presentation or user interface logic from business logic. Creating boundary classes early in the development lifecycle provides clear separation between user interface and business logic. As we progress, we'll see that boundary classes make it easier to allocate behavior appropriately.

choices than to create a boundary class. Boundary classes typically aren't difficult to identify, and it usually holds true that associations connecting actors and use cases are the most likely candidates. At this point, we can comfortably state that all communication between an actor and a use case must go through a boundary class.

The Boundary classes identified are shown in Figure 7.2.

7.2.2   Entity

The entities represent our initial concepts. They are our domain objects, and as such, their behavior typically is the most interesting. In addition, entity classes are the most likely candidates for persistence—that is, the data within these classes is most likely read from, and written to, a persistent data store, such as a relational database. Early in the lifecycle, however, we're most interested in establishing only high-level behaviors. We aren't necessarily concerned with

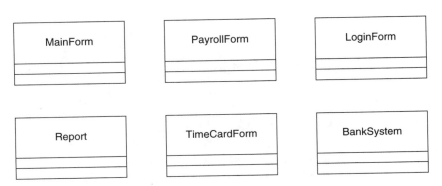

Figure 7.2   Payroll System Boundary Classes

how these classes will be persisted. In fact, the initial concepts already identified serve as an excellent set of entity classes. Therefore, we'll carry forward the initial concepts identified in Figure 7.1 and use them as our initial set of entity classes. In the next chapter, we begin the process of associating behavior to these classes.

In reality, the identification of our initial concepts, which we now call *entity classes*, and of the boundary and control classes, discussed in the following sections, takes place virtually simultaneously. We've separated them into separate activities only because when identifying initial concepts, we treated them as business entities. At this point, we treat these initial concepts as software classes.

7.2.3   Control

Control classes most often cause the most confusion. It's quite typical to find less-experienced developers struggling to come to grips with the purpose of a control class. Stated in simple terms, a control class serves as the medium through which boundary classes and entity classes communicate. This, however, begs an interesting question. Why can't our boundary classes speak directly to our entity classes? This is a plausible alternative to using control classes. However, were we to allow boundary classes to talk directly to entity classes, it's inevitable that our classes would suffer from a lack of cohesion.

Boundary classes serve as the mechanism through which actors and use cases communicate. Entity classes, on the other hand, are the classes containing business logic. It's certain that we'll find behaviors that are specific to a business process. Should we decide to place business process–specific behavior in an entity class, we'll limit the usability of that entity class in other business processes. Similarly, if we place this behavior in a boundary class, we might find it difficult to allow other actors to initiate the business process in situations where those actors can't interact directly with the boundary class encapsulating

Mediator Design Pattern

The concept of a control class is similar to the Mediator Design Patterns discussed in [GOF95]. Mediators are responsible for encapsulating how a society of objects interacts. Control classes encapsulate use case–specific behavior. Because many classes work together to fulfill a use case's functionality, the Mediator pattern is a useful implementation mechanism for control classes. We elaborate on this topic in Chapters 8 and 9.

the business process–specific behavior. This is exactly the situation where a control class is most useful. Consequently, we can state that control classes should encapsulate business process–specific behavior.

Again, considering our requirements from Chapter 6, we realize that in addition to payroll being run at set times throughout the month, a human resources representative also must be able to initiate the payroll process for a selected set of employees. Placing this process-specific behavior in a boundary class limits our ability to initiate this process from multiple contexts. In addition, placing this behavior in an entity class may limit the usability of that class in other business processes. This is an excellent situation in which to use a control class, and we elaborate on this process in Chapter 8. For now, let's concentrate on how we identify the control classes.

Control classes initially are easy to identify. Because use cases represent business processes, we begin by creating a separate control class for each use case. As we progress, we find that some control classes lack interesting behavior. In these cases, the logic can be placed into the appropriate boundary or entity class.

In other cases, we may find that some business processes have extremely interesting behavior. We also may discover that we don't want to associate some system-level processes with either our boundary or entity classes, even though these system-level processes aren't represented as use cases. As we refine our design, and discover these interesting situations, control classes can be introduced.

Figure 7.3 shows a class diagram representing the control classes identified early in the development effort. We have chosen to create a control class for each use case. Later, if we find that some of the control classes are not needed, or that they have uninteresting behavior, we'll remove them.

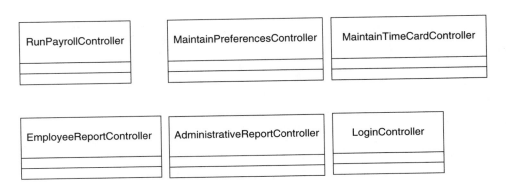

Figure 7.3 Payroll System Control Classes

7.3   Establishing Architecture

Up to this point, we have identified, at least at a high level, some of the classes that compose our system. Classes, however, don't exist in a vacuum but must reside in packages. Therefore, any industrial-strength application must consider the packages that will contain the many different classes. It certainly isn't a good idea to place all classes in the same package, even early on, because doing so promotes bad practices. While Chapter 10 is devoted exclusively to architecture, we discuss it briefly in this chapter due to the significant role that architecture plays in the overall development lifecycle.

Each of our boundary, entity, and control classes has quite specific purposes. As such, it makes perfect sense to create an initial package structure that follows along these same lines. In Figure 7.4, we see three initial packages that we've defined dependencies between. As discussed in Chapter 1, a dependency between two packages implies that the contents of one package, call it the *reliant package*, can use the contents of another package, call it the *dependent package*, but not vice versa. Therefore, the contents of the user interface package can use the contents of business services, but not vice versa. Similarly, the contents of business services can use the contents of business objects.

Figure 7.4 depicts our first pass on defining our high-level system architecture. As we progress through more detailed design, we must make sure that we adhere to these package dependencies. Therefore, as we begin to associate behaviors to various classes, and identify relationships between these classes, all relationships must be consistent with the relationships between packages. If we find inconsistencies, it's extremely important that we consciously resolve the

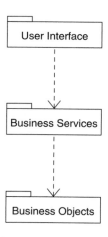

Figure 7.4   Payroll System Initial Package Diagram

violation. The resolution may be new dependencies between packages or a more flexible class design. In each case, many advantages and disadvantages must be considered. When considering these options, we should take into account the principles discussed in Chapter 1.

7.4 Allocating Classes

We've created a set of classes to house the behavior our system will ultimately realize. We've also identified some packages to contain these classes. Our next activity, prior to focusing on the allocation of behavior to classes, is to allocate our different classes to their appropriate packages. In most cases, this activity is a simple, but important, one. It's simple in the sense that our boundary classes are allocated to the user interface package, our control classes to the business services package, and our entity classes to the business objects package. These allocations are illustrated in Figure 7.5.

This allocation is important because we now have attempted to identify which classes can communicate. Boundary classes can talk to other boundary and control classes, and control classes can talk to other control and entity classes. Entity classes can talk only to other entity classes. At this point, however, any other communication is forbidden. Again, whether this process carries forward through more detailed design is yet to be seen, but by taking these small steps, and consciously allocating classes to appropriate packages, we've moved one step closer to creating an application that is resilient, robust, and more maintainable.

7.5 Conclusion

This chapter serves as the gateway from requirements into analysis and design. We begin by analyzing our requirements artifacts and transforming them into an appropriate set of specification artifacts. At a low level, these specification artifacts are the boundary, entity, and control classes discovered by analyzing the requirements artifacts. At a higher level, these artifacts are the packages that contain each of these individual types of classes. After completing this activity, we have a robust set of specification elements that should serve us well as we move into more detailed analysis and design activities.

Planning our system's architecture is vital. A flexible, resilient architecture survives as the needs of the system change. All of our activities in this chapter work toward the goal of establishing architecture and ensuring that the architecture can accommodate the behavior. At any point in time that we feel our architecture is compromised, we must work to achieve a comfortable resolution. Not doing so compromises our system's integrity.

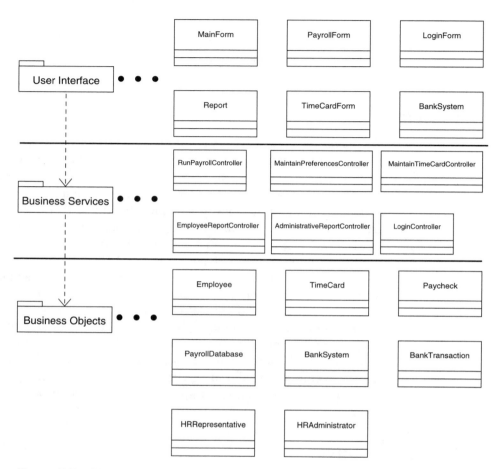

Figure 7.5   Allocation of Classes to Packages

While the architecture is important, we must not fall prey to overanalysis. Architectures tend to grow naturally. The activities, and the best practices they encompass, are important. Simply because we produce artifacts doesn't ensure architectural resiliency. If we find that artifacts produced during requirements aren't of value, we must question their inclusion and further refinement in later iterations. We should feel comfortable moving to the next activity, not when we are convinced we've produced an appropriate set of artifacts, but when we're comfortable that the artifacts we have produced will provide the most value in the next activity. In addition, we must be cautious not to try doing too much, too early.

CHAPTER 8

Behavioral Modeling

*Allocating responsibilities to our classes may be the single
most important activity we perform as developers.*

In the previous chapter, we identified some high-level classes and packages that
compose our system. However, we didn't identify any of the class responsibilities. Behavioral modeling is the process of allocating responsibilities to these
classes. It's the most important activity we perform throughout the lifecycle
because the behavior dictates our system's structure.

Unfortunately, many development efforts tend to move directly from
requirements to structural modeling, skipping the modeling of behavior. This
approach is flawed because we haven't consciously determined the responsibilities of our classes. While we eventually may end up with classes and their associated responsibilities, behavioral modeling makes this determination an
explicit activity. The result is a much more robust set of classes and associated
behaviors, something that will most likely not occur if we don't consciously
model behavior.

The resiliency of our application ultimately is based on the degree to which
we are able to manage the dependencies between classes. Much of the material
in Chapter 1 focused on the reduction of coupling between classes by abstractly
coupling the relationships and managing the dependencies between our packages. These flexible dependencies are the heart of a flexible system. However,
the identification of these dependencies is extremely difficult when we don't
know how our objects talk to each other. If an object talks to another object, the
classes must have a structural relationship. Therefore, by modeling behavior,
not only are we able to determine what a class does, but we're also able to see

how it will interact with other objects when instantiated. As we'll see in this chapter, our behavioral models serve as the artifacts from which we'll decide our system's structure.

As we've mentioned previously, and as we remind ourselves in this chapter, activities typically aren't performed in a vacuum. While behavioral modeling emphasizes allocation of responsibilities, it doesn't imply that we work only with behavioral diagrams. In fact, the activities discussed in this chapter are performed virtually simultaneously. The time period separating these activities is measured in hours, if not minutes.

The static view of software probably contributes less than half to the overall specification. Software is all about behavior, and therefore, the dynamic view is more valuable than the static view. Unfortunately, few developers recognize this fact, and even fewer actually model the dynamic aspects of a system. In this chapter, we practice using the behavioral diagrams and gain an appreciation for behavioral modeling.

8.0   Notation

Let's now explore the fundamental elements present on sequence and collaboration diagrams, two of the most commonly used behavioral diagrams. This material can also be found in Chapter 3.

8.0.1   Object

Object:Class

An *object* is an instance of a class and is represented by a rectangle. An object can be named in three different ways. First, and probably most common, we can specify the class that this object is an instance of. We specify the class name, preceded by a semicolon and underlined, in the object rectangle. Second, we can specify only the object name, neglecting the class name. We do so by omitting the class name and semicolon and simply typing the object name and underlining it. In this naming scenario, we don't know the class that this object is an instance of. We'll see an example of this method in Chapter 11. The third way to represent an object is to combine the two previously discussed approaches.

An object also can be thought of as a physical entity, whereas a class is a conceptual entity. At fist glance, it may seem odd that an object doesn't have a Java language mapping. In fact, it does. An object in the UML maps directly to an object in Java. However, when developers create Java applications, they're creating Java classes, not Java objects. Developers never write their code inside a Java object. Thinking about objects a little differently, we can think of objects as existing at runtime and classes existing at design time. Developers create their code and map UML elements to Java at design time, not runtime. Therefore, while a UML object maps directly to an Java object, no Java language mapping represents a UML object.

8.0.2 Message

A *message* is graphically represented using a solid directed arrow. While this representation is similar to that of an association on a class diagram, messages are used to represent the communication that occurs between objects, not the structural relationship present between classes.

8.0.3 Sequence Diagrams

Sequence diagrams are a form of behavioral diagram that enable us to specify the interactions that exist between a set of objects. While other behavioral diagrams may prove valuable, sequence diagrams are used most often, primarily because they enable us to see how objects use each other. Based on this information, we more accurately can determine why two objects are related, and no structural diagram can provide this information.

Because sequence diagrams are always read top to bottom, they provide an illustration of the order in which messages are sent between objects. This enables us quickly to determine the subsequence of events associated with any message sent. This subsequence, or subflow, is important because it enables us to examine many sequence diagrams, identify common subflows, and determine if these subflows are reuse candidates.

It's perfectly acceptable to suppress certain messages that may participate in the present flow of events if the message isn't significant in the context of the sequence diagram. While complex diagrams are impressive, they don't do much for communication. Sequence diagrams should be kept as simple as possible, and any message that is insignificant need not be shown.

Figure 8.1 shows a sample sequence diagram, the primary components of which follow:

- **Object:** The objects on a sequence diagram always are listed across the top of the diagram, which makes it easy to identify the classes (assuming the class notation is used) that participate in the interaction.
- **Message:** Messages are represented as directed arrows. In the diagram in Figure 8.1, we say that `SomeObject` sends `aMessage` to `Class`. Above the directed arrow is text informing us of the message sent between the objects. Messages can be numbered, indicating the order that the

messages are sent. On sequence diagrams, this numbering is somewhat
redundant because the ordering of the messages always is determined
by the order, from top to bottom, in which they appear on the diagram. In addition, it's possible to show an object sending a message to
itself using a reflexive message, which the message marked as "2" in
the diagram in Figure 8.1 illustrates. There is no restriction on the
direction of messages. Messages on sequence diagrams can flow from
either left to right or right to left.

- **Focus of control:** This illustrates the period of time during which an
  object is performing an action. The actual amount of time, measured in
  some unit such as seconds, isn't relevant. In this context, we're interested only in knowing the period that a particular method has control
  of the sequence of events. Indicating the focus of control is optional.
  This focus of control can be rendered graphically on sequence diagrams by placing a rectangle on top of the object lifeline.

- **Object lifeline:** This represents the life of an object in the context of the
  sequence of events. Objects that are created late in the sequence don't
  necessarily appear at the top of the diagram but may appear at the
  point they're created. In addition, the lifeline can end at the point the
  object is destroyed or a reference to the object is lost. Similarly, object
  creation can be represented by simply sending a `create` or `new` message
  to an object.

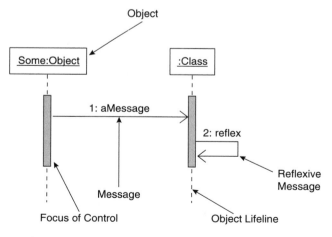

Figure 8.1   Syntax of a Sequence Diagram

8.0.4 Collaboration Diagrams

Semantically, collaboration diagrams are equivalent to sequence diagrams. They too illustrate the interactions among a group of objects. Thus, collaboration and sequence diagrams can be referred to as *interaction diagrams*. Interaction diagrams illustrate the flow of events for a society of objects.

Visually, however, sequence and collaboration diagrams are quite different. Whereas sequence diagrams are effective at illustrating the ordering of a sequence of events, collaboration diagrams are best suited to specifying how a group of objects are interconnected. This spatial layout can be useful when we must determine system structure. Because of the semantic equivalencies, structure also can be derived from sequence diagrams, and we use sequence diagrams as our primary interaction diagram throughout this book.

The numbering on collaboration diagrams is a bit more important than on sequence diagrams. Because collaboration diagrams are more spatial in nature, nothing dictates where objects must reside nor the order in which messages are sent. In addition, flow of control can be difficult to determine on collaboration diagrams. The Dewey Decimal System can be used to represent flow of control. For information on flow of control on collaboration diagrams, refer to *The Unified Modeling Language User's Guide* [BOOCH99].

Figure 8.2 shows a sample collaboration diagram. The primary components of this diagram follow:

- **Object:** The objects on a collaboration diagram are laid out in a manner that indicates how object are connected. This makes it easy to derive the relationships between the classes (assuming the class notation is used).
- **Message:** A message on a sequence diagram is represented by a directed arrow above a link. In the diagram in Figure 8.2, SomeObject sends the

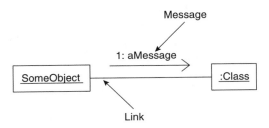

Figure 8.2 Syntax of a Collaboration Diagram

aMessage to Class. Semantically, a message on a collaboration diagram specifies the same thing as a message on a sequence diagram.

- **Link:** Links represent the connections between objects. In UML terms, a link is an instance of an association, just as an object is an instance of a class. Because a link is an instance of an association, it's easier to derive the structural relationships that exist between classes from collaboration diagrams rather than from sequence diagrams.

8.1   Use Case Realizations

As mentioned previously, we model our system's behavior to allocate responsibilities to the classes we identified during problem analysis. Based on this behavior, and how objects interact, we can determine the structure of our system. Tackling the system in its entirety, however, can be an overwhelming task. We should begin by allocating responsibilities for use cases on an individual basis, an activity we call *use case realization.*

When realizing use cases, we're actually transforming the behavior specified in the use case model to behavior in the design model. Recall that our use case model describes the system from a user's perspective. Use cases are excellent at showing what the system must do, but they don't specify how the system does anything. Identifying the initial concepts in Chapter 7 was a first step at performing this transformation by creating structural entities, namely by using the boundary, entity, and control stereotypes that were applied to the appropriate classes. When we realize use cases, we combine the behavior in the use case model with our initial structural entities. Interaction diagrams are a natural way to combine this behavior and structure into a group of interacting objects. This concept was discussed in detail in Chapter 4.

Breaking down each individual use case as a group of interacting objects enables us to focus on significant business processes independently, which enables us to manage the complexity associated with large system development. Eventually, we'll examine each of our use case realizations, looking for common sequences of messages that might exist across use cases. As we identify these common sequences, we'll extract these common behavioral elements, organize them into more generic packages, and use them within each use case.

When we identified our use cases, we created use case specifications that document the flows of events associated with that use case. As we realize our use cases, we rely heavily upon these flows of events. As a starting point, we'll create a single interaction diagram for each flow of events. Using our flows of events to derive our interactions represents a significant aspect of a process driven by behavior. If we don't use these specifications during the realization process, we must question the value of the specifications in the first place.

8.2   **Responsibility Allocation**

In this section, we'll illustrate the concepts by example. In Chapter 6, we presented a use case model that captured the requirements for a payroll system, and in Chapter 7, we identified initial classes we derived from the use case model. In this section, we transform our system into a set of interacting objects by combining the behavioral requirements with the structural boundary, entity, and control stereotypes we applied to the appropriate types of classes. Let's begin with the Run Payroll use case's primary flow of events.

The following reviews the primary flow of events presented in Figure 6.5 in Chapter 6 for the Run Payroll use case:

1. The system retrieves a list of employees with signed time cards for the pay period.

2. The system calculates pay for each employee, based on the time card information or based on the commission rate for a commissioned employee.

3. The system generates a pay stub and prints it.

4. The system creates a bank transaction.

5. The bank transaction is sent to the bank system for processing and subsequent deposit in the employee's specified account.

6. When employees have been processed, the system shuts down.

In Figure 8.3, we see an initial sequence diagram that represents the primary flow of events for the Run Payroll use case. Let's examine the decisions made as the sequence diagram was created.

First, we must identify the classes that participate in this flow of events. From the problem statement from Chapter 6, we see that the payroll process is initiated at specified times during the month: "It is important that the payroll process run on the fifteenth and last day of each month at 12:00 a.m." This statement tells us that we need a boundary class that either monitors the system clock or is initiated by some job scheduler at the specified time. Unfortunately, we didn't identify a boundary class to satisfy this need. Therefore, we should update our class diagram in Figure 7.2 to represent the addition of this new boundary class named SystemClock. The new diagram is shown in Figure 8.4, and we now have a boundary class that can receive external, time-sensitive, events. The SystemClock now notifies the PayrollController that it's time to run the payroll process.

At this point, we might question the need for our SystemClock class. Isn't it true that we could allow the payroll controller to serve as both the control and boundary classes? While we certainly could, there's good reason not to do so. In

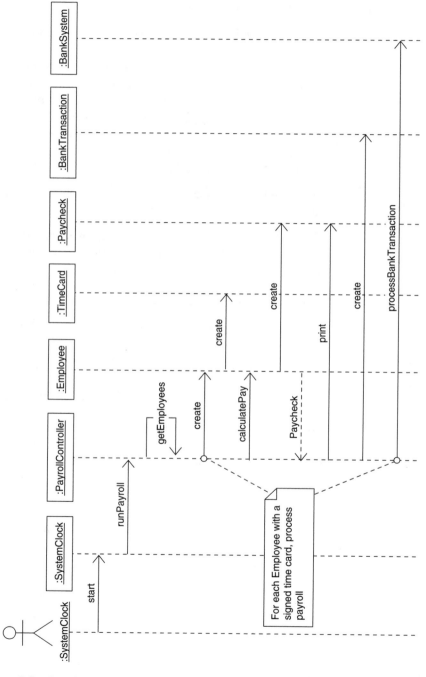

Figure 8.3   Run Payroll Batch Sequence Diagram for Primary Flow of Events

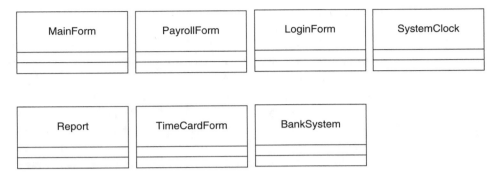

Figure 8.4   Run Payroll Boundary Classes

addition to the previous statement, recall the following statement from the requirements documentation: "A human resources representative must have the ability to initiate the payroll process on demand based on a selected list of employees."

This statement should serve as a good indication that the behavior of the Run Payroll use case must be initiated by two separate actors, one of whom is human and the other is not. Attempting to use our `PayrollController` as both a boundary class and a control class violates class cohesion because our `PayrollController` class performs multiple responsibilities. This violation of cohesion should become more clear as we analyze the important responsibilities of the `PayrollController`.

In our flow of events, we see next that the system must retrieve a list of employees with signed time cards—our first significant behavioral design decision. Which class is responsible for retrieving and managing this list of employees? The `Employee` class itself can't do it because it doesn't make sense for an `Employee` instance to manage a list of all other employees. An `Employee` should be responsible only for managing itself.

The obvious candidate for this task should be the `PayrollController` class, which illustrates more clearly the importance of having a control class. Were this control class not to exist, it would be easy to place the responsibility of managing the list of `Employee` objects within one of the two boundary classes. However, just as our control class shouldn't serve as a boundary class, as mentioned previously, our boundary classes shouldn't serve as control classes. Doing so creates an obvious disadvantage. After creating the first boundary class to run the batch payroll process, we would have to accommodate human initiation of the payroll process by duplicating the code within the form that the human resources representative actor interacts with. Therefore, in this case, the importance of separating our boundary responsibilities and control responsibilities should be apparent.

Note that we don't necessarily care at this point how the list of employees is obtained; instead, we care only that the `PayrollController` is the class responsible for obtaining the employees. While we might deduce that the `PayrollController` will retrieve this list of employees from a relational database, and that we'll filter out employees with signed time cards via a SQL where clause, we choose not to elaborate on this implementation right away. For now, we're more concerned with what an object is responsible for doing, not how it gets the work done. If we want to concern ourselves with this issue right now, the best thing to do would be to place a note next to the `getEmployees` reflexive message stating that only employees with signed time cards can be retrieved.

Upon obtaining a list of employees, we must calculate pay based on time card information for each of those employees. In Figure 8.3, we've enclosed all messages that must participate in the pay calculation loop within the confines of a note that has been attached to each message existing at the boundary of the loop. Doing this makes it clear which messages must be performed as part of the loop and which of those messages are external to the loop.

The first step in performing the actual pay calculation is to create an `Employee` object. After creating the `Employee` object, a `TimeCard` object also is created. Next, `PayrollController` sends the `calculatePay` message to the `Employee` instance, which might seem odd at first glance. Let's consider a few of the alternatives. We certainly could allow `PayrollController` to calculate pay. However, the calculation of pay may not be a straightforward computation. This computation will be dependent on some important information within the `Employee` object. An `Employee` knows whether pay should be calculated based on `TimeCard` information or commission. If pay is calculated based on time card information, the `Employee` should know whether the calculation is based upon an hourly or salaried rate. Thus, if we allow `PayrollController` to calculate pay, `PayrollController` will need to obtain all information from `Employee` and `TimeCard` and use this information to calculate the pay. The need to obtain all of this information from multiple sources should send a red flag as a violation of encapsulation. If the behavior and data don't reside on the same class, we must have a good reason for it. It makes more sense in this case for an employee to calculate his or her own pay. Unlike true employees in the real world, we need not worry about dishonest objects. All `Employee` objects are from the same mold—the `Employee` class.

At this point, `Employee` is responsible for calculating his or her own pay. Upon calculating pay, `Employee` creates a paycheck, which seems reasonable because if an `Employee` should be responsible for calculating pay, then why not have the `Employee` generate the `Paycheck`? Upon creating the `Paycheck`, we see

Controller Classes

We should be aware that controller classes can be a violation of encapsulation. We should always try to keep data and related behavior together. Sometimes, for simplicity and elegance, controllers are required. A classic situation is a VCR and videotapes. Ideally, a tape contains its own controller, negating the need for everyone to own a VCR to watch a movie. However, because of the expensive nature of the controller and its complex behavior, it's more feasible to separate the controlling functionality and create a separate controller class. Therefore, the controller exists separately, as a VCR. Another similar analogy where the controller and entity have been combined is a disposable camera. Before the invention of a disposable camera, a separate camera controller class was needed because of the expensive nature of this controller class.

this `Paycheck` is returned to `PayrollController`. `PayrollController` then prints the `Paycheck`.

This sequence of actions is interesting. While nothing is obviously incorrect about the sequence, we should question why the `Employee` creates the `Paycheck`, only to pass it back to the `PayrollController` who is responsible for printing it. Something about the print method on the `Paycheck` must determine that we want only the `PayrollController`, and not the `Employee`, to know about it. Unfortunately, this requirement isn't documented anywhere on the diagram, and the result is simply an extra degree of coupling that isn't necessarily needed. It makes more sense if the object responsible for creating the `Paycheck` were also the object responsible for printing it. This helps reduce coupling because only a single class will be dependent on the `Paycheck` class. Which way is correct? Well, it depends.

At this point, the problem with choosing the most appropriate relationship is that it may be driven by how other use cases will use and interact with our `Employee` class. If we find that the relationship between `Employee` and `Paycheck` is pervasive in that many other use cases have similar interactions, then it's desirable to allow our `Employee` to create the `Paycheck` and print it. However, if this use case is the only one in which `Employee` interacts with a `Paycheck`, then it is desirable for our `PayrollController` to mediate this interaction. After all, the purpose of the `PayrollController` is to encapsulate use case–specific functionality. In this situation, we have decided that it should be the responsibility of the `PayrollController` to mediate this behavior. Our new sequence diagram can be found in Figure 8.5.

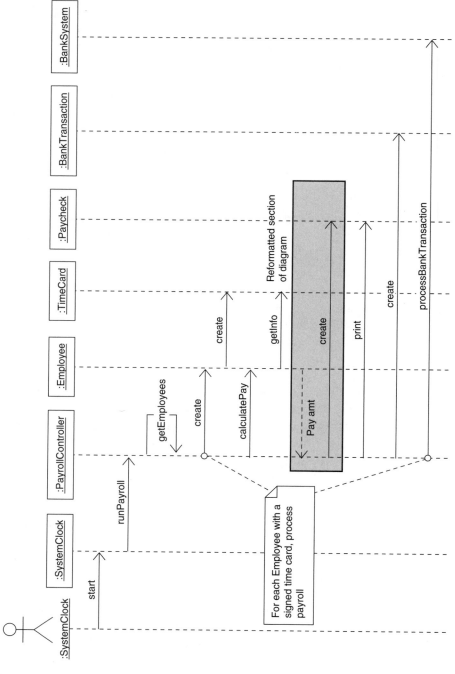

Figure 8.5   Revised Run Payroll Batch Primary Flow Sequence Diagram

The modeling of the last couple of interactions is based on the decision that interactions with a BankTransaction are specific to this use case. We can only deduce this because the PayrollController is the class that communicates with a BankTransaction instead of the Employee class.

8.2.1   Decentralized versus Centralized Flow of Control

As mentioned previously, it's important to consider which object is in charge at any given point in time. This decision ultimately will be determined by how other interactions within other use cases are realized. Previously, we decided that the PayrollController should be responsible for managing the creation of a Paycheck and printing it. This decision was based on the assumption that other interactions with Employee most likely won't duplicate this sequence of events.

In the diagram in Figure 8.3, our Employee was responsible for creating the TimeCard object as well as obtaining information from the TimeCard. In this sequence, no other object sends a message to the TimeCard object. This decision was based on the assumption that in many other use cases in which the Employee participates, the Employee will interact with TimeCard. In fact, we can deduce from the diagram in Figure 8.5 that each time an Employee object is created, the Employee time card information also will be created and encapsulated in a TimeCard object.

The decisions that we've made when allocating responsibilities to our objects can be characterized as centralized versus decentralized flow of control, and these decisions impact a class' granularity. When many messages originate from the same object, we can say that the sequence of messages is centralized. However, when a single message causes a cascading set of other messages to originate from within the operation called, the flow of control is decentralized. Thus, PayrollController communicating to Paycheck represents a centralized flow because PayrollController relies upon Employee to calculate the pay amount that then is used to create Paycheck. On the other hand, Payroll-Controller communicating with Employee, which subsequently communicates with TimeCard, is decentralized because PayrollController has no knowledge of time card information. Instead, PayrollController knows only of Employee.

8.2.2   Controllers as Mediators

The Mediator design pattern enables a society of objects to interact, while ensuring that the society maintains loose coupling. The Mediator pattern does so by encapsulating the behaviors that are the result of the object interactions. Therefore, because the Mediator pattern encapsulates this functionality, the objects themselves don't have to reference each other directly; instead, these objects allow the `Mediator` to manage, and add to, the collective behavior.

In [GOF95], the authors tell us to consider using Mediator in the following situations:

- A society of objects interact in complex, but well-defined, ways.
- Reusing an object is difficult because of its dependencies on other, not needed, objects.
- Behaviors spread across many classes should be customizable, without subclassing.

Figure 8.6 shows the class diagram for the Mediator pattern.

Without `Mediator`, our `ConcreteColleague` classes would be dependent on each other. If, for some reason, this dependency isn't desirable, we can introduce a `Mediator` that manages their interactions. Using the Mediator pattern in this context is strikingly similar to our previous discussions on whether we should centralize or decentralize control. In fact, applying the Mediator pattern centralizes flow of control for the objects that the `Mediator` manages. Some of the consequences, both pro and con, of using the Mediator pattern include:

- **Limits subclassing:** Because a `Mediator` manages how a society of objects interact, it can be easy to change the interaction by simply subclassing the `Mediator` class, instead of attempting to subclass many different colleagues.
- **Decouples colleagues:** Because the `Mediator` manages the interactions of colleagues, individual colleague classes now can be used in other contexts that might not require the presence of colleagues specific to the interaction the `Mediator` manages.
- **Manages object interaction:** Encapsulating the interaction knowledge within the `Mediator` creates a focal point for the behavior, which clari-

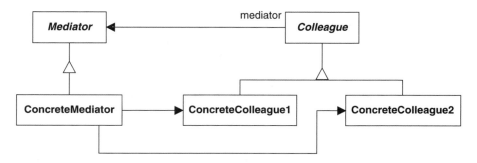

Figure 8.6   Mediator Design Pattern

fies the understanding of the number of objects that are used together as part of a greater whole.

- **Centralizes control:** Because a `Mediator` encapsulates the interaction knowledge, the `Mediator` itself can grow in size and complexity, creating a `Mediator` that becomes a god class. This makes it more likely that the `Mediator` will become a pit into which we throw behaviors that might not necessarily belong.

As stated previously, early in the life of the project, we typically create a control class for each use case, the purpose of which is to encapsulate use case–specific functionality. Initially, the control class might be simple and contain little interesting behavior. However, as our design progresses, we find that new and unpredicted behaviors will surface that we don't feel comfortable associating with our entity or boundary classes. In these situations, our control classes tend to fill up with functionality, and we should consider the consequences associated with the Mediator design pattern.

In reality, all control classes are a degenerative form of a `Mediator`. In Figure 8.6, were we to omit the abstract `Mediator` class, choosing only to create a `ConcreteMediator`, we would have a design that is eerily similar to our `PayrollController` and the responsibilities that it manages between our `Employee` and `Paycheck` class.

So why didn't we simply call our control classes `Mediators` instead? The Mediator pattern solves a general type of problem, which is how a society of objects interact. A control class, on the other hand, encapsulates use case–specific functionality, in addition to managing the communication between boundary and entity classes. Though the context in which we've discussed control classes and Mediators might make it seem as if they're the same, this is

Lazy Instantiation

Lazy instantiation is a technique where objects are created only when they are needed. Lazy instantiation is a useful technique in situations where the number of objects in memory at any given time might be quite large but the number of objects that we currently are working with is small. In our example, where we are working with only a single `Employee`, but we are enumerating through a large set of `Employee` instances, we could consider managing the collection of `Employee` instances within a separate class and creating `Employee` objects only as they are needed. Chapter 9 contains an example of how to use lazy instantiation.

untrue. Mediators have a variety of applications. They can be used to manage complex user interface issues, where certain user interface widgets are enabled or disabled based upon the state within others. Therefore, applying the Mediator design pattern to our control class is just one context in which the Mediator can be used. In addition, our control class serves other roles. It facilitates communication from our boundary to our entity classes, which is something not present, nor stated, in the Mediator pattern. We also may find that we apply other patterns to our control class, such as the ability for it to observe objects that have been registered with it. This is the nature of patterns, in that they're rarely ever used in a vacuum, and they're always slightly tailored to solve the interesting problem at hand. Thus, where control classes are used, the consequences of `Mediator` should be measured. However, in other situations where `Mediator` might be used, the characteristics of a control class rarely need be considered.

8.2.3   Managing Collections

Another important decision that we must make is which object is responsible for managing sets of other objects. In Figure 8.5, our `PayrollController` was responsible for managing a collection of `Employee` objects. Managing collections isn't necessarily a trivial task. We must consider not only how we store the collection, but also how the individual objects within the collection are instantiated.

Again, the decision is based upon how the `Employee` class is used in other contexts. In other use cases, if we find we commonly work with only a single `Employee`, then managing the collection of `Employee` instances with `Payroll-Controller` is acceptable. However, if we find that we're constantly writing code that manages a list of employees, we might consider a class that manages a list of employees for us. Not only might this class manage the collection, but it also might also be responsible for knowing how to create the objects within the collection.

Consider that's it's highly likely that `Employee` objects will be retrieved from some persistent data store. In this case, our `EmployeeCollection` might know how to retrieve this collection of employees from the database and return individual `Employee` objects on demand. Doing so enables us to perform lazy instantiation of the actual `Employee` objects. We elaborate on this topic in Chapter 9.

8.2.4   Accessor and Mutator Methods

While not used on any of the diagrams we've produced to this point, it's very common to see objects with accessor methods present. Accessor methods also are commonly referred to as simply `get` and `set` methods. These methods enable us to obtain the value of an object's attribute (the get), as well as change the value of an object's attribute (the set).

Most developers are familiar with encapsulation, and it's quite common to see classes with all instance attributes declared as private. Accessor methods that allow other objects to access these attributes also are common. On the one hand, it's good because various rules can be associated with the get and set methods to ensure that the attribute is not altered incorrectly. For instance, consider an Employee class with a Salary attribute. Were the Salary attribute public, it would be easy for any other object to access that Salary attribute, setting it to any desired value. However, if the salary attribute is private, and wrapped with accessor methods, we can prevent the setting of that attribute if it doesn't fall within a certain range. For instance, if a rule states that an employee's salary must be between $15,000 and $75,000, the setSalary method can contain a rule that enforces this restriction. At this point, no other object in the system can change the employee's salary to any amount not within this range. Consider the following accessor methods:

```
private void setSalary(float salary) {
if ( (salary < 15000.0F) || (salary > 75000.0F) ) {
    throw new SalaryOutOfRangeException("Employee salary must " +
"be between $15000 and $75000");
} else {
    this._salary = salary;
}

private float getSalary() {
    return this._salary;
}
```

While using accessor and mutator methods is certainly advantageous, it also can be problematic. It still allows another object to access the internal attributes of Employee, perform some function on that attribute, and then change the value of that attribute on that Employee. Therefore, in a sense, accessor methods can be seen as a violation of encapsulation. While not all accessor methods are violations, examining the object interactions in many systems typically results in the discovery that a number of accessor methods are violations. If we find that a single class has accessor methods for each of its attributes, we should question it. It's likely that one of the two following conditions are present when we find accessor methods present:

- The attribute might not belong to the class in which it currently resides and should be moved to the class that is using the accessor method.
- The behavior might not belong to the class in which it is currently defined and should be moved to the class that contains the attribute.

One of the problems with an accessor method might be in name only. For instance, consider our `Employee` class discussed previously. If we really do desire to set an `Employee` instance salary, it might be best if we incorporate a bit more meaning into the reason we're setting the salary. For instance, if the salary is being adjusted to provide the employee with a raise, we may consider changing the name of the method to the following:

```
private void adjustSalary(float salary) {
if ( (salary < 15000.0F) || (salary > 75000.0F) ) {
    throw new SalaryOutOfRangeException("Employee salary must " +
"be between $15000 and $75000");
} else {
    this._salary = salary;
}
```

While this change is certainly subtle, it's simply a much better practice, and it communicates to other developers who might be using the `Employee` class what the method actually does much better than what we previously had. Therefore, be guarded against blindly creating accessor methods simply because you suspect another class needs that attribute. Question whether the attribute or method is placed correctly. As we've stated previously, any time we associate a new responsibility with a class, it should be a conscious decision, and even simple accessor and mutator methods fall under this guideline.

Guard Conditions

Guard conditions on sequence diagrams should be used with caution. While they enable us to model conditionals, they also tempt us into creating sequence diagrams that are overly complex. If we find that a single sequence diagram is littered with guard conditions and has become difficult to read, we should consider dividing the sequence diagram into multiple diagrams. In fact, a sequence diagrams with many guard conditions may be an indication that another flow of events has been discovered that wasn't previously considered when analyzing requirements. At this point, we should consider consulting the customer to unearth these additional requirements.

8.2.5 Additional Diagrams

Figure 8.7 shows a sequence diagram for the Maintain Time Card use case's primary flow of events. Many of the considerations discussed previously also hold true here. We see that an Employee interacts with his or her TimeCard. However, we don't see the need for Employee instances to interact with a Paycheck. Each of these situations supports our decisions in the sequence diagrams we created previously, such as that in Figure 8.5. Thus, while it's important to consider each use case independently to manage complexity, it's also important to consider use cases as a collective whole representing our system because coupling is impacted by those classes that participate in more than one use case.

In the diagram in Figure 8.7, when our LoginForm creates the Employee object, we don't show the creation of the TimeCard object as we did in Figure 8.5. The creation of the TimeCard object is implicit in the creation of Employee instances and was omitted in Figure 8.7 purposely. In fact, looking at both diagrams simultaneously, a question that begs to be answered is how we instantiate TimeCard objects. Do we need to instantiate multiple TimeCard instances? For the Run Payroll use case, we're primarily interested in creating TimeCard instances for a pay period where the TimeCard objects for that pay period are signed. However, for the Maintain Time Card use case, it might be necessary to create TimeCard objects that haven't been signed or to obtain a listing of all time cards based upon some period specified by an employee. Subsequently, Run Payroll and Maintain Time Card use cases may create TimeCard instances based on two periods of time. These two periods may be different and quite possibly may require different criteria be used to instantiate the appropriate time cards. Needless to say, all these decisions are important, and without at least considering how the Employee will use TimeCard instances and the context in which TimeCard instances will be used, it's unlikely that any solution can be as robust as a decision we reach when carefully considering our alternatives.

We've also chosen to annotate the diagram in Figure 8.7 with guard conditions. Guard conditions are used on sequence diagrams to specify simple conditional statements. In Figure 8.7, we'll get the timecard information if it exists; otherwise, we'll create a new TimeCard object and initialize it appropriately.

Other issues must be considered in the scenario in Figure 8.7. When displaying time card information on the TimeCardForm, do we wish to pass a reference to the TimeCard object back to the form, or use some other object that encapsulates the time card information? A flexible alternative is to create a separate class that maps to the individual fields on our form. This new class might contain the data that needs to be displayed, as well as the logic that knows how to bind the information to the appropriate form fields. This removes the logic from the form, which is beneficial in keeping our boundary classes separate from our entity classes. It also removes the logic from the TimeCard object, which we certainly don't want dependent on our boundary classes. The special types of classes that map data elements to form fields might be created for each form displaying data. While we need not solve these challenges here, we should make note of them to ensure they're addressed in the future.

Also, note the addition of the PayrollDatabase class, which wasn't present on our class diagrams resulting from problem analysis in Chapter 6. We introduced this class to facilitate interaction with the payroll database, and we should consider updating our class diagrams to reflect the addition of the PayrollDatabase class. It's likely that this class would be a boundary class because it interacts with a system external to the system under development.

8.2.5.1   Object References

At some point, we must consider how references to objects will be obtained. Do we simply create the object when we need to use it, or do we need some other, more elaborate creation mechanism. In the diagram in Figure 8.7, our Maintain-TimecardController object obviously needs to interact with Employee objects. How does this controller get a reference to the Employee object? It's unlikely that the controller will be able to create the Employee object when it needs it. Attempting to do so will unveil the need for the controller to know information about which Employee object to instantiate, such as an employee ID.

While not explicitly modeled in the scenario in Figure 8.7, we can deduce that because LoginForm is responsible for creating the Employee object, each subsequent object in the scenario will use this same instance of the Employee object and thus will obtain its reference to the Employee from this LoginForm, whether directly or indirectly. How exactly the LoginForm creates the Employee object isn't illustrated; however, by examining the Login use case, it's likely that this creation could be more clearly specified. We choose to suppress the details of this in Figure 8.7 because we don't want to confuse our scenario with the details encapsulated within another. Examining the Login use case might show that we create the Employee object using an object factory, and that we then store this object in a structure accessible from anywhere, such as the Session object (if we're using Java's Servlet API to build Web applications). The point here is not that we want to know how the Employee object is created, only that we did give careful consideration to where it will be created, and that other objects will be involved in its usage.

Many of these issues will be discovered only when we begin coding. Creating simple prototypes simulating the behavior illustrated in our designs is extremely valuable. In the next section, we do just this using the Run Payroll diagram in Figure 8.5 as our basis.

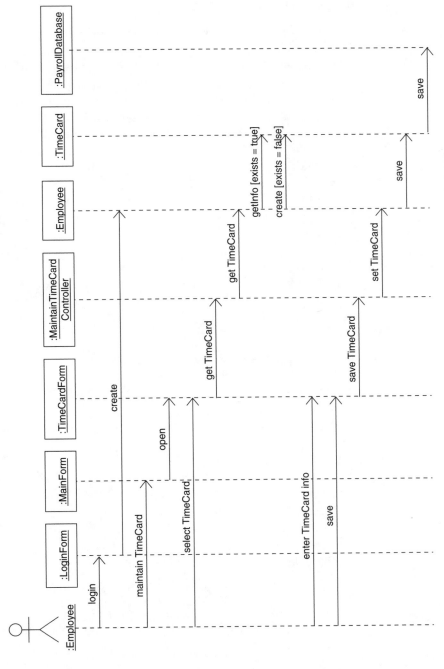

Figure 8.7 Maintain Time Card Primary Flow Sequence Diagram

8.2.6   Simple Prototypes

At this point, the sequence diagram for the primary flow has been discussed and is fairly straightforward. Let's write a little bit of code to see how easily it can be implemented. Remember, one of the best practices that we wish to adhere to is the creation of simple prototypes. While many people and processes may not advocate writing simple code this early in the development lifecycle, it's something that can be helpful in earlier iterations. If we can't easily implement a working skeleton of our design, then we can't be convinced that the design isn't flawed. We're primarily interested in determining whether the responsibilities we've allocated to our classes make sense, though we may choose to create a simple class diagram, which is the topic of the next chapter. We may find that much of what we do in this section is create throw-away code.

Realistically, there's no reason to wait before implementing our design, at least in a simple form. If we can prove it in code, and we are comfortable with it, we can move on to the next task in the process. However, if we find we're uncomfortable with the code, it's a good time to refactor our design immediately. The following illustrates the sample code produced as the result of our first attempt at design. Note that we take into consideration only the Run Payroll use case. We leave the implementation of the Maintain Time Card use case as an exercise for the reader. Go ahead, try it!

```java
public class SystemClock {
    public static void main(String args[]) {
        SystemClock initiator = new SystemClock();
        initiator.start();
    }

    public void start() {
        PayrollController pc = new PayrollController();
        pc.runPayroll();
    }
}
```

```java
import java.util.*;

public class PayrollController {
    public void runPayroll() {
        System.out.println("running payroll");
        Iterator employees = getEmployees();
        while (employees.hasNext()) {
            Employee emp = (Employee) employees.next();
            float f = emp.calculatePay();
            Paycheck paycheck = new Paycheck(f);
```

```
                    paycheck.print();
                    BankTransaction trans = new BankTransaction();
                    BankSystem bank = new BankSystem(trans);
                    bank.processBankTransaction();
                }
        }

        private Iterator getEmployees() {
            System.out.println("getting employees");
            //do i create the employee objects here and store
            //them in a collection, or do I store the resultSet
            //and loop through that to create each Employee as I
            //need to work with it? Let's create a collection now!
            ArrayList employees = new ArrayList();
            employees.add(new Employee());
            employees.add(new Employee());
            return employees.iterator();

        }
}
```

```
public class Employee {
    public float calculatePay() {
        System.out.println("Calculating Pay");
        return 2000.0f;             //hardcoded value. That's fine,
it's just a proof of concept.
    }
}
```

```
public class Paycheck {
    private float _amt;
    public Paycheck(float amt) {
        this._amt = amt;
    }

    public void print() {
        System.out.println("Printing paycheck");
    }

}
```

```
public class BankTransaction {
//this class doesn't do anything yet. Do we really need it? Proba-
bly too early to tell.
}
```

```
public class BankSystem {
    private BankTransaction _trans;
    public BankSystem(BankTransaction trans) {
        this._trans = trans;
    }

    public void processBankTransaction() {
        System.out.println("Process Bank Transaction");
    }
}
```

8.3   Model Structure

As we may now suspect, a single system can contain many sequence diagrams. The way that we organize these sequence diagrams definitely contributes to the likelihood that our model lives and grows with the system, versus it becoming a monolith that is difficult to maintain and eventually is discarded.

As discussed in Chapter 4, it may be beneficial to create collaborations for each use case. As described earlier, we call this collaboration a *use case realization*. It's named appropriately because the sequence diagrams (and in Chapter 9, the class diagrams) specify the behavior of individual use cases as a set of interacting objects (of course, the class diagrams specify the structure). Therefore, we'll organize our model by associating each of the diagrams with their appropriate use case realization, which works well because each sequence diagram represents a flow of events for an individual use case. For further discussion on this topic, refer to Chapter 4.

8.4   Conclusion

As we've seen, the allocation of responsibilities to our classes is an important step in designing our applications. The messages sent between the objects help

Modeling Tools

Realistically, the structure of our model most likely will be dictated by some modeling tool, if in fact, we are using one. If we are, we should first determine if our tool supports creating a collaboration. If it does, we should create one for each use case and associate the diagrams with that use case with the collaboration. If the tool doesn't support collaborations, consider using a package stereotype as use case realization.

flesh out the structure that exists between our classes. Attempting to determine system structure without first understanding how objects interact is extremely difficult and error prone. It's unfortunate that the behavioral aspect of most systems is so often taken for granted. While behavior allocation is important, it's one of the most difficult design challenges we're faced with. The sheer number of decisions that must be made, in conjunction with the ramifications that each decision has on many other areas of the system, makes behavioral modeling difficult.

We discussed a number of the important decisions that were made in creating the diagrams in the figures in this chapter. Because of the unique nature of each project, the decisions we face vary widely, and it's likely that many of the decisions we'll face in the future will be different than many we've made in the past. As long as careful thought goes into each decision, our design will benefit.

Keep in mind that not all behavioral decisions need to made immediately. However, the decisions that we do make must be conscious ones, and the alternatives must be carefully considered. If we're unsure of the ramifications or feasibility of a decision, a simple prototype often can answer many of our questions. This prototype need not be elaborate in nature and may be taken only to a level that enables us to gain a certain degree of comfort with the design decisions that we've made. In addition, behavioral modeling, while discussed in this chapter as a separate activity, is typically performed in conjunction with problem analysis, discussed in Chapter 7, and structural modeling, discussed in Chapter 9.

CHAPTER 9

Structural Modeling

*System structure really is only about flexibly managing the dependencies between our classes.
The behavior of our system indicates the need for flexible dependency management.*

We've discussed the design decisions that must be made when establishing the dynamic aspects of our system. The allocation of responsibilities determine how objects interact, which dictates the structural relations that must exist among our classes. While the allocation of responsibilities and the way that objects interact is extremely important, the flexibility with which we manage the relationships between our classes determines the resiliency of our system.

In this chapter, we turn our attention to designing the static structure of our system. We'll learn how we can flexibly manage the structural relationships among our classes to help create highly flexible systems. Simply establishing structure based on the interactions among objects doesn't result in a resilient system. We must consider how we define these relationships to ensure we can easily extend our system in the future without making rampant modifications throughout. To do so, we'll analyze the behavior of our classes, searching for similar responsibilities and areas that will probably change, and we'll take advantage of the power of object orientation to create a flexible design. This power is realized by using the strengths of object orientation such as inheritance, polymorphism, and composition, which we emphasize in this chapter. As we'll see, the manner in which we use these powerful constructs in Java can vary widely, based on various conditions. Because each problem is unique, we'll find that individual design challenges can be solved in many ways. Needless to say, the approach we take should be carefully calculated, and similar to behavioral modeling, the creation of static relationships also should be the result of conscious decisions that are precisely calculated and carefully evaluated.

9.0   Notation

At this point, most notation on class diagrams should be familiar. We've seen a few diagrams and have discussed some of the common elements. Let's briefly review. For more detail on class diagrams, and the components on them, refer to Chapter 3 where we introduce the fundamental elements, or Chapter 6 where we discuss additional structural notation.

9.0.1   Class Diagrams

Many of the fundamental elements we use on class diagrams were formally introduced in Chapter 3 and have been previously discussed. In this section, we provide a brief review of these elements. The diagram in Figure 9.1 is a sample class diagram derived from a set of requirements for a course registration system.

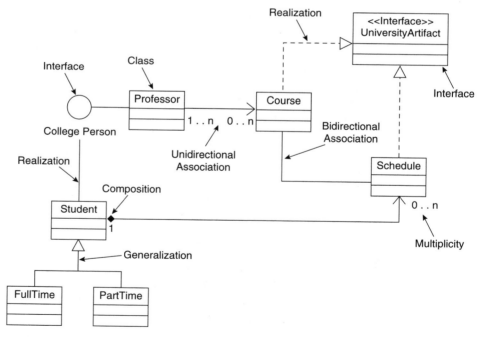

Figure 9.1   Syntax of a Class Diagram

9.0.2 Structural Elements

As seen in Figure 9.1, a class is represented as a simple rectangle with three distinct compartments. The first compartment contains text representing the class name and is required. The two remaining compartments, both optional, represent the attributes and operations of the class, respectively. In Figure 9.1, `Student`, `FullTime`, and `PartTime` are all class names. An interface can be represented different ways. As seen in Figure 9.1, we can use the iconic form or the stereotyped form. `CollegePerson`, which represents an interface, is drawn as a simple circle, whereas `UniversityArtifact` is represented as a class with an interface stereotype. While other structural elements, such as packages, can appear on a class diagram, classes and interfaces are the most common.

9.0.3 Relationships

A total of four different types of relationships are depicted on the class diagram in Figure 9.1. Two of these relationships translate into variable declarations in Java code, whereas the other two translate into forms of inheritance. An association relationship, whether it be a unidirectional or bidirectional association, always translates into an instance variable in Java code. Composition, represented as an association with a filled diamond closest to the class containing the variable, also translates into an instance variable in Java code but with a stronger form of semantic meaning. Two other forms of relationships, dependencies and aggregations, not shown in Figure 9.1, are also interpreted as variable declarations in Java. Again, refer to Chapter 3 for a detailed discussion of each of these types of relationships.

Associated with each of these first two relationships are several important adornments. Navigability, represented by a directed arrow at one end of an association, dependency, aggregation, or composition, represents the direction of the instance relation. For example, in Figure 9.1, a `Professor` can call methods on the `Course` class, but a `Course` class cannot call methods on the `Professor` class. The navigability on class diagrams enable us to determine where the variable declarations should be placed. The `Professor` class has an instance variable of type `Course` but not vice versa.

Multiplicity specifies the instance relationships between the classes. For instance, in Figure 9.1, we see that an instance of the `Professor` class can contain zero or many instances of the `Course` class. A `Course` instance, on the other hand, can belong to one or more `Professor` instances. Interpreted differently, we can say that a professor can teach many courses and that a single course can be taught by many different professors.

The remaining two types of relationships, realization and generalization, represent a form of inheritance. Realization translates into the use of the `implements` keyword in Java and should be used in UML to attach a class to an interface that it implements. This realization relationship represents pure interface inheritance. Generalization translates into use of the `extends` keyword in Java and is the more traditional mixture of interface and implementation inheritance. For more information on the differences between interface and implementation inheritance, refer to Chapter 1. Neither realization nor generalization include adornments such as navigability or multiplicity.

9.1   Coupling and Cohesion

Of all of the fancy terms associated with object orientation, two of the simplest are too often forgotten. In fact, any discussion on inheritance, polymorphism, or composition is really talking about *coupling* and *cohesion*. Informal definitions for these terms follow:

- **Coupling:** The degree to which classes within our system are dependent on each other.
- **Cohesion:** The measure of how much an entity supports a singular purpose within a system.

Our goal when designing a system should be to reduce coupling and increase cohesion. A system that is loosely coupled implies the number of relationships among all classes in our system has been kept to the minimum. Obviously, classes must have relationships to each other; otherwise, it would be difficult to actually get anything done. But if we can reduce the relationships among classes to the fewest possible, it's much more likely that classes that we want to reuse in other contexts actually can be used. In addition, if we have a highly cohesive system, we have classes with individual responsibilities, which contributes to ease of maintenance. By crisply defining what individual classes do, it's more likely we'll know which class a behavior affects when a behavior changes. Remember, a class should do one thing and do it well.

Coupling was discussed briefly in Chapter 1. Coupling is about the structure between our classes. Flexible structures help increase reusability. As we saw in Chapter 1, when we use a class, we also are indirectly using all classes upon which it is dependent. As we progress through this chapter, we pay careful attention to the coupling between our system classes and, in many situations, utilize abstract coupling. (Abstract coupling was introduced during our discussion of object-oriented principles in Chapter 1.)

In object orientation, there are three different degrees of coupling. For purposes of our discussion in this chapter, we'll call them *tight*, *nil*, and *abstract*, each of which is illustrated in Figure 9.2. Tight coupling implies a concrete class has a direct relationship to another concrete class. Nil coupling implies that two classes have no relationship to each other. Abstract coupling implies that a class has a relationship to some other abstract class. Figure 9.2 illustrates these degrees of coupling. In abstract and tight coupling, the `Service` class is an instance variable in the `Client` class.

Cohesion is primarily about responsibilities, which we discussed in Chapter 8. We've stated previously that whenever we assign a new responsibility to a class, we must carefully evaluate whether the responsibility is being allocated to the correct class. That is, our decisions about allocating responsibilities to classes should be conscious decisions.

9.2   Useful Class Diagrams

When we design a system, many different types of class diagrams can be useful. The type of a diagram is determined by the intent it's communicating. Each of these diagrams can exist at different levels of abstractions. One diagram may

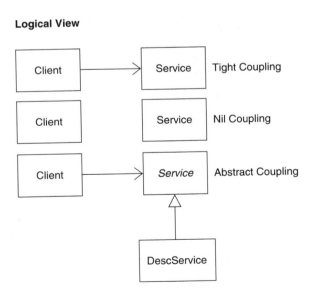

Figure 9.2   Degrees of Coupling

communicate high-level system structure, whereas another might communicate a lower-level implementation. Regardless of the diagram's intent, it's important to keep diagrams at a consistent level of abstraction. When we decide to combine high-level system constructs with lower-level implementations on a single diagram, we should have a good reason for doing so.

9.2.1   Package Diagrams

Package diagrams are useful when we need to communicate and understand the structure of the system from a higher level of abstraction. As discussed in Chapter 1, relationships between packages are represented by drawing a dependency relation between two packages. In Chapter 1, we discussed a number of package relationship principles, such as acyclic dependencies principle, stable dependencies principle, and stable abstractions principle. The diagram in Figure 9.3 shows a relationship between two packages and the restrictions that it imposes on our Java code. As seen in the figure, package A has a dependency on package B, which implies that our classes in package A can use the classes in package B but not vice versa. For additional information on package relationships and

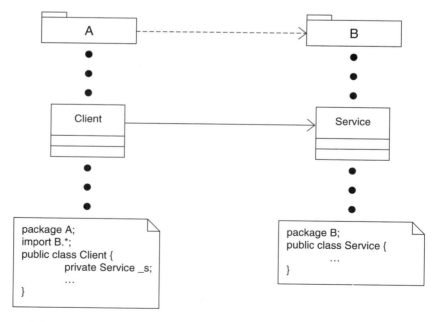

Figure 9.3   Implications of a Package Relationship on Class Relationships

principles, refer to Chapter 1. We provide additional discussion on designing package relationships, and their impact, in Chapter 10.

9.2.2 Interface Diagram

An interface diagram is a type of class diagram where we model primarily interface data types. In this sense, an interface diagram also is a more abstract diagram. Interface diagrams are most useful when we wish to generically model frameworks, class libraries, or other aspects of our system that are open for extension. When creating interface diagrams, we typically model only the interfaces and the primary classes that implement those interfaces. It's quite common to model the extension points of a framework, possibly with a default implementation to serve as a sample, on an interface diagram. In this regard, interface diagrams represent an external view of a society of classes, as shown in the diagram in Figure 9.4.

The diagram in Figure 9.4 shows a sample interface diagram for an error-handling framework, developed internally, that many applications might use. This framework, and the means through which the diagram in Figure 9.4 came about, is the focus of our discussion on frameworks and class libraries in Chapter 10. Notice that not all of our classes on this diagram are interfaces. However, the classes that do appear on this diagram are the primary classes participating in the usage of our error handler. An interface diagram typically is accompanied by a sequence diagram illustrating the dynamic behavior of the classes represented. In fact, interface diagrams are similar in nature to the specification model, discussed in Chapter 5.

Class and Sequence

Remember from our previous discussion in Chapter 4 that using class diagrams and sequence diagrams in conjunction with each other is much more powerful than using one without the other. Class diagrams don't show us why the relationships exist, but sequence diagrams do. On the other hand, sequence diagrams aren't good at showing the hierarchical or multiplicity relationships between our classes. As a general rule, consider always using these diagrams together.

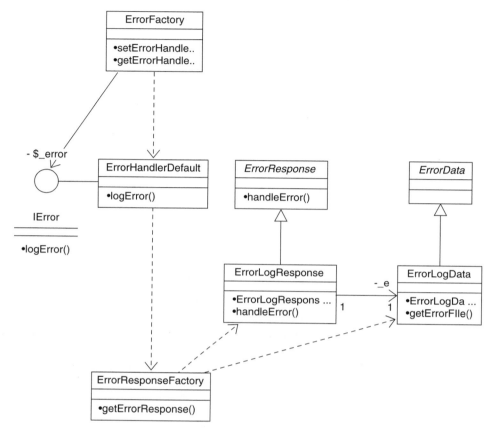

Figure 9.4   Error-Handling Interface Diagram

9.2.3   Implementation Diagram

Implementation diagrams emphasize the illustration of detail, including all attributes and methods residing on individual classes, as well as all classes of a particular society. The diagram in Figure 9.4 doesn't show all the classes that make up our error-handling framework. If interface diagrams are similar to modeling at the specification level, then implementation diagrams are similar to modeling at the implementation level. Diagrams at this level of abstraction are very precise and very detailed. Many of the classes on implementation diagrams are concrete classes, and we'll probably see attributes and operations modeled as well.

It's common to find that those people who are new to modeling try to use implementation diagrams exclusively, which can be problematic for a couple of different reasons. In fact, it's more valuable to use the other three diagrams types instead of implementation diagrams. Some of the challenges with using implementation diagrams follow:

- Implementations change more often than interfaces or package relationships. Unless we are using an automated tool that manages the synchronization of source code with our model, we're forced to manually synchronize or risk an outdated model.
- If we're truly interested in viewing our system from such a detailed level, we should consider perusing the source code, versus a lower-level implementation model, which we can't necessarily guarantee is synchronized with the source code.
- Implementation diagrams are very difficult to create correctly during the initial stages of analysis and design. Attempting to predict all of the interesting challenges that occur during coding is virtually impossible. Therefore, when we try to create implementation diagrams before writing code, we run the risk of writing code that doesn't exactly represent our model, resulting in the first bullet point in this list. Creating implementation diagrams based on existing source code is easier, but at that point, we must question their true value, considering our discussion in the second bullet.

9.2.4 View of Participating Classes (VOPC)

The View of Participating Classes (VOPC) is a type of diagram that can be represented as either a package, an interface, or an implementation diagram. However, it's most common to use an interface diagram with default implementation when representing the VOPC.

The VOPC is useful for representing the classes that participate in the realization of a use case. Use case realizations were introduced in Chapter 4 and reviewed in Chapter 8. They're structured around a collaboration element. In this chapter, we create a VOPC class diagram and then eventually progress to the creation of interface diagrams.

9.3 Identifying Structure

Our first attempt at identifying our system's structure is a straightforward activity. We only need examine the sequence diagrams already produced to determine the basic relationships. Consider the sequence diagram produced for the Run Payroll use case primary flow of events in Chapter 8 and seen again in Figure 9.5. From the sequence diagram in Figure 9.5, we can derive our first VOPC class diagram.

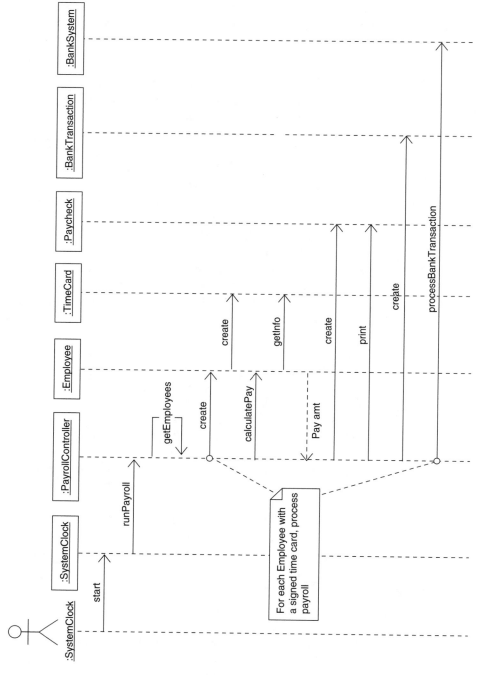

Figure 9.5   Sequence Diagram for Run Payroll Primary Flow of Events

In a sense, we are combining the static representation existing on the conceptual diagrams produced in Chapter 7, containing our boundary, entity, and control classes, with the dynamics of our system, represented as objects on our sequence diagrams. We can see a VOPC class diagram in Figure 9.6.

Note the obvious omission of the actor in Figure 9.6. Whereas on the sequence diagram in Figure 9.5, we included the actor to illustrate interaction and initiation of the use case, we don't need to do so on a class diagram. Because class diagrams illustrate structure, not behavior, actors have no significance on class diagrams.

In Figure 9.6, we've also chosen to include the initial responsibilities for the individual classes. Doing so is optional. While it does serve to easily communicate the responsibilities of the various classes, including the initial responsibilities for the individual classes, it also could easily be determined by browsing the associated sequence diagrams for the use case realization. Some automated tools manage the synchronization of messages sent to objects with the responsibilities associated with individual classes. Many of these same tools enable us to suppress attributes and operations as well. Inclusion of operations and attributes on class diagrams should be done when it brings clarity to the diagram. At

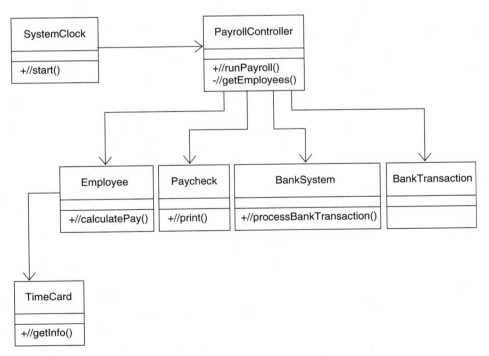

Figure 9.6   View of Participating Class for Run Payroll Use Case

times, the number of classes appearing on our diagrams are such that inclusion of the attributes and operations provide clutter rather than clarity. This choice is entirely a personal modeling preference.

9.3.1   Complex Structure

The diagram in Figure 9.6 is a fairly simple class diagram. It represents only the initial set of responsibilities allocated to the classes that we've identified as participating in the Run Payroll use case. However, it isn't representative of what we might expect our final design to look like. We've not included much information beyond that which we derived from the behavioral sequence diagrams. A final class diagram such as the one in Figure 9.6 doesn't provide any more benefit than the sequence diagram because the class diagram depicts a very straightforward translation of messages to associations. We must perform many more activities to endow our class diagram with more meaning. For instance, we should take a shot at defining the multiplicity associated with the instance relationships. We also may wish to define various role names that elaborate on the various relationships shown in Figure 9.6. Inheritance, one of the most important decisions that we'll make, isn't depicted in Figure 9.6, and it's highly unlikely that we'll build any Java application that doesn't take advantage of inheritance in some way, whether it be through extending some base class or implementing an interface. At this point, we should discuss these more complex structural relationships and how we design for them.

9.3.1.1   Inheritance

As stated previously, inheritance is one of the most important decisions that we'll make when designing our system. Unfortunately, the importance of the decision is derived more from the misuses of inheritance in our applications rather than from the power that can be realized when inheritance is used correctly. Inheritance certainly is a powerful construct. As we saw in Chapter 1, inheritance enables us to comply with many of the class principles discussed in Chapter 1. However, inheritance also makes systems inflexible, brittle, and short lived. When we use inheritance, we must make sure we're using it appropriately and with a distinct purpose in mind. We must avoid using inheritance in situations where its flexibility may not be needed. Let's discuss some situations where inheritance is applicable and others where its use is open for debate.

We should consider a number of issues when determining whether inheritance should be used. The complexity of a particular process can be a good identifier. Complex processes can be abstracted to a high level, such that we easily can maintain the process should it be required. This implies we utilize tech-

Inheritance Misuse

Inheritance is the most misused, overused, and poorly applied object-oriented technique. Many technologists equate object orientation with inheritance, and languages that don't support some form of inheritance typically aren't considered object oriented. Thus, object orientation and inheritance are almost synonymous.

For those new to object orientation, the most confusing and difficult aspect to understand is centered around inheritance. Almost all advanced object-oriented concepts such as polymorphism, dynamic binding, and abstract operations require inheritance. Because of the complexity, developers often try to solve complex problems using inheritance without first considering other, possibly more appropriate, alternatives. They do so probably because of the false assumption that inheritance and object orientation are virtually equivalent.

In addition, many developers believe that the promise of reuse when using objects is centered around inheritance. Inheritance's complexity coupled with its mystique leads developers to believe that they must use inheritance if their classes are to be reusable. Therefore, we feel that if we don't use inheritance frequently, our systems won't exhibit high degrees of reuse. While inheritance is powerful and does contribute to more flexible designs, it's entirely possible to design flexible systems without using inheritance at all. For more discussion on inheritance, refer to Chapter 1.

niques such as abstract coupling. In many situations, we'll flesh out interesting inheritance relationships as we begin to identify the attributes of our classes. Classes with many attributes, with potentially complex conditional logic based on the values of those attributes, are good candidates for utilizing inheritance as well.

To begin identifying good candidates for inheritance in our payroll system, we start by looking at the sequence diagram and identifying those processes that are complex in behavior and are dependent on the attributes of the class. While we haven't talked much about how we identify attributes of a class, this activity is similar to that of identifying classes. In fact, any classes that we may have identified earlier that don't have interesting behavior associated with them may be good candidates for attributes. Let's begin by examining the `calculatePay` responsibility of the `Employee` class, which is fairly complex in that we know that salary is calculated in three ways, based upon the type of employee we are working with. Therefore, one of the attributes on the `Employee` class may be an employee type because we need this information to determine how we calculate salary. Were we to simply define an employee type attribute on this class, it's likely that we would require conditional logic to calculate salary based on the type of employee we're working with. While this solution is plausible, doing so violates the Open Closed Principle (OCP—introduced in Chapter 1). If we need to add new employee types in the future, we would have to modify the Employee class to accommodate this enhancement, which is undesirable. Therefore, we must explore ways to ensure that we can flexibly add new types of employees without having to modify the Employee class directly.

Whenever we are considering the use of inheritance, we have the following three primary options:

- **Simple attribute:** This option doesn't utilize inheritance at all. Instead, we forego the use of inheritance to encapsulate the logic directly in the class itself. If the value of this attribute at any given point in the life of an object impacts behavior, we'll find conditional logic present that is based on the value of this attribute. While simple conditional logic may not be cause for concern, as the system grows, it's likely that this simple logic will become more complex and that new behaviors will be realized as different attribute values are introduced. As mentioned previously, this scenario violates OCP.

- **Subclass directly:** In this scenario, we subclass directly based on the variant cases. Consequently, what was previously a conditional statement when using a simple attribute is deferred to the individual subclasses. While this approach can help rid the class hierarchy of complex conditional logic, it introduces a different problem. If we find that other attributes impact behavior in a way that isn't consistent with our subclasses, we'll be forced to introduce potentially complex conditional logic based on this attribute or subclass again. We'll explore some of the interesting challenges with this scenario later in this section.

- **Composition:** We apply the Composite Reuse Principle (CRP—also introduced in Chapter 1) to achieve reuse through composition. While this solution may be the most complex of the three, it's probably the most flexible. This scenario also results in the most classes being produced, which adds to the complexity.

Let's examine each of the preceding solutions using our Employee class in the context of salary calculation. From the requirements, we know that salary is calculated based on the type of employee we're dealing with. Each of the three types of salaries, for hourly, salaried, and commissioned employees, is calculated differently.

Let's examine the solution using a simple attribute. Figure 9.7 shows an `Employee` class with a single private instance attribute named `_empType`. The value for this attribute is set within the constructor when the `Employee` instance is created. When the `calculatePay` method is invoked, the value of this attribute is checked, and salary is calculated for the appropriate employee type.

This approach has a few disadvantages. First, new types of employees or new salary calculations require a change to our existing `Employee` class, which is an obvious violation of OCP. Second, the employee type is not type safe. For instance, if a value of four were passed to the constructor, the `Employee` instance would blindly set the value of `_empType` equal to the invalid value of four. Of course, we can always put some code in the constructor to ensure that the value passed in is within the appropriate range, but this solution only adds to the OCP violation. Using this solution, for new types of employees or salary calculations, we not only have to update the `calculatePay` method with an additional conditional, but we also have to make sure we remember to modify the constructor to allow the `_empType` instance attribute to accommodate this new value within its range of values. As the functionality grows and evolves, the `Employee` class will become unwieldy to work with. All of these problems are the result of a simple violation of OCP.

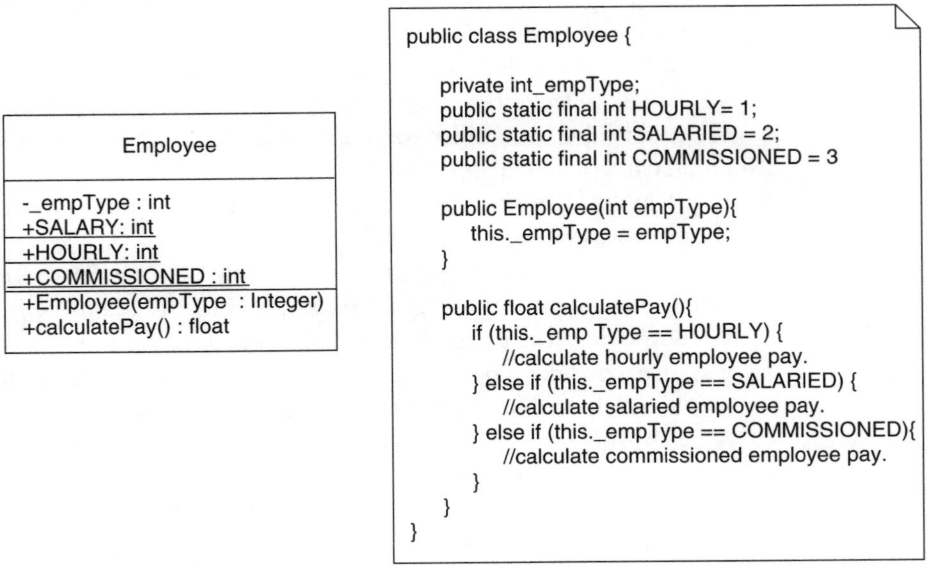

```
Employee

-_empType : int
+SALARY: int
+HOURLY: int
+COMMISSIONED : int
+Employee(empType : Integer)
+calculatePay() : float
```

```java
public class Employee {

    private int_empType;
    public static final int HOURLY= 1;
    public static final int SALARIED = 2;
    public static final int COMMISSIONED = 3

    public Employee(int empType){
        this._empType = empType;
    }

    public float calculatePay(){
        if (this._emp Type == H0URLY) {
            //calculate hourly employee pay.
        } else if (this._empType == SALARIED) {
            //calculate salaried employee pay.
        } else if (this._empType == COMMISSIONED){
            //calculate commissioned employee pay.
        }
    }
}
```

Figure 9.7   Employee Class with Simple Attributes

Object Factories

Object factories enable us to decouple the instantiation of an object from the object that actually uses the instance. A more detailed discussion on object factories can be found in Section 9.3.2, later in this chapter.

The diagram in Figure 9.8 illustrates an equivalent solution using subclasses. In this diagram, we subclass an abstract `Employee` class with three subclasses representing each employee type. Whereas in Figure 9.7, we instantiated an `Employee` class, passing the appropriate type to the constructor, in Figure 9.8, we rely on some client to create the appropriate instance of the descendent class directly, possibly using an object factory. In this situation, though, we no longer have any conditional logic based on the type of employee because all of this logic is now deferred to the appropriate `Employee` descendent. Common attributes and behaviors can be easily implemented on the ancestor `Employee` class. In addition, any class referencing any of the descendents of the `Employee` class actually hold a reference to the `Employee` class data type directly. Due to the nature of inheritance and dynamic binding, we should be able to substitute descendents anywhere the ancestor is referenced. Thus, we've achieved OCP, and in doing so, we've adhered to the Liskov Substitution Principle (LSP), which we essentially just restated.

We've also solved our type safety problem identified when using simple attributes. In this situation, we have only three classes that can be instantiated. We don't have the ability to create an instance of any other type of class that could cause a similar problem.

While a bit more complex, this approach certainly is more flexible than the solution illustrated in Figure 9.7. However, it doesn't come without its disadvantages. First, inheritance is a very static solution space. Were we to identify additional behavioral variants that didn't fit into the realm of our subclasses, we would be left with a structure that doesn't accommodate our behavior. For instance, consider a new or changing requirement that states that employee benefits are deducted from paychecks based upon the status of the employee. Unfortunately, the employee status may not fall along the same lines as the employee type; our employee status may fall into one of three categories—full-time, part-time, or on-leave. If this new requirement impacts how salary is calculated, or impacts any behavior on the `Employee` class, we might find we're relegated to using a simple attribute with conditionals. Let's examine some of our options.

First, we can try subclassing each of our employee descendents directly and create separate status classes for each employee type subclass, which would

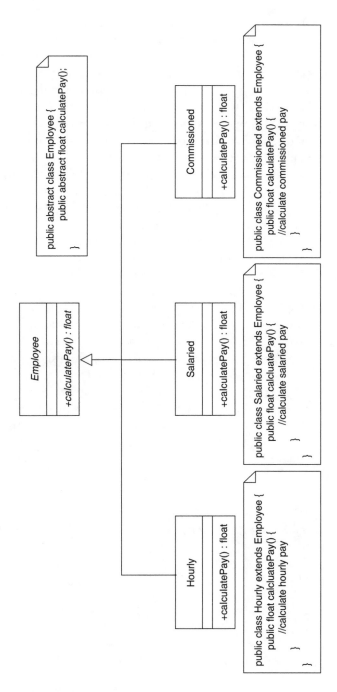

Figure 9.8 Employee Class with Descendent

result in a proliferation of classes and a high probability of duplicate code. In essence, we would have a full-time, part-time, and on-leave set of subclasses for each employee descendent, resulting in nine new classes. This option is extremely inflexible with many disadvantages.

Second, we could define default status behavior in our ancestor `Employee` class and override this behavior in descendents with variant behavior. This option, however, is not without its problems. For instance, this solution doesn't work well if a salaried employee has different calculations for salaries depending on the status, which would result in complex conditionals for salaried employees based on whether they are full-time, part-time, or on-leave.

Another problem with using this subclass approach becomes apparent when we ask, "What happens if an employee can switch types in the middle of a pay period?" For instance, the first two days of the week, the employee's status is full-time, and the remaining three days, the employee is commissioned. Or perhaps an employee receives a small salary plus commissions. The approach in Figure 9.8 assumes that we have a single descendent instance for each `Employee`. Doing so results in overhead if we have common attributes defined on the `Employee` class because each of these attributes will be loaded and stored in memory twice. Therefore, our system shouldn't represent a single employee with multiple `Employee` instances in the system.

If it's not yet apparent that our system shouldn't represent a single employee with multiple `Employee` instances in the system, we need only consider some of the other uses of our `Employee` class within our system and across use cases. When maintaining a time card, an employee is required to log on to the system by entering a user ID and password. Part of the authentication and later authorization process of that employee in accessing various functions of the system might be to store the `Employee` instance on a context object within the applica-

Discriminator

The *discriminator* is a term used to describe the single variant that is the cause for our creation of subclasses. The relationship between any descendent and ancestor should involve only a single discriminator. If we find that a ancestor-descendent relationship has multiple discriminators, we should carefully consider an alternative solution, such as composition. Sometimes, however rare, subclassing the descendent based on another discriminator works, too. This solution, however, isn't without its problems either.

tion, such as the `Session` object in a Java Web application. If an employee is both salaried and commissioned, we wouldn't want to store two objects in memory representing that single employee—that doesn't make sense, nor does it work out very well.

In summary, while this second approach works well for simple situations, it doesn't scale well as complexity increases or if we use the `Employee` class itself to store common attributes and behaviors. Any time we decide to use inheritance, we should fully understand the discriminator that exists that is the cause for the creation of the descendents.

Figure 9.9 shows our final alternative. It depicts a single `Employee` class that's composed of an `EmployeeType` abstract class. We again see that upon instantiation of the `Employee` class, the `EmployeeType` is passed to the constructor. While a bit more complex, this solution is much more flexible. We certainly have the ability to extend `EmployeeType` and create new types of employees without modifying the `Employee` class directly. Hence, we have achieved OCP.

In addition, were a new requirement introduced that necessitated incorporating employee status into the structure, we easily could create a new `Employee-Status` abstract class with the appropriate descendents to satisfy status-specific behavior. In other words, our inheritance hierarchies are very small and involve only a single discriminator.

This approach is actually a direct application of CRP, which we view as the most flexible solution. However, it should be used only in those situations that require this degree of flexibility, due to the associated complexity.

9.3.2 Factories

Object factories are specialized design classes whose intent it is to create instances. Factories are useful when we want to decouple the process of creation from the classes that ultimately will use the created instance. Factories typically are used in situations where we deem the creation of objects to be fairly complex algorithmically, or we wish to decouple classes from a particular implementation. We certainly have this second case in the diagram in Figure 9.9.

Structurally, the `Employee` class is not dependent on any of the concrete `EmployeeType` classes. However, we must ask ourselves how we intend to create concrete instances of the `EmployeeType`. In Figure 9.9, an `EmployeeType` instance is passed to the constructor of the `Employee` class. This implies, however, that the class using `Employee` must be aware of the various `EmployeeType` subclasses, which may be undesirable because the class using `Employee` most likely has other responsibilities. For instance, one of the classes in our Run Payroll use case is the `PayrollController`, and referring to the sequence diagram in Figure 8.5 back in Chapter 8, we see that this `PayrollController` creates an

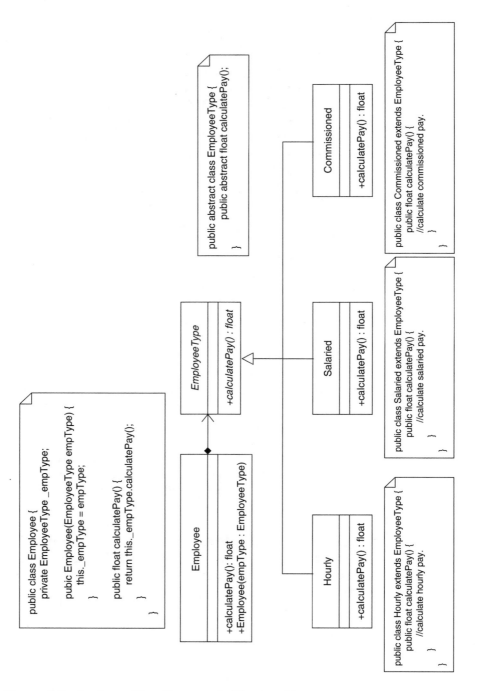

Figure 9.9   Employee Class Composed of EmployeeType

`Employee` instance. We can assume that we'll pass the `EmployeeType` descendent to the constructor of the `Employee` class. Of course, this scenario implies that the `PayrollController` must create the appropriate `EmployeeType` instance.

The creation of `EmployeeType` instances certainly isn't overly difficult. However, examining the sequence diagram in Figure 8.7 in Chapter 8, we see that the `LoginForm` also instantiates an `Employee`, which implies that we must also create the appropriate `EmployeeType` here. Again, this task isn't difficult; however, stepping back and examining the overall picture, we see a subtle violation of OCP. If it's necessary to extend the system with new `EmployeeType` subclasses, we must ensure that both `PayrollController` and the `MaintainTimecardController` be modified to create the new `EmployeeType` subclass appropriately. Thus, we've achieved closure within the `Employee` class because it need not be modified when we subclass `EmployeeType`. However, the remainder of the system is wide open to maintenance difficulties.

A case certainly can be made for the `Employee` class containing the responsibility for creating its own `EmployeeType` subclass. The problem with this option is that the `Employee` class would no longer be closed to modification, which is the situation we've been trying to avoid all along and is the reason we created the `EmployeeType` hierarchy. Therefore, we require an approach that results in closure for both the `Employee` class and the classes using `Employee`. To implement this approach, we'll use an object factory.

The diagram in Figure 9.10 is an updated version of that in Figure 9.9 and includes a new class named `EmployeeTypeFactory`. The intent of this class is to create `EmployeeType` subclass instances. Another key change has been made to this diagram as well. We no longer pass the `EmployeeType` to the constructor of the `Employee` class but instead pass the employee ID. This employee ID is obtained within the `PayrollController` when it retrieves a list of employees for which payroll must be processed. If we pass this employee ID to the constructor of the `Employee` class, the `Employee` class can be responsible for retrieving its own internal data set, which includes an indicator that informs this instance of the type of `Employee`, which we'll assume is a simple numeric field on a relational database table. The `Employee` class invokes the static `getInstance` method on the `EmployeeTypeFactory`, passing this indicator. Based on this indicator, the `getInstance` method returns the appropriate `EmployeeType` instance.

We've achieved closure for our entire system in regard to `EmployeeType`, aside from the `EmployeeTypeFactory`, which is perfectly acceptable because creation must occur somewhere, implying that it's virtually impossible to achieve closure systemwide. However, because of the cohesive nature of the `EmployeeTypeFactory`, it should be apparent to maintainers that new `EmployeeType` descendents require an update to our `EmployeeTypeFactory`. While this class

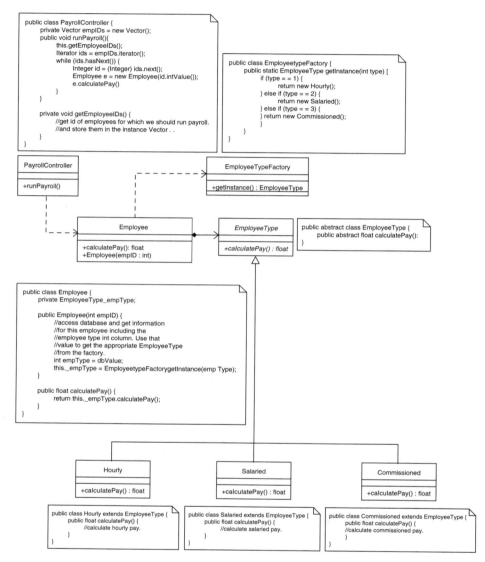

Figure 9.10   Employee Usage of an Object Factory

isn't closed to modification, the remainder of our system is, including `Employee`, `PayrollController`, and `MaintainTimecardController`.

The tradeoff we've made is an additional class and some additional complexity for increased maintainability and system closure. In the majority of cases, we should be willing to make this tradeoff. Should we need to extend the system with an additional `EmployeeType` in the future, we need only make one small change to `EmployeeTypeFactory`. We don't have to search the entire system looking for classes that create the appropriate `EmployeeType` and make the change there as well. Nor do we have to search the `Employee` class itself.

While ease of maintenance certainly is a benefit of the approach we've just described, there's another, less obvious, benefit. Whenever we need to extend our system, the less existing code that we have to change, the less likely we are to introduce new bugs into our system. Considering the small change we have to make only to `EmployeeTypeFactory`, we're virtually guaranteed that we won't introduce new errors into the system—except for errors in the new `EmployeeType` subclass. When we run our test cases, if we find that we've introduced a bug, we know that it is either in the `EmployeeTypeFactory` class, which is unlikely because of the simplistic nature of the change, or the new `EmployeeType` subclass. However, because the remaining classes in the system worked before, they still work because they have not been changed.

Quite a few variations of object factories are available. [GOF95] discusses five types of object factories, which are categorized as creational patterns. Depending on the flexibility required, we may wish to utilize one of these more advanced creational designs to further improve the maintainability of our system. These additional creational patterns are, however, beyond the scope of this book.

9.3.3 Collections

In our previous discussion on factories, as well as in Chapter 7, we realized that `PayrollController` must retrieve a list of employee IDs for which we'll process payroll. In its simplest form, this list of employee IDs can be stored as a simple `ArrayList`. However, the `PayrollController` still is responsible for retrieving the list of employee IDs and storing them on `ArrayList`. As we realize other use cases, if we find that we're repeatedly writing code to manage a list of employees, we might find that a custom collection class is a better approach.

In our situation, we might create a custom `EmployeeCollection` class that manages a list of employees. It's quite possible that this custom collection class is simply a thin wrapper around one of the Java collection classes, such as `ArrayList`. A number of benefits are associated with a custom collection class:

- Other classes that must work with employee collections no longer have to manage the collection internally. Instead, they can use the collection class, which reduces the likelihood that we'll have multiple classes in our application with duplicate collection management code.

- The internal management of the list can change very easily. We can start by managing only a simple list of employee IDs. If necessary, we can change the implementation to manage a list of Employee objects in the future.
- If the list of objects in the collection is quite long, we can employ lazy instantiation. In this case, the collection isn't really managing a list at all but actually is creating the appropriate instances as needed. Clients of the collection, however, still see it as a list.

Let's take a look at how this custom collection class might be designed. Figure 9.11 is an updated version of the diagram in Figure 9.10. In Figure 9.11, we've introduced our EmployeeCollection class. The PayrollController class is no longer responsible for managing the list of Employee instances. Instead, this work is the responsibility of the EmployeeCollection class, and the PayrollController simply takes advantage of this behavior.

As can be seen from the code example in this diagram, the EmployeeCollection constructor retrieves a listing of all the Employee instances that the collection must manage. The PayrollController simply calls the next method to retrieve the next Employee.

A couple of interesting behavioral traits of the EmployeeCollection class deserve discussion. First, notice the return data type of the next method. Because the EmployeeCollection class is responsible for managing only a list of Employee instances, we perform the cast before we return the instance to the

Java Collection API

The Java Collection API is a set of classes focused entirely on enabling us to manage sets of objects. The simplest, most efficient way to manage a collection of objects is to use an array. Arrays in Java, however, are static and cannot grow dynamically. In other words, an array's size must be specified when the array is created. In most situations, this requirement isn't flexible enough. An ArrayList is a Java class that represents a dynamic array. Consequently, the size of an ArrayList need not be specified upon creation, and the size grows as new objects are added to the list. Vectors, which may be more familiar to many of us because of their longer inclusion in the Java API, are a synchronized version of an ArrayList. Vectors, while less efficient, are thread safe. In situations where we need a dynamic array and aren't concerned with thread safety, an ArrayList should be used.

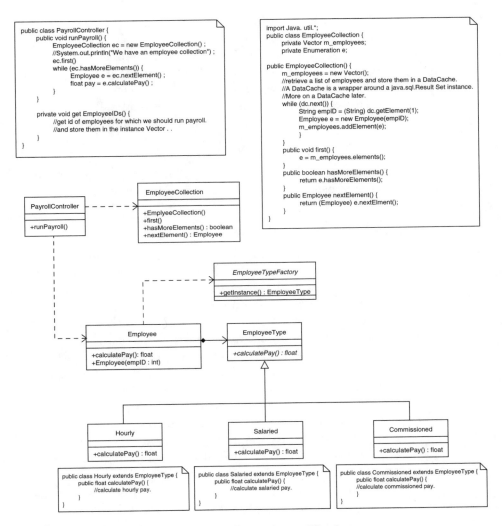

Figure 9.11 Employee Collection to Manage Lists of Employees

calling object. When using a standard Java collection class, a cast typically must be performed each time we get elements off the list. Because we know we're dealing with only Employee instances, there's no reason not to make this cast the responsibility of the EmployeeCollection.

More interesting, however, is determining which class should contain the responsibility of determining whether an Employee is ready to have salary calculated. Were we to make this calculation a function of the EmployeeCollection, we would limit the use of this class because it would manage only those employees who are ready for their salaries to be calculated. Other contexts wishing to use the `EmployeeCollection` may be limited by this requirement. Associating this behavior with the `PayrollController` increases the likelihood that the collection can be reused. In determining the best solution, we must carefully evaluate how we desire the collection class to be used. That determination is a matter entirely of allocating responsibilities to classes, which, as we've mentioned earlier, is one of the most important decisions when designing our classes. In fact, much of the discussion lately has been about responsibility allocation, even though the discussion has been in the context of determining system structure. Based on this important point, it should be more apparent that a system's behavior is responsible for determining our system's structure.

9.3.4   Structural Notes

We've spent quite a bit of time progressing through the design of our system. Quite a bit of code is associated with the diagrams we've produced. As we progressed through the discussion, we might have noticed that our design has evolved from a simple conceptual model (in Figure 7.1) into a model (in Figure 9.11) that contains some design classes, such as the collection and factory classes, not existing in our business domain. By carefully evaluating requirements, we were able to design a UML structure that satisfied the immediate need. In doing so, we wrote quite a bit of code. We used very short design-code feedback loops to ensure our design worked properly. We took advantage of the sequence diagrams produced earlier to flesh out our initial structure and to drive the design decision-making process. The code we've produced provides a simple prototype of the payroll-processing portion of the system.

During the process of architectural modeling, discussed in Chapter 10, we'll put some finishing touches on our system's design. For instance, while we have many of the classes that might be needed to focus on the construction of our Run Payroll use case, we've not devoted any time to discussing the package structure of our application. It's unlikely that all of the classes we've discussed to this point belong in the same package. Among other things, this topic is the focus of Chapter 10.

9.4   Model Structure

In addition to the sequence diagrams that we'll create to design our system, we'll likely create a number of class diagrams. The way that we organize these diagrams definitely determines whether our model lives and grows with the system or becomes a monolith that is difficult to maintain and eventually is discarded.

As discussed in Chapter 4, it may be beneficial to create collaborations for each use case. We'll call this collaboration a *use case realization*. It's named appropriately because the sequence and class diagrams specify the behavior and structure of individual use cases. Therefore, we'll organize our model by associating each of the diagrams with their appropriate use case realization, which is effective because each sequence diagram we produce represents a flow of events for an individual use case. For further discussion on this topic, refer to Chapter 4.

9.4.1 View of Participating Classes

Let's take another look at a VOPC class diagram, which is associated with each use case. Its purpose is to illustrate the structural relationships among all of the classes that participate in a use case. This class diagram commonly exists at the specification level. Unlike many of the detailed diagrams, which showed methods with method signatures, presented in our discussion of identifying structure, VOPC diagrams typically show classes, relationships, and a few adornments such as multiplicity, navigability, and role names. However, attempting to specify methods with method signatures on VOPC diagrams typically results in a situation where the VOPC diagram must be continuously synchronized with the system. This situation is neither desirable nor beneficial.

Based on our discussion of structural design in this chapter, we can produce the VOPC class diagram in Figure 9.12. While much of our attention was focused on the interesting `PayrollController`/`Employee` and `Employee`/`EmployeeType` relationships, we could have the same discussions regarding the remaining relationships, and if space and time permitted, we would. Note also that we've specified multiplicity for the `Employee`/`EmployeeType` composition, from which we can interpret that an `Employee` must be of at least one `EmployeeType` and can be up to all three.

Most interesting on this diagram, however, is the regression made in the specification of detail. As mentioned previously, the VOPC typically is a specification diagram, focusing mainly on relationships and high-level responsibilities. If we question this approach, considering that in our previous diagrams we specified more detail, we should take a number of issues into account. If we really need to understand a system at such a fine level of detail, we should consider using the diagram to guide us through the source code. In fact, in the previous examples, was it the diagram that provided the most information or the accompanying code? It's likely that we used the diagram to guide our understanding of the code. In addition, taking this approach helps ensure that our diagrams require little maintenance to remain synchronized with the code.

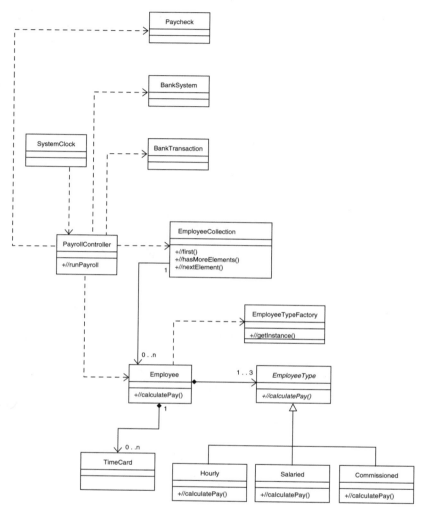

Figure 9.12   View of Participating Classes for Run Payroll Use Case

9.5   Conclusion

Designing a system is a much more involved process than simply writing code. Many important decisions must be carefully calculated. Each method defined and each relationship introduced must be the result of a conscious decision in which the ramifications are carefully considered. In this chapter, we discussed many of the decisions that must be made when designing our system's structure.

Ultimately, our system's behavior drives the creation of our structure. Complex and indefinite behaviors require more flexible structural relationships. Always considering the application of various principles and patterns, where warranted, contributes to a system design that is more resilient and maintainable.

If the line between behavioral design, structural design, and coding is blurred, there's good reason. While each of these tasks is a separate activity, with its own set of important decisions, the most effective way to perform these activities is virtually in conjunction with each other.

CHAPTER 10

Architectural Modeling

A series of elegant, yet independent, design solutions does not ensure a system is architecturally stable.

When modeling our Java applications, it's paramount that we seriously consider our software's architecture. Decisions about the architecture that guide our development effort can be the most important technical decisions that we make. Architectures that are resilient and accommodate change enable a system to grow as our business grows and as requirements change. On the other hand, rigid architectures resist change, eventually contributing to our system's demise. A software system's architecture goes far beyond the implementation of a set of efficient, though independent, designs.

In this chapter, we discuss how we can use the UML to establish a clear and concise architectural vision. This vision should instill a pattern to which we can adhere as we extend our system to support new requirements or modify it to support changing requirements. Therefore, our discussion in this chapter is twofold. First, we focus on how the UML can be used to create consistent views into our system's architecture. Second, we discuss mechanisms that can be employed to ensure our architecture is resilient and consistent. In fact, the majority of our emphasis on design to this point stresses the importance of creating a resilient architecture.

10.0 Defining Architecture

Because much already has been written on what software architecture is, our intent isn't to duplicate this effort. It is important, however, that throughout our

201

discussions, we understand the implications of software architecture. This understanding provides a foundation for our discussion of using the UML to effectively model our architecture, resulting in an architectural implementation that complements the Java development environment. In [BOOCH98], architecture is defined as follows:

> *Software architecture encompasses the set of significant decisions about the organization of a software system: the selection of the structural elements and their interfaces by which a system is composed, together with their behavior as specified in the collaborations among those elements, the composition of these structural and behavioral elements into progressively larger subsystems, and the architectural style that guides this organization.*

This definition implies that we must identify the aspects of the system having a higher probability of change and make conscious decisions regarding how we can accommodate it. These decisions are significant because our selection of these various elements and their interactions will directly impact how well our system supports growth. Finally, the decisions we make to resolve these challenges will serve as a guide to help architects, designers, and developers make consistent and correct decisions, ultimately guiding us through our development effort.

This architectural style we choose also will impact the extensibility, flexibility, reusability, and robustness of our application. We strive to achieve these technical goals when constructing an application. The degree to which we achieve these technical goals ultimately will contribute to the functionality, maintainability, performance, and resilience of our application. Our software ultimately will be judged on such characteristics by the project's stakeholders. Therefore, solving the technical challenges presented by the system contributes to the solution of the business objective for which this system is being developed. Because achievement of our technical goals drives the measurement of our system's success, establishing an architecture that's clear, concise, and crisp may be one of the most important decisions we make.

10.1   Establishing Architecture

An application can be constructed in literally an infinite number of ways. Assigning the same application to two different developers often produces two radically different results. While each of these applications may satisfy the system's requirements, it's highly likely that various aspects of each will accommodate change with varying degrees of success. It's not uncommon, however, for

Evaluating Probability of Change

In attempting to assess areas of the system that are most likely to change, we typically pay close attention to how users respond to questions on topics such as system requirements. If they seem sure that a requirement is static and not likely to change, we feel assured that this area is not one of high risk. If, on the other hand, the users seem hesitant, or different users provide different responses, it's an indication that this area may be of higher risk and therefore is more architecturally significant. We want to focus on such areas from an architectural standpoint, attempting to create seams in our application. These seams will be realized concretely in the form of interfaces, which serve as the contract between the client, who is dependent on this requirement, and the service that provides the implementation.

software development teams to do what we have just described. They may not assign developers the same task, but they might assign them separate tasks within a single development initiative. While coding standards and peer reviews can help ensure consistent naming conventions and adherence to basic principles, they don't ensure a consistent software architecture. In order to ensure robust architectures, we need to establish an architectural vision.

This architectural vision needs to serve many purposes. On one hand, it should be flexible enough to accommodate change easily, yet simple enough that individuals can understand it. From another perspective, our architecture needs to enforce restrictions. A flexible architecture should not be so flexible that it allows developers to roam freely in structuring the application. An architecture needs to be flexible so that it can accommodate change in those areas where we see the highest possibility of change. Therefore, while flexible, an architecture should also impose constraints on individuals, providing guidance on how best to structure individual pieces of the same application.

Many items must be taken into consideration when establishing this architectural vision. We must evaluate our system and determine where the highest probability of change lies. We must identify the areas of our system that have the highest degree of complexity. Understanding the business priorities driving the development effort contributes greatly in determining which aspects of the system must be most resilient. We should focus on these architecturally significant elements. Each system is different, and thus, each will have different architecturally significant elements. However, the mechanisms we use to support and enforce our vision typically are reused on all development efforts.

10.2   Architectural Mechanisms

On most software development projects, we use fundamental mechanisms to contribute to developing a resilient architecture. As we gain more experience in designing systems, it's common to reuse from previous systems aspects that we have found effective. These mechanisms are the architectural patterns helping to drive our system's growth. We won't necessarily employ the exact architectural pattern across applications, but likely will utilize various aspects of it, morphing the pattern to fit the needs of our present system.

Fortunately, many architectural patterns have been proven effective on a wide variety of systems. In our Java development efforts, it's common to begin establishing our architectural vision using these various patterns. Throughout our iterations, we refine these patterns to more closely reflect our requirements and help in solving challenges the system poses. An entire book could easily be devoted to a discussion of the many architectural patterns, and obviously, our discussion in this chapter is limited. Two patterns can be utilized on most every system: the Layers pattern and the Partitions pattern. While we won't discuss these patterns in great detail, we strive for a basic understanding of them in this chapter because they are essential to our discussion on architectural modeling. We encourage those readers who wish to obtain more information about these patterns to research them.

10.2.1   Layers

Conceptually, layering our application is a simple task; in practice, however, a number of challenges present themselves. Before discussing these challenges, let's discuss the goals and benefits of a layered architecture. Our goal in layering an architecture is to identify the various levels of granularity of which our sys-

Stable Abstractions and Stable Dependencies Principles

In this chapter, we revisit our discussion in Chapter 1 on the Stable Abstractions Principle (SAP) and the Stable Dependencies Principle (SDP) in the context of modeling our system's architecture. While these principles define the desired relationships between packages, in this context, we discuss them in terms of class relationships. Regardless of the context, these principles should be applied. In fact, as we discussed in Section 9.2.1 and will elaborate upon further in Section 10.3, the relationships between the packages is of utmost importance.

tem is composed and create an acyclic dependency structure between these levels, which creates relationships as depicted in the class diagram in Figure 10.1. In this figure, we see the domain classes that represent a payroll system. The top layer defines the user interface or the forms that make up our application's graphical user interface. The second, or middle, layer represents the classes that coordinate various payroll processes, and the lowest layer represents the business classes, such as `Employee` and `Timecard`.

In this layered scenario, it's important that our business classes be independent of the services that control them, in addition to being independent of the user interface that displays the information the business classes encapsulate. Therefore, the associations and, subsequently, the messages must flow in one direction, which is consistent with our desire for an acyclic dependency structure. If, on the other hand, we were to create a cyclic dependency between any of these layers, the reusability of our application's components would be severely limited. For instance, if our `Employee` class in Figure 10.1 were dependent on the `PayrollController` class, this bidirectional relationship would limit the usage of our `Employee` class and would reduce the likelihood that it could be used in other use cases, such as the maintenance of a time card where the calculation of payroll for our employees wasn't an issue. Or consider a dependency between `Employee` and `PayrollFrame`, which would place limitations on our ability to replace the form-based user interface with a browser-based front end. Contrarily, it is perfectly acceptable for classes within a higher layer to depend on classes within lower layers, which is the intent of a layered architecture. Therefore, in identifying and implementing a layered architecture, we must give careful consideration to the granularity that exists at each layer. More simply, we must recognize the role each layer plays in our application and allocate behaviors to layers that satisfy the role.

Levels of Granularity

In Chapter 8, we discussed the importance of allocating responsibilities to classes. Associating the correct responsibilities with a class ensures class cohesion. In this chapter, we discuss the levels of granularity associated with a layered architecture. Assigning the appropriate responsibilities to a layer is as important as assigning the responsibilities to a class. If done successfully, each results in a higher degree of cohesion. In Chapter 9, we focused on class cohesion, while in this chapter, we focus on the cohesion of a particular layer, a different level of granularity.

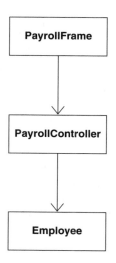

Figure 10.1   Class Layering

In addition to the acyclic dependency constraint, additional issues should be taken into consideration when establishing our layers. As seen in Figure 10.1, we have enforced a strict layering scheme, which is evident because of the dependency relationships that exist between our classes. We also could have created a more relaxed layering scheme, which would allow higher-level layers to communicate directly to any layer that exists at a lower level of granularity. This second approach has the advantage that if a high layer needs the services contained within a layer not directly beneath it, that layer can communicate directly with the classes in the lower layer. Without using relaxed layers, our middle layer would have to serve as a pass-through to the lower layers, which eventually could result in the intermediate layers becoming very large, with many delegate methods. This second approach has some disadvantages, however. For instance, if we are working in a distributed environment, where a lower layer resides on a separate server, we couldn't directly communicate with it unless we built the communication mechanism directly into the accessing layer. The problem with this approach is that we would have multiple responsibilities associated with a single layer in our application. In essence, multiple levels of granularity would exist within the same layer. The scope of this book doesn't include a discussion of the advanced design challenges that are at play in such a scenario. Suffice it to say that when layering our application, we carefully must take into consideration the granularity existing at each layer. Not doing so will haunt us when we try to grow our application.

As we've seen, layering an application, which is conceptually a simple task, abounds with pragmatic challenges. For instance, what happens if a class existing in a lower layer needs to send a message to one in an upper-level layer? Assuming we can identify appropriate layers, it's inevitable that when we move into the construction phase of the development lifecycle, unexpected requirements will emerge that dictate the need for a lower layer to depend on a layer existing at a higher level of granularity. Fortunately, taking advantage of a common design pattern enables us to accommodate this need.

10.2.2 Observing

Our management of the notification of events that go against the acyclic dependency structure has a major impact on our architecture. We have to be cautious with this process. If we allow ourselves to violate dependency relationships between architectural layers, we no longer have a layered architecture. Therefore, simply stated, we cannot violate architectural layers. Instead, as we identify a change in our layers, we should define some other mechanism that enables us to maintain our architectural layers, while still satisfying our requirement. One common way to solve this challenge is to use a variation of the Observer pattern [GOF95].

In Figure 10.2, we see our new class structure with the addition of an important class. The Observer class is a Java interface that has a single method

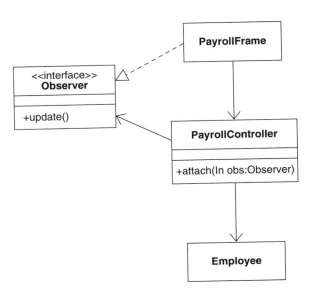

Figure 10.2 Observer Design Pattern Class Diagram

named `update`. Via the realization relationship, we see that our `PayrollFrame` implements this interface. Thus, our `PayrollController` has an `attach` method on it, allowing the `PayrollFrame`, which implements the `Observer` interface, to register itself with the `PayrollController`. Now our `PayrollController` can send a message to our `PayrollFrame` without violating our defined layers.

If desired, we also could have defined an `attach` method on `Employee`, allowing any class implementing `Observer` to register itself with this class, creating the same message notification scheme. The Observer pattern has many variations. An important decision that must be given careful consideration concerns the semantics associated with the update message sent to `Observer` instances. Because of the generic nature of the `Observer`, which increases its usability, it can be challenging to devise a scheme that allows the objects responsible for notifying `Observer` objects to inform the `Observer` why it's being notified. For further discussion on this topic, I encourage you to study the Observer pattern as described in [GOF95]. The flexibility in using the Observer pattern is our present concern. As we've seen, using the Observer enables us to send messages up our layered hierarchy. In fact, the Observer pattern presented in Figure 10.2 is a variation of the Model-View-Controller (MVC) pattern.

10.2.3   Model-View-Controller (MVC)

The class diagram in Figure 10.3 differs slightly from that in Figure 10.2. The diagram in Figure 10.3 is a pure representation of the MVC pattern [POSA96]. In Figure 10.3, `View` has an associative relationship with both `Model` and `Controller`. When running, our `View` attaches itself to the `Model` as an `Observer`. As events in our `View` occur, the `Controller` notifies `Model`, causing a change in state. Because of this change in state, the `Model` notifies each of its `Observer` instances. The advantage is that we can modify `Model`, `View`, or `Controller`, independent of each other, which contributes to a much higher degree of maintainability for each class.

Lest we mislead, we must make it clear that Layers and MVC are different patterns, each having unique characteristics. We certainly can layer an architecture without utilizing MVC, and we also can employ the MVC pattern without layering our architecture. However, we must remember the level of granularity that exists at each layer. If our application consists of three layers, and each is granular at the MVC level, then MVC and Layers are synonymous, but that isn't always the case. The point is that a layered architecture focuses on defining distinct levels of granularity, typically among packages, and creating an acyclic dependency between them. The intent of MVC is to separate classes implementing the user interface from its controlling component and model components. Recall that when we use patterns, we create variations of a pattern definition to

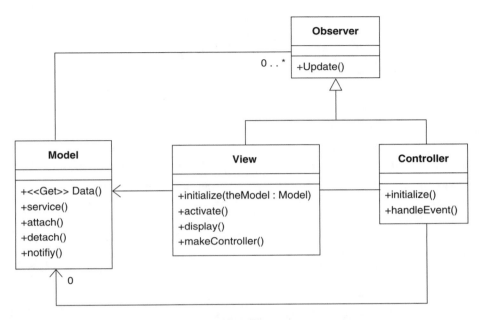

Figure 10.3   Model-View-Controller Class Diagram

fit our particular need. In this variation, MVC and Layers have very similar structure, yet each is focused in solving a particular challenge. Reduced to its simplest form, Layers focus more on the relationships between packages, whereas the focal point of MVC is to reduce coupling among our classes. Each of these patterns is central to our discussion on architectural modeling.

10.2.4   Partitions

Before we discuss architectural modeling, let's discuss one more useful architectural pattern. As we've seen, layering our application involves identifying the levels of granularity and creating an acyclic dependency between these various levels. Within each of these levels of granularity, we can further refine our architecture. By identifying and separating various behavioral categories, the potential for reuse increases. In Figure 10.4, we have created partitions within each of our individual layers. The classes contained within each partition are singularly focused on accomplishing a cohesive task. These tasks have been separated vertically and horizontally. In fact, Figure 10.4 depicts a slice through our layers, such that our partitions exist horizontally within each layer, which run vertically. This perspective can be seen more clearly in Figure 10.5. For simplicity, we have omitted the BusinessService layer in Figure 10.5. We clearly can see the

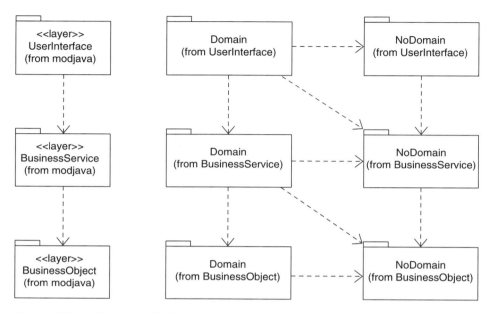

Figure 10.4   Separating Packages into Partitions

direction of the relationships in this diagram. In fact, we have turned our focus to the relationships that exist between various packages in our application. Turning our attention back to Figure 10.4, we see we have a package structure that is compliant with the primary responsibilities of MVC. This structure allows a very natural separation in the general responsibilities of an application at both the class level, using MVC, and the package level, by layering and parti-

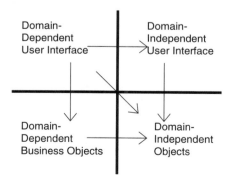

Figure 10.5   Common Architectural Partitions

> ### Common Closure Principle
>
> A principle discussed in Chapter 1 is again at the root of our discussion. Partitioning our application helps us adhere to the Common Closure Principle (CCP). By separating domain-dependent and domain-independent responsibilities, we ensure the classes that change together, stay together.

tioning. Now, each of our classes in Figure 10.1 have a natural allocation to their containing packages in Figure 10.4.

Our partitions typically separate the concerns between those behaviors that are domain dependent and those that are domain independent. The classes composing the domain-independent partition are those whose intent it is to be used across applications. Those classes composing the partition dependent on the domain encapsulate the behaviors specific to our application under development. By combining the use of layers and partitions, we can build complex, yet elegant, architectures that easily can be extended without having to modify the existing functionality contained within them. Layering and partitioning helps us define our architecture, is the framework upon which our architecture grows, and is the vision upon which our system is built, ultimately contributing to our system's evolution.

10.3 Views of Architecture

Let's look at how our previous discussions in this chapter fit into the realm of modeling. We use modeling to drive the creation of our architectural vision. Based on the two simple patterns discussed in the preceding sections, the many variations of each pattern, and the numerous architectural patterns not discussed, establishing an architecture for a large system can't be done spontaneously. This section demonstrates by example how we use models to communicate ideas, devise variations of common patterns, and problem-solve difficult challenges.

As discussed previously, a fundamental difference exists between Layers and MVC. An application can be layered only if it's done according to the physical unit of release, which, in Java, is the package. MVC, on the other hand, still is centered around how the classes are structured in relation to each other, not necessarily taking into consideration the packages within which they reside. This implies that we can implement the MVC pattern, even if we place all of our classes in the same package. However, an application of the Layers pattern dictates that our packages exist at different levels of granularity.

Release Reuse Equivalency Principle (REP)

As discussed in Chapter 1, the REP principle states that "The granule of reuse is the granule of release." As we've seen, this chapter discusses many of the principles associated with packaging our application. Up to this point, our discussion has been in regard to putting these principles in the context of the relationships that exist between classes. Turning our discussion to the package relationships is easy at this point because we know a class can't use another class in a different package without importing that package. Doing so creates a dependency between the two packages. We now turn our focus to the higher-level package view of architecture and the lower-level class view of our system. Up to this point, we've seen a number of common patterns utilized in numerous systems. At the root of each of these patterns are fundamental principles, which brings us back to an important point made in Chapter 1: Most patterns are simply an application of these principles.

At this point, we have discussed layering from strictly a class perspective. Conceptually, our application is layered, but until we layer according to the physical unit of release (in Java, the package) within our programming language environment, our system is not physically layered. If we were to place each of these classes in the same package, attempting to reuse one of the classes would imply a dependency on each of the other classes also residing within that package. We might argue that we can import only a single class; however, doing so does nothing to ensure that during a maintenance phase, another developer won't decide to import additional classes from that package or use the wildcard import to gain access to all classes. In reality, this argument goes far beyond placing restrictions on the use of certain classes in a package. It is centered on deployment and reuse. In Java, we deploy at the package level, and regardless of whether a class imports just a single class from another package, we still need to deploy all classes in that package, creating potential dependencies.

So how do we begin to establish our architectural vision, and how can we use the UML in helping us do so? As we begin establishing our architectural vision, it becomes important that we specify its structure. This specification can exist at many different levels of abstraction throughout our system. At its highest level, we may see the layers that compose our architecture. At a more well-defined level, we might illustrate relationships among classes or document patterns used to solve complex challenges. The level of detail to which we model our architecture is best left to our judgment and will typically vary across systems. In determining this level of detail, we must constantly consider which elements are architecturally significant; these elements should be modeled when establishing our architecture. We also know that some models exist at different levels of abstraction, and along with these varying levels of abstraction, as we progress through the design of our system, comes a system of checks and balances that enable us to guarantee a certain degree of architectural stability. *Phrased differently, our models, while focused on communicating different aspects of a system, still represent the same system; therefore, each of our models should be consistent in what it communicates, regardless of at what level of abstraction it exists.* These different perspectives are extremely valuable. By defining the relationships that exist among the packages in our application, as well as the relationships that exist among our classes, we have two different views into our system, each at different levels of abstraction. Thus, if the diagrams in Figure 10.1 and Figure 10.6 represent the same system, each of these diagrams must communicate the same thing but at different levels of abstraction. The relationships between the packages, and the relationships between the classes, must be consistent based on the packages in which the classes reside. Therefore, giving careful consideration to the packages that compose our application, and their relationships and responsibilities, is of equal importance as carefully considering the relationships and responsibilities of our classes.

In addition to the modeling that takes place, we've seen that simple prototypes also bring great value in helping prove the validity of the design. These prototypes serve as proofs of concept, helping to ensure that relationships and designs exhibited within our models can be implemented in Java. These proofs also enable us to prove that higher-level package dependencies are consistent with the lower-level class relationships.

In Figure 10.6, we see a sample class diagram illustrating the layers of which our payroll application is composed. Based on this class diagram, we can assume that these dependencies hold true throughout our application. While this diagram exists at a fairly high level, it can be used to validate the diagram in Figure 10.7, which represents the relationships among the contained packages within each layer. In this simple representation, the first three layers also contain classes and are duplicated. The `dataaccess` package, however, contains two additional packages; one containing the interfaces that the higher-level packages are dependent upon, and the other containing the actual implementation of our data access interfaces. These two different diagrams communicate the system at a different level of abstraction. In a more complex scenario, each of our layers also might contain additional packages, at which point our diagram in Figure 10.7 would illustrate these contained packages. For instance, in Figure 10.6, we see that the `userinterface` package has a dependency to the `businessservices`

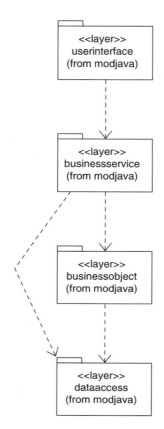

Figure 10.6   High-Level Package Diagram Illustrating Architectural Layers

package. In addition, userinterface is dependent only on businessservices and awt.

The diagram in Figure 10.8 represents the classes that compose this same payroll system; it represents a refinement of the diagram in Figure 9.12 in Chapter 9. Can you see how this diagram might have been further revised based on the requirements? Based on these relationships, we can assure ourselves of a few important architectural restrictions.

- The classes in the userinterface package can be dependent only on the classes in these other two packages, which is the purpose of using a dependency relationship. If we identify a situation where a class in userinterface requires the service of a class not in these other packages, our class relationships violate our package relationships, and we must refactor our model to accommodate this need.

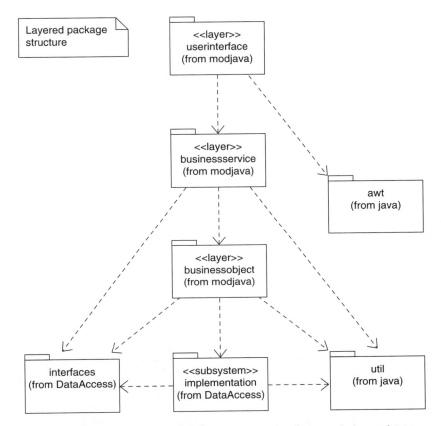

Figure 10.7   Package Diagram Illustrating Architectural Package Relationships

- We also can see in the diagram in Figure 10.7 that our implementation subsystem contained within the dataaccess package has a dependency only on the interfaces package. Therefore, we know that this implementation package can be used in any other system, as long as we make sure that the interfaces package also is deployed.
- No packages in our application are dependent on implementation other than the containing dataaccess package, which is an important distinction and a qualifying characteristic of what constitutes a subsystem. (Subsystems are discussed in Chapter 11.) At this point, however, we see that we can easily replace the implementation package with another package providing a similar set of functionality because we haven't coupled any other package to it. The only stipulation is that the replacement package must implement the interfaces that our

application is dependent upon. (Again, Chapter 11 discusses subsystems.)

When working with our class diagram, it's important that the relationships that exist among our classes be consistent with the relationships that exist among the packages that contain these classes. Therefore, the relationships in

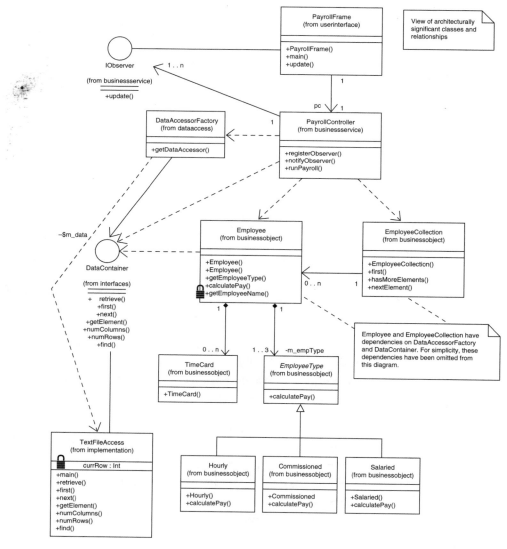

Figure 10.8   Class Diagram Illustrating More Complete Payroll System

Figure 10.7 must be consistent with the relationships in Figure 10.6. Aside from applying the common architectural patterns mentioned previously, this goal is the single most important one in establishing our architectural vision and, consequently, in architectural modeling. Making sure that the relationships among classes are consistent with the relationships that exist among packages ensures a maintainable, robust, and resilient architecture. These different views, existing at different levels of granularity, validate each other, serving as a system of checks and balances. They're the result of the application of our architectural mechanisms. To help clarify our established architecture, Figure 10.9 is a sequence diagram that details the collaboration between instances of the classes depicted in Figure 10.8.

10.4   Frameworks and Class Libraries

Object orientation has been promising reuse for many years, but only now are we beginning to realize this promise. Identifying various business processes and workflows is the means to writing reusable code. Assuming we've identified solid reuse candidates, our next challenge is determining a strategy for achieving reuse. This strategy should involve the establishment of an architectural vision, which may involve growing a framework or a class library.

Framework and *class library* often are used synonymously. However, a framework isn't the same as a class library. The two concepts differ on a fundamental level. Frameworks help us resolve challenges through inheritance, whereas class libraries do so through composition. Class libraries, which usually perform some set of similar behaviors, are an excellent way to achieve reusability. Class libraries can vary in size, from a relatively small number of classes to libraries with more than 1,000 classes. These classes are treated as black boxes and aren't typically open for extension. Based on the simplistic nature of class libraries, we focus our discussion in the following section on frameworks.

10.4.1   Frameworks

Frameworks are an excellent way to help enforce our architectural mechanisms. A common misunderstanding regarding frameworks is that only a single framework can exist for an application. In fact, an application may be composed of multiple frameworks, each focused on solving different design challenges and each helping to enforce a different set of restrictions. For instance, we may have a framework for data access, another for error handling, and yet another for performing business rule validation. Each of these frameworks is used in conjunction with the other to compose an application and may be used to design a

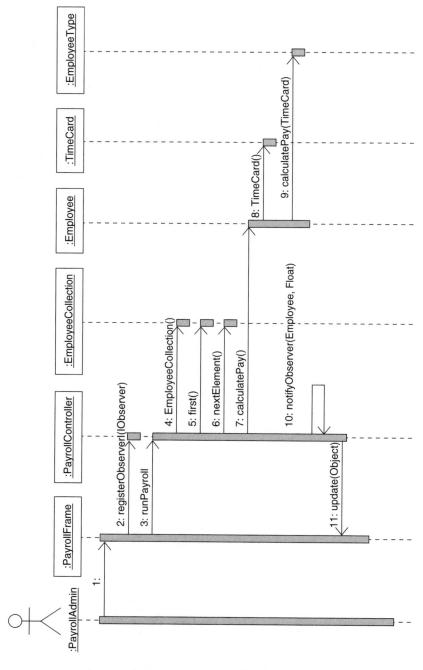

Figure 10.9   Sequence Diagram Illustrating the Run Payroll Use Case

higher-level, application-specific, architectural framework. Framework design has many of the same goals as designing any architecture. However, one especially important goal in designing a framework is identifying the extension points. These extension points are the points at which developers add customized behavior to the framework, which is done via interfaces and abstract classes. Recall that one of the goals of establishing an architectural vision is to enforce certain restrictions that developers who extend the architecture must adhere to. Frameworks accommodate this goal nicely because the variations in behavior that must be achieved exist only at our framework's extension points. So how do we define these extension points and actually design a framework? Let's look at an example.

10.4.1.1   *Framework Example*

Most systems require some form of error handling. Different systems often follow the same process in handling an error, yet the actual implementation may vary across systems. For instance, one system may wish to log errors to a database, while another system may log errors to a file. Our goal must be to identify the common behavior that exists across all uses of our error-handling mechanism, encapsulate this behavior into a set of classes that realize our error-handling mechanism, and then allow for variations of the implementation based on application-specific needs. We also strive to make sure that other developers who need to use our error handler can do so in as simple a manner as possible. In addition, the internal design of our error-handling system must be flexible enough to grow because we should be able to add new features to the error handler without having to make rampant modifications. Therefore, we have the following four primary goals in designing our error handler:

- Ease of use
- Provision of default error-handling behavior
- Customization by clients, overriding default behavior
- Easy maintenance by developers, adding new internal features as desired

Figure 10.10 is a sequence diagram that illustrates how we want these other developers to use our error handler. As can be seen, the error handler is simple to use and can be done with just a few lines of code. Note that in the diagram in Figure 10.10, we have opted not to illustrate the type of object that invokes our error handler, which isn't important in this context. In fact, were we to show an object type in this diagram, it might cause confusion as to where the error handler could be used. By omitting this information, we allow the error clients to be any object that imports the package containing the error-handling classes. In

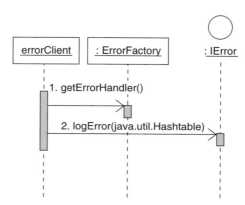

Figure 10.10   External Error-Handling Sequence Diagram

addition, the package containing the error-handling classes can be marked
"global," indicating that any other package within the application also can use
the error handler.

Obviously, the implementation of our error handler must go beyond what
we see in the simple diagram in Figure 10.10. Behind this high-level diagram is
another sequence of actions that detail how the internal behavior is realized.
Figure 10.11 illustrates another sequence diagram that shows how the error
handler handles an error when the logError method is invoked by an error
client. This diagram doesn't model the concrete implementation of the error
handler because the actual implementation may not be known, especially if the
framework has been extended with custom classes via the framework's extension points. It models only the abstract flow that the error-handler framework
always performs, regardless of how the error is handled. This distinction is subtle but important. Modeling in this fashion clearly illustrates the points at which
our error handler can be extended internally. It also easily accommodates the
many variations of implementation that our framework may support. From a
modeling perspective, modeling at this higher level of abstraction ensures that
our model won't need maintenance with each variation. In essence, the diagram
in Figure 10.11 details the flow for our error handler but does not couple it
directly to any concrete implementation.

This is not to say that a concrete representation of our error handler might
not be useful. In fact, we probably will define some default behavior that any
system can take advantage of. In doing so, we don't force each system using the
error handler to provide implementations for each of the extension points.
Instead, each system need only provide custom extension points at the place
that the application wishes to override this default behavior. In fact, by provid-

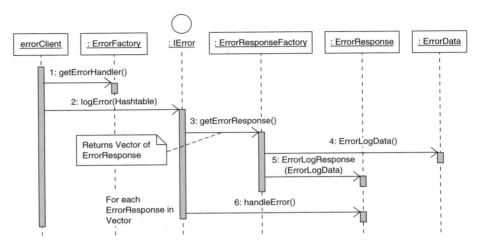

Figure 10.11   Internal Error-Handling High-Level Sequence Diagram Indicating Usage

ing default behaviors, our error-handling framework functions out of the box as a class library but, because of these extension points, has the advantage of extension because it has been designed as a framework. Figure 10.12 illustrates this default behavior provided out of the box for the error-handling framework.

Figure 10.13 illustrates the extension point provided by our error-handler framework. In this figure, external clients can manually set the default ErrorHandler class that will be used by our framework. The only stipulation is that this new class must implement the IError interface because our error-handler framework is bound to this interface, which again, is of utmost importance.

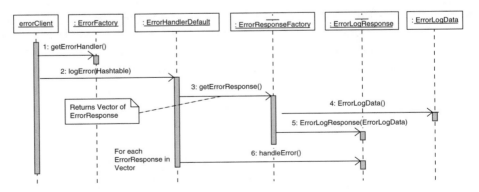

Figure 10.12   Internal Error-Handling Detailed Sequence Diagram

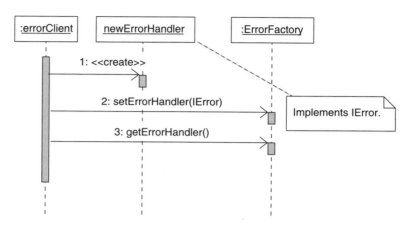

Figure 10.13   External Error-Handling Sequence Diagram Indicating Creation

By coupling our framework to an interface instead of a concrete implementation, we can easily vary implementations by providing new implementations of the interface. We also may wish to define other methods that enable us to alter additional behaviors within our error handler. For instance, creating a setErrorResponse method would allow an application to use the existing ErrorHandler class, extending the framework by defining only a new response.

Finally, in Figures 10.14 and 10.15, we see the package and class diagrams that contain our error-handling framework. In the simple example in Figure 10.14, we have only a single package. Note, however, that this package is marked "global," which indicates that all other packages have an implicit dependency to the error package and can therefore take advantage of its functionality. We add this notation for the simple reason that we don't want to confuse our package diagrams with a bunch of dependencies to this error-handling framework. It's important to note, however, that while our error handler exists within the same package, it may not accommodate all future needs. For instance, how does this error handler accommodate a multitier application consisting of a Java GUI client and a Java server? If our client needed to use the

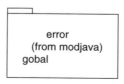

Figure 10.14   Error-Handling Package Diagram

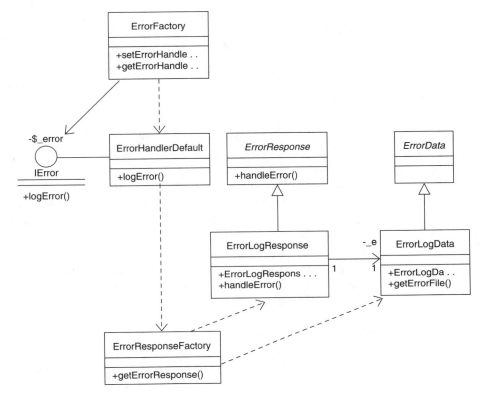

Figure 10.15　Error-Handling Class Diagram

error handler to log errors, but we always wanted the errors to log themselves on the server, this model requires some overhead. Because we have only one package, our unit of reuse is the unit of release, and therefore, we must release the entire package. However, we still need network communication, which this model doesn't take into consideration. Therefore, when designing frameworks, it's important to consider future needs and not just those of the present. As we've seen previously, the class diagram is invaluable in helping to understand the structural relationships that exist among our classes. By using each of these diagrams in conjunction with each other, we have a consistent and more easily understandable representation of our error-handling framework.

10.4.1.2　*Framework Example Notes*

Architectures that take advantage of frameworks have many advantages, including the ability of developers to define custom behaviors that extend the framework, as well as enabling developers to utilize a set of default behaviors defined by the framework itself. This concept has been the main focus of our discussion on frameworks.

When designing frameworks, we also must keep in mind many of the rules associated with architectural modeling. The internal representation of our framework must be robust and resilient so that it's easily maintainable by developers who need to maintain and extend the framework. Because of this requirement, we can apply many of the architectural patterns previously discussed when designing our frameworks.

Because frameworks must be extensible, they typically are more difficult to design. We have to consider not only how our framework will be used and possibly extended by clients, but also how our framework may need to grow in the future. In this sense, we can think of frameworks as small systems in and of themselves. Therefore, it's common to treat a framework as a subsystem. Subsystems are discussed in Chapter 11.

The example in Section 10.4.1.1 is a simple illustration of how we might design an error-handling framework. We have chosen to model it at a fairly high level. Some implementation-specific details haven't been modeled at this point, which is the nature of an iterative development lifecycle. At this point, we are primarily interested in understanding what our error handler needs to do and how we are going to accomplish it in an architecturally sound way. As we progress through construction and encounter new challenges, our model will grow with our source code, solving these difficult challenges as they're presented. Because our model grows with our code, we have a more accurate specification of how the significant elements within our system interact. As such, it would be beneficial to create some simple prototypical code, similar to that produced in 8.2.6 for the Run Payroll use case. This code will help ensure that our design is robust and that the code and model work together to verify the integrity and validity of our design. At a practical level, some issues aren't discovered until we write code. By writing the code as we model, the discovery process is much richer. Keep in mind that any source code written at this point can exist at a fairly high level. In many situations, exceptions may not be handled appropriately, nor are many classes provided with a meaningful implementation. However, as stated previously, doing things this way helps ensure that our design is consistent and pragmatic at many different levels.

10.4.2   Class Libraries

Many of the challenges we've discussed in regard to frameworks also exist when developing class libraries. We still need to make sure that the behaviors associated with the classes within our class library are highly reusable. This high degree of reuse can be achieved only if we assure ourselves that the functionality exhibited by the class library is so granular that it can be used by many different applications, yet not so granular that we have to duplicate functionality across applications in order to use our class library.

One common approach that is useful when developing class libraries is to design them in a framework-oriented manner. In doing so, we identify the areas within the class library that are most likely to change in the future. We must design a flexible extension point for these areas. However, because it's likely that most applications using this library will do so in a consistent manner, we might consider providing a class implementing some default behavior, and have the class library use that class at that extension point, unless told to use some other class by the application using this library. In doing so, we gain the advantage of having a fully encapsulated set of functionality that can be used as a black box, while also being able to override this functionality with another class should the need arise. We have done this with the error-handling framework discussed previously.

10.5   Component Architectures

We've not discussed another side to architecture so far in this chapter. Up to this point, we've focused on architecture in the context of class and package design. While the relationships between classes and packages are very important, higher-level constructs deserve discussion. When we deploy Java applications, the minimal unit of deployment is the package. However, it's unlikely that we'll ever deploy an individual package by itself. Instead, we typically deploy some higher-level unit, such as Enterprise JavaBeans (EJB), Java Archives (JARs), or Web Archives (WARs) file. In addition, it's quite likely that when we develop Java applications, we'll take advantage of some of the code that was written by others, which typically is deployed in a JAR file as well. Therefore, while the relationships between the classes and packages in our system are important because they increase maintainability and system resiliency, the relationships between these higher-level deployable units are equally important because they impact reuse. We'll call these higher-level elements, such as JAR files, *components*.

10.5.1   Components Defined

In his book *Component Software*, Clemens Szyperski defines a component as the following:

A software component is a unit of composition with contractually specified interfaces and explicit context dependencies only. A software component can be deployed independently, and is subject to composition by third parties. [COMP97]

Based on this definition, we can't exclude classes. However, not just classes can be components. Examining the definition further, we see no mention of object orientation whatsoever. Common libraries such as Windows DLL files can be considered components. One of the forces of components is that they aren't coupled to objects. Because we're primarily interested in object orientation, however, our discussion of components is centered around object orientation.

A component typically is composed of many classes and packages. A component is composed of everything that it needs that allows it to be independently deployable. In the previously cited book, Szyperski also states that a component has the following three characteristic properties:

- A component is a unit of independent deployment.
- A component is a unit of third-party composition.
- A component has no persistent state. [COMP97]

While we've already discussed the first of these items, the remaining two can be a bit confusing at first. For example, let's consider a JAR file; one of its reuse benefits is that we don't necessarily know how it was written. Instead, we know only the public methods available on the public classes within the JAR file. These public methods compose the JAR file's interface. Because we care only about the public interface, we consider the use of a JAR file as being similar to using any other component that might have been developed by a third party.

Many of the classes we develop are created with state in mind. The state typically contributes to the behavior of its instances, and it's because of the interesting state-related behavior that we create multiple instances of the class. A component, however, has no state-related behavior because we never instantiate more than a single instance of the component. If at first this seems strange in light of the fact that individual classes can also be components, then we only need to ask ourselves if we would ever need to deploy multiple JAR files for a single application. A JAR file deployed with our application is the single instance of the component represented by that JAR file.

10.5.2   Components and the UML

In the UML, we model components using a component diagram. A component diagram is similar in nature to a class diagram, except we use the component fundamental element. Relationships can be modeled between components on a

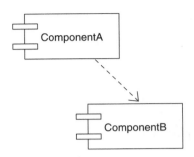

Figure 10.16   Syntax of a Component Diagram

component diagram using dependencies. Figure 10.16 illustrates a sample component diagram.

In this diagram, ComponentA has a structural relationship to ComponentB, which implies that ComponentA can't be deployed without ComponentB. While it also implies that elements within ComponentA use elements in ComponentB, because components represent black boxes, we're really primarily concerned only with deployment.

10.5.3   Component Sample

Components can exist at many levels. Entire systems can be components if desired. Of course, this implies that entire systems will be reused in other contexts, which may not be very likely. In Chapter 11, we discuss subsystems, which are, in fact, excellent component examples.

We just completed a sample where we designed an error-handling framework. We designed it in such a way that it can be extended by subclassing at the appropriate extension points. It also would be quite useful if we could create a unit of deployment that's separate from the rest of our application. Therefore, if needed, we could use this error handler in other contexts. Hence, our error-handling component is seen as a third-party piece of software by all systems.

10.6   Conclusion

As we've seen, establishing an architectural vision is of utmost importance. Systems with a robust, resilient, and extensible architecture are more likely to accommodate growth. This architectural vision consists of much more than simply a series of elegant, yet disjointed, designs. It must encompass the system in its entirety, focusing on those elements that are most architecturally significant. These architecturally significant elements may be those that are of the highest risk, are most functionally complex, or are tightest in terms of scheduling.

In establishing our architectural vision, we can take advantage of many proven mechanisms to help us achieve our architectural goals. These mechanisms serve as patterns that are customized to our application's needs based on the context in which our application exists. Centering our application architectures around the concepts of frameworks and class libraries contributes to flexible systems that enable us to accommodate our system's growth.

CHAPTER 11

Designing Subsystems

*To effectively achieve any degree of reuse, we must emphasize interfaces,
not implementation. Subsystems enable us to emphasize interfaces.*

We haven't spent much time talking about reuse. In fact, we've downplayed the concept of reuse in favor of emphasizing architecture and dependency management. We've done so because in order for us to effectively reuse, we must define classes with the appropriate level of granularity and manage the dependencies between these classes. Emphasizing flexible dependencies contributes positively to a more resilient software architecture, and if we can design resilient systems with flexible dependency management, it's easier to create more independent units of deployment. These units of independent deployment can be componentized, and subsystems are a very effective means of doing so.

11.0 Defining Subsystems

A subsystem can be thought of as a small system in and of itself. Subsystems, as defined in this book, focus on a reusable asset that other components within our application use. These other components, however, are bound to a well-defined interface that the subsystem exposes, which enables us to effectively alter implementations without modifying those elements dependent on the subsystem interface. A subsystem typically is the result of identifying some aspect of a system that exhibits largely independent characteristics from that system. Let's examine the following characteristics of a subsystem:

- <<subsystem>> stereotyped package
- Well-defined interface

- Interface implemented by public proxy class
- All classes package scope except proxy

Let's explore these four characteristics independently; then we'll take a look at how these characteristics are translated to Java.

The first of these characteristics is a simple mechanism that enables us to organize the classes of a subsystem in a cohesive manner. A single package, which can contain nested packages if desired, represents a subsystem. Next, each subsystem has a well-defined interface. This interface is how the external components see and interact with the subsystem. All external classes communicate with the subsystem through this well-defined interface. Thus, we can clearly separate the implementation details, which may be complex, from the simpler usage of the subsystem. Obviously, an implementation of the operations defined on the interface must be behind this interface. The proxy class represents this implementation. Last, we want to ensure that elements outside the confines of the subsystem package can't access the internal elements of the subsystem. Therefore, all classes residing in the subsystem package must be marked so that they aren't accessible outside the scope of the subsystem package. The only exception in this case is the proxy class, which provides the implementation for the subsystem interface. The reason for this exception is because some other object must be responsible for creating an instance of the proxy class. If it were package scope, we wouldn't be able to instantiate the proxy class.

To really understand why these special restrictions are placed on subsystems, we must first examine the goals of subsystems and what their creation can bring to the development effort. Because of these restrictions, developing subsystems certainly is going to be more complex than creating regular packages. Part of this complexity is because we can communicate with the subsystem only through the subsystem's well-defined interface, which implies that no other element within our application, save a factory class, should access the elements internal to the subsystem. We've discussed the advantages of using factories in Chapter 9 and how they can help ensure adherence to the principles we discussed in Chapter 1. While we don't intend to repeat that discussion in this chapter, we do want to examine the importance of this subsystem interface and the subsystem dependencies.

11.0.1 Subsystem Dependencies

The purpose of the subsystem interface is to serve as a contract between the subsystem and the outside world. Any interaction with the subsystem always should go through the subsystem interface. Of course, as we just mentioned, a factory class probably will need to access at least one internal element, which is the proxy class that serves as the implementation of our interface. Therefore, combining the four characteristics listed previously implies that a subsystem must restrict incoming dependencies. A subsystem represents strict adherence to both the Stable Dependencies Principle (SDP) and the Stable Abstractions Principle (SAP).

However, the four characteristics of a subsystem don't provide any implications as to the outgoing dependencies of the subsystem package. If necessary, we can allow the classes inside the subsystem package to use the contents of another package. Of course, we should try to adhere to our package principles discussed in Chapter 1 because any outgoing dependencies we create certainly increase the coupling between the subsystem package and the dependent package. Regardless, no restriction is placed on outgoing dependencies as there is with incoming dependencies. Therefore, we can state the following:

> *A subsystem must restrict incoming dependencies. A subsystem need not restrict outgoing dependencies.*

The importance of these statements may not be apparent because of their subtlety. Because the subsystem has a clear and crisp boundary, it should be a highly reusable component within or across systems. We can reuse the behaviors of the subsystem and any of its dependent packages wherever needed. However, the true value of a subsystem is the simplicity associated with its replaceability. Because the subsystem restricts incoming dependencies, and the external elements know only about the subsystem's interface, we can replace the existing subsystem implementation with a new subsystem implementation, as long as the new implementation adheres to the predefined interface. Consequently, we can state:

> *The true value of a subsystem is the simplicity of its replacement with a new subsystem adhering to the well-defined interface.*

Because of this unique characteristic of a subsystem, not all packages require the flexibility a subsystem offers. A subsystem is more difficult to design because of its unique characteristics, and the use of subsystems should be driven by necessity, rather than by any other desire.

Figure 11.1 illustrates the relationships between external elements and a subsystem. In this figure, we see client classes in the `client` package use the subsystem `subsystem` package. The only class in the `client` package that accesses any class that is internal to the subsystem is `Factory`. Any other class that needs to interact with the subsystem requests an instance of the `SubsystemInterface`

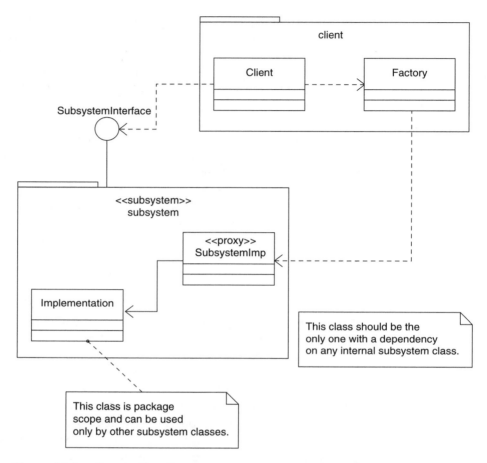

Figure 11.1   Sample Class Diagram Illustrating Primary Class and Package
Relationships

interface implementation. This request results in the `Factory` creating an
instance of the `SubsystemImp` proxy class and returning it as a `SubsystemInter-`
`face` type, which the `SubsystemImp` implements.

11.1   Subsystems in Java

We now understand some of the basic characteristics of a subsystem. Not sur-
prisingly, however, a number of implementation-specific details are encountered
when we try to implement subsystems in Java. Not because Java doesn't provide
support for the basic characteristics of subsystems, but because the nature of

programming always offers interesting twists we don't often foresee when discussing concepts. After all, this is why one of our best practices is to develop simple prototypes and to develop and design simultaneously. So let's take a look at implementing a subsystem in Java.

When implementing subsystems in Java, it's obviously important that we adhere to the four basic characteristics listed in Section 11.0. Because we already have a class diagram in place in Figure 11.1, let's write the sample code associated with it to see what sort of interesting twists we encounter. We'll start with the subsystem internals. The following code is for the subsystem package itself, with rather uninteresting behavior:

```java
package subsystem;

public interface SubsystemInterface {
    public void doSomething();
}

package subsystem;

public class SubsystemImp implements SubsystemInterface {
    public void doSomething() {
        System.out.println("SubsystemImp.doSomething");
    }
}

package subsystem;

class Implementation {
    public void doImp() {
        System.out.println("Implementation.doImp");
    }
}
```

This code includes three classes. First, the SubsystemInterface defines the contract the proxy class guarantees to carry out. The second class is the proxy class that provides the implementation for the interface. Finally, the third class depicts a class that is package scope, because it omits the public modifier from the class declaration and therefore can be accessed only by the other classes in the subsystem.

The following illustrates the client classes:

```java
package client

import subsystem.*;

public class Factory {
    public static SubsystemInterface getSubsystem() {
        return new SubsystemImp();
```

```
        }
    }

    package client

    import subsystem.*;

    public class Client {
        public static void main(String args[]){
            SubsystemInterface s = Factory.getSubsystem();
            s.doSomething();
        }
    }
```

Note that the factory class is responsible for creating the subsystem proxy, SubsystemImp. The Client class doesn't refer to SubsystemImp but instead references the SubsystemInterface class. If either of these classes tried to reference the Implementation class in the subsystem package, a compiler error would occur.

This code may seem uninteresting at this point, but let's further examine it and some of the ramifications of our decisions. Most significant is the location of the SubsystemInterface class. One of the characteristics of a subsystem is its replaceability. If we actually decide to place the SubsystemInterface in the subsystem and if we tried to replace the subsystem package with a new package that implements this interface, we wouldn't be able to. The problem isn't necessarily because the SubsystemInterface is in the subsystem package, but because our Client class in the client package has to import the subsystem package to refer to the SubsystemInterface class. If we were to create a new subsystem package named newsubsystem, with intentions of removing the old subsystem package, a compiler error would occur in our Client class. Of course, one would also occur in the Factory class, with similar ramifications, but it has been designed to accommodate changes more easily. Our desire to achieve system closure hasn't occurred at all because any new subsystem package implies potentially widespread modifications, whereas if only the Factory class refers to internal subsystem classes, the rest of our application is closed to changes, leaving only the Factory open.

Stated simply, the class serving as the interface to which external elements are bound can't be a class that is placed in the subsystem. Instead, this SubsystemInterface class should be moved to a separate package. In addition, we might consider moving the Factory class to this new package, to ensure that any subsystem modifications are local to only this new package and the remainder of the system is closed to such changes, which, in fact, is adherence to the Common Closure Principle (CCP) discussed in Chapter 1. However, if we move the

Factory to the new interfaces package, we find that the package relationships between subsystem and interfaces is now cyclic in nature, which is a violation of the Acyclic Dependencies Principle (ADP). We may consider a more flexible Factory implementation, such as an abstract factory. (For further information, see [GOF95].)

Figure 11.2 illustrates this solution, in which we now have three packages. Because the code is essentially the same, we've chosen to illustrate this solution using a class diagram. Our client package no longer has to import any of the classes in the subsystem package. The only package that can peer inside the subsystem package is the interface package, which contains the Factory class responsible for creating the subsystem proxy class, SubsystemImp. In this situation, if we decide we need to replace the subsystem package with a new

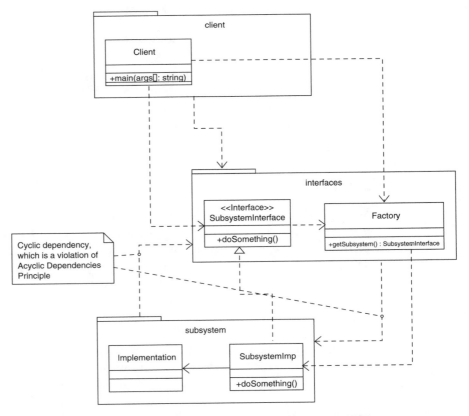

Figure 11.2   Subsystem Implementation with a Package Containing the Interface and the Object Factory

implementation, we simply create the new package, define a new proxy that implements `SubsystemInterface`, and modify `Factory` to create the new proxy class. No changes need be made to our client classes.

The only real concern in Figure 11.2 is the violation of ADP, and a few alternatives are available. First, as mentioned previously, we might opt for a more flexible `Factory` implementation, such as using an abstract factory (as discussed in [GOF95]). However, examining this option a bit further, the violation may not be a major cause for concern. First, if we decide to use the subsystem elsewhere, the interface package is a required package because our proxy class is dependent on the `SubsystemInterface` it implements. Therefore, we also would have to deploy the interfaces package, which, because it contains the `Factory` class, will still ensure that any new client packages can use the `Factory` to create the appropriate `SubsystemImp`. Also, because all other classes in our `subsystem` package are package scope, it's unlikely that classes outside this package can ever access these package scope classes. They can access only the proxy class.

The primary goal of our subsystem has been accomplished, which was to reduce dependencies of the client that uses the subsystem from the `subsystem` package itself. Therefore, the `subsystem` package easily is replaceable by simply replacing the `subsystem` package with a new subsystem and making the appropriate change to the `Factory`. As an exercise for the reader, we encourage exploration of additional flexibility by using an abstract factory to reduce the cyclic dependency.

11.2   Subsystem Specification

When modeling subsystems, it's useful to create a diagram illustrating the interaction between clients and the subsystem as well as the structure and behavior of the internal elements, which we'll refer to as the "external" and "internal subsystem specifications," respectively. When specifying a subsystem using the UML, it's important that we use both behavioral and structural diagrams, just as when we specify the design for a system. Let's examine an example using our payroll system discussed throughout the book.

One of the requirements for the Run Payroll use case was that, after the system calculates salary for an employee, the system must create a bank transaction and deposit the appropriate amount in the employee's bank account. Were we to examine our list of initial concepts identified in Chapter 7 when performing problem analysis, we would find that we created an entity class named `BankSystem`, the purpose of which was to communicate with our external bank system. The process that communicates with an external bank system is an ideal candidate for a subsystem for a number of reasons. First and foremost, we want to manage the incoming dependencies to the set of behavior to ensure that we easily can incorporate new external system interfaces in the future.

Assuming we decide to take the subsystem route with our bank system, we should apply all of what we've learned to this point. In this chapter, we concentrate on how to most effectively represent the external and internal specification of the bank system subsystem.

Figure 11.3 shows the package diagram illustrating the various package relationships. We're most interested here in how we've managed the incoming dependencies. Only the classes in the factory package have access to the internal class in the banksystem package. As we'll see, this is because the factory class must instantiate the BankSystem proxy class. This relationship is the only incoming reference we'll find. In addition, the banksystem package has a few outgoing dependencies. Most notable here is the dependency on the business-object package.

The four diagrams in Figure 11.4 through Figure 11.7 illustrate the external and internal views of the subsystem. Figure 11.4 illustrates how developers can use the bank subsystem. On this diagram, the first object represented is a generic object, which implies that we aren't concerned with the type of the object using the bank subsystem, only that some object invokes the getBankSystem method on the factory. Figure 11.5 shows the external view class diagram. For those developers who need to use the bank subsystem, this class diagram illustrates all

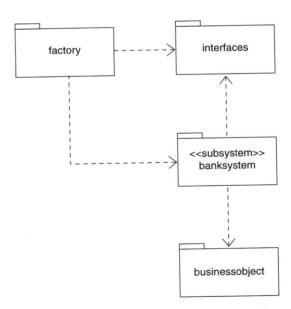

Figure 11.3   Package Diagram Illustrating Subsystem Relationships

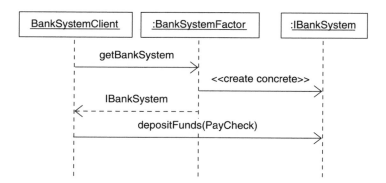

Figure 11.4   Sequence Diagram Showing Client Usage of Bank Subsystem

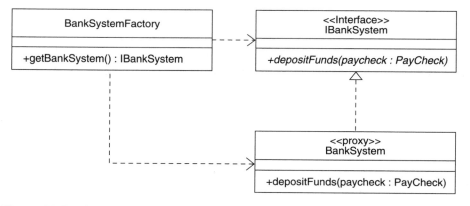

Figure 11.5   Class Diagram Showing Client Usage of Bank Subsystem

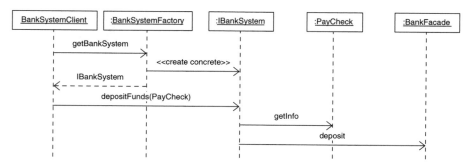

Figure 11.6   Sequence Diagram Showing Detailed Bank Subsystem Processing

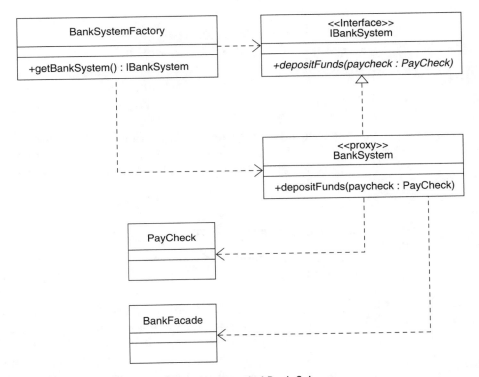

Figure 11.7 Class Diagram Showing Detailed Bank Subsystem

the classes that a developer needs to know about. In fact, while we show the proxy class on the diagram in Figure 11.5 for the sake of completeness, a developer needn't necessarily know much about this class because only the factory and the interface have to be referenced in the bank subsystem clients.

The remaining two figures represent the internal behavior and structure of the bank subsystem. What may be most interesting here is how our proxy class within the bank subsystem is very similar in role to the controller classes that we discussed previously in the context of our individual Use Cases. We'll find this to be a common trend when designing subsystems.

11.3   Subsystem Identification

We can determine whether a set of classes are good candidates for subsystems in a number of ways. First, examining our structural model might yield situations where a grouping of classes perform a cohesive set of responsibilities. While this set of classes may have a high degree of coupling, we might find that classes that use them are coupled to only one or two of the entire set, which is a likely indication that a subsystem could be used. In such a case, the design of the subsystem is probably made easier because of the natural dependency structure that currently exists.

Another situation that is a good candidate for a subsystem is one in which we're fairly confident that a certain portion of the system will have to be replaced at some point in the future. For instance, if a set of classes currently serve as a facade to the underlying operating system, but we suspect that our application will have to run on another platform in the future, we should seriously consider minimizing the incoming dependencies on these classes by encapsulating them inside a subsystem.

11.4   Subsystem Development

Essentially, we can think of subsystems as minisystems in and of themselves. Because of this, when we are designing subsystems, we should perform each of the significant activities we would perform when developing a system. Of additional interest, however, is that subsystems promote parallel development. Because a subsystem emphasizes the management of incoming dependencies, and all other classes in our system are dependent only on the subsystem interface, after we've specified the interface for the subsystem, the implementation is only a concern for those constructing the internal components of the subsystem. Those developers who need to use the subsystem, however, can work as if the subsystem already had been developed.

In this case, creating a mock object that serves as some degenerative implementation of the subsystem enables other developers to work with the subsystem, even though the internals haven't been completely developed. The advantages are obvious, because we're able to streamline the development process. Of course, if we decide to develop subsystems in parallel with other system components, management and communication are two key aspects to our effort. Changes to the subsystem interface can have major ramifications on those developers using the subsystem. While not ideal, it's certainly more desirable than these other developers being dependent on the implementation details. It's likely that the implementation will change more often than the interface.

11.5   Subsystems as Frameworks

While our discussion on subsystems has been solely focused on the various relationships between client and subsystem classes, it's quite possible that a subsystem can evolve into a flexible framework. We briefly discussed frameworks in

Chapter 10 and provided a sample error-handling framework. A framework offers flexibility in that it enables classes to be plugged into the framework at various extension points. In fact, the development of frameworks and subsystems is complementary.

We'll find that frameworks typically focus on identifying the extension points that must be customized on a situational basis. Subsystems, on the other hand, are focused more on how we package our classes and define the appropriate relationships between these classes.

11.6   Conclusion

Subsystems virtually are minisystems in and of themselves. In designing subsystems, we should elicit the requirements of the subsystem, understand the behavioral aspects, and create flexible structures. Subsystems, however, add a unique perspective in that we not only consider what the subsystem must use, but also what must use the subsystem.

Subsystem design involves looking at the problem a bit differently from how we typically look at other design challenges. Instead of focusing on the outgoing relationships that may exist among our subsystem classes, we focus more on the incoming relationships. Considering both the incoming and outgoing relationships helps to reduce coupling and manage dependencies throughout our entire package and class structure. The result is a much more flexible and resilient system.

The topic of subsystem development, however, does not exist independent of many of the other topics we've considered in previous chapters. In fact, subsystems complement each of these topics. As discussed, frameworks and subsystems are a complementary approach to design. Using subsystems judiciously can help contribute greatly to the overall flexibility of our systems. When designing subsystems, and treating them as small systems in themselves, we can take advantage of the power of convergence associated with using object orientation, the UML, software process, and Java as a cohesive whole. This complementary approach enables us to apply each of these technologies when designing subsystems in a fashion similar to what we've discussed throughout this book.

APPENDIX A

Rational Unified Process (RUP) and Extreme Programming (XP)

Much of our discussion throughout this book has been focused on the software development process. The software process we use when developing an application guides us in performing the appropriate activities at the appropriate times, directs us to the creation of an appropriate set of artifacts, and ties the many activities associated with software development into a cohesive whole. All software processes must exhibit the following fundamental characteristics:

- Support the traceability of any artifact produced as the result of one activity to another artifact produced during a separate activity
- Embody various best practices of software development
- Help ensure that we produce high-quality software

Processes that don't exhibit these basic characteristics likely lack a certain degree of ceremony—that is, they don't emphasize creating a sense of cohesion associated with the individual software development activities.

Two of the more common software processes today are the Rational Unified Process (RUP) and Extreme Programming (XP). There is much debate among industry experts as to which of these approaches is most likely to ensure success. After stressing the importance of process throughout this book, we would be remiss if we didn't devote some time to a discussion of these two industry giants. During this discussion, we point out the differences and similarities between each approach.

A.0 Rational Unified Process (RUP)

While commonly categorized as a software development process, in reality, RUP is a process framework. One of the driving forces behind an adoption of

243

RUP is to devise a customized development case, or *RUP instance*, that fits within an organization or development team. In fact, any attempt to adopt RUP "out of the box" is virtually futile because of its scope. In the attempt to define a process framework that is universally applicable, RUP provides a robust set of practices that must be carefully examined. Those aspects that are most pertinent to our team must be applied to our custom instance of RUP. In fact, many of the activities performed and artifacts produced throughout this book were gleaned from RUP. Because of the framework nature of RUP, when we say "process," we imply "process framework" in the following sections.

A.0.1 Characteristics of RUP

First, RUP is an iterative process. The iterative approach to software development advocates system growth through a series of iterations that enable us to understand the problem in a stepwise fashion. The result is an incremental growth in our system's functionality. As such, it's common to refer to RUP as iterative and incremental.

RUP is an architecture-centric process. A system's architecture should be emphasized early in the development process, paying careful attention to those aspects of the system that are considered architecturally significant. Architecturally significant aspects may include areas of the system that encapsulate critical business functions, are needed sooner rather than later, or include a high degree of technical risk.

When developing an application using RUP, all activities are use case–driven. A strong emphasis is placed on building a system that satisfies user requirements. As we've seen throughout this book, use cases define various business processes, which are elaborated upon as we progress throughout the software development lifecycle.

Based on these three primary characteristics, RUP typically is referred to as a *use case–driven, architecture-centric, and iterative and incremental* software

Iteration Duration

A lot of books discuss iterative and incremental development. Unfortunately, not many of them tell us how long an iteration should be. Depending on the complexity of the application, and the phase of the software lifecycle, a typical iteration should last between three weeks and three months.

development process framework. Of course, RUP has many other significant, yet more detailed, aspects that must be discussed to obtain a deeper understanding of its use. However, these three characteristics form the foundation upon which it is built.

A.0.2   Workflows and Phases

The use case–driven, architecture-centric, and iterative and incremental nature of RUP is captured in its phases and workflows. The diagram in Figure A.1 illustrates these workflows and phases. The workflows illustrated in this figure represent the more traditional stages of the typical software development lifecycle. The phases, on the other hand, represent a certain area of emphasis that is dependent upon our overall point in the life of the system.

The Inception phase marks the beginning of the software development effort. During this phase, the business case and project scope for the system is established. The end of the Inception phase is marked by the Lifecycle Objective milestone, where we determine the overall feasibility of the project and whether we should continue with its development.

The Elaboration phase emphasizes establishing a sound project plan and system architecture. During this phase, we should focus on mitigating the highest risk aspects of the system that may jeopardize future development efforts.

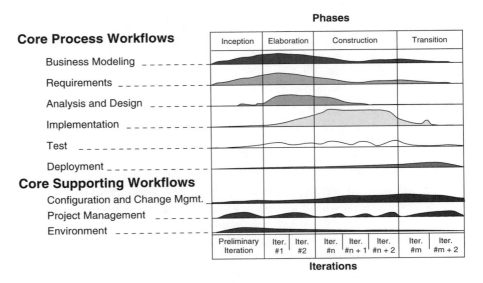

Adapted from Kruchten, Philippe, *The Rational Unified Process*, Addison-Wesley, 1999.

Figure A.1   The Rational Unified Process (RUP)

The completion of the Elaboration phase is marked by the Lifecycle Architecture milestone, where we assess our system's architecture, ensuring we've mitigated the primary risks.

The Construction phase stresses the development of the system into a complete product that is useful to its end users. The end of the Construction phase is marked by the Initial Operational Capability milestone, where we assure our system meets its specified requirements.

The Transition phase is when we deploy the application to the end user. The Product Release milestone is the point at which we determine if the system objectives were met and whether we should start another development cycle.

An iteration represents traversal through the core workflows. Each iteration should result in an executable version of the system, whether it be an internal or external release. Most interesting is the regularity with which we perform the workflows. Note that even during the Inception phase, when our emphasis is placed on establishing the business case for the system, we still consider more technical implementation issues, which is an important consideration because it enables us to continuously evaluate the risk associated with the system. Were we to concentrate only on eliciting requirements during the Inception phase, it's unlikely that we could adequately measure the risk associated with various technologies. Regardless of iteration or phase, however, RUP places a strong emphasis on the mitigation of risk. Higher-risk areas of the system should be the focal point of earlier iterations. A single iteration accommodates this risk throughout all workflows. This risk is managed using the six best practices that RUP promotes, discussed in Table A.1.

Phases versus Workflows

A different way to view phases and workflows is by considering the macro versus the micro aspects of the development lifecycle. The macro aspect encompasses the major decision points of the development effort, embodied within the phases. These decision points include overall project scope, multiple iteration planning, and high-level project planning. The micro aspect emphasizes the day-to-day activities of the development effort, addressed by the workflows, which includes many of the core challenges faced by developers on a daily basis such as design challenges, technical challenges, and constantly changing requirements.

Table A.1   Software Development Best Practices Identified by RUP

Best Practice	Description
Develop iteratively	Iterative development focuses on growing the system in small, incremental, and planned steps. At the beginning of each iteration, a well-established set of goals must be established. At the end of each iteration, these goals should have been realized. If not, we need to accommodate for them in subsequent iterations. Iterative development requires continuous planning to help mitigate risk. When developing iteratively, we don't try to identify at the beginning of the project all requirements the system must eventually support. Instead, shorter cycles enable us to almost continuously identify requirements and design effective solutions.
Manage requirements	Changing requirements are a constant in software development. Not only must we be able to effectively elicit requirements, but also we must have activities in place that help us effectively manage them.
Model visually	In Chapter 2, we discussed the importance of the UML in the software development effort. The advantages of the UML can be realized by visualizing our software systems and using this model as a communication and problem-solving tool throughout the entire development lifecycle. The UML is a way to help us maintain our architecture-centric views throughout development. *(continues)*

Table A.1   Software Development Best Practices Identified by RUP *(continued)*

Best Practice	Description
Use component architectures	A heavy emphasis must be placed on the architecture of our software systems. The architecture contributes greatly to our system's ability to accommodate change and evolve gracefully.
Verify quality	The inability to ensure that our system adheres to its requirements ultimately results in a system that doesn't fulfill user needs. We must be able to continuously verify our system's behavior.
Control change	Change can result in a system that doesn't fulfill requirements. Managing these requirements is very important. In addition, we must manage change at all levels of software development, which includes not only requirements, but also such things as source code, release units, and other supplemental artifacts.

A.0.3   Tailoring RUP

Because of the customizable nature of RUP, it's quite easy for almost any software development team to claim that they're using it on their software development project. However, any tailored instance of the process must conform to a few fundamental characteristics. RUP defines six fundamental software development best practices, described in Table A.1, to which all instances must conform. RUP is quite clear on this issue, as seen in the following:

> *The Rational Unified Process encourages tailoring. However, tailoring is not license to bypass the process altogether. The essentials of the Rational Unified Process are embodied in its best practices. Follow the spirit of these best practices, while tailoring the activities and artifacts to fit your needs. [RUP00]*

To tailor RUP, we adhere to these six best practices and glean from it only the artifacts and activities that best fit our development environment.

A.1 Extreme Programming (XP)

The foundation of XP is built on a single, fundamental concept of software development: If performing an activity while developing software is considered a worthwhile task, then let's perform that activity so often that it's considered extreme. For instance, if testing is a good thing to do, let's test our code after each change that we make. Of course, XP espouses other principles, and we discuss them in the sections that follow, but this single, fundamental concept captures the essence of XP.

A.1.1 Characteristics of XP

XP considers 12 principles so important that they should be applied at an extreme level. These principles are described in Table A.2.

Table A.2 XP Principles

XP Principle	Description
Planning game	Examine and determine the scope of an upcoming release by evaluating business priorities and development estimates.
Small releases	Develop aspects of the system of highest priority as quickly as possible, in a very short release cycle.
Metaphor	Establish a consistent vision of how the entire system is structured and how it functions.
Simple design	Avoid any complexity that does not contribute to the immediate highest priority tasks.
Testing	Developers create unit tests that are continuously run to verify the system. These tests must run completely for new

(continues)

Table A.2 XP Principles *(continued)*

XP Principle	Description
	development to continue. Customers write acceptance tests to validate system features.
Refactoring	Developers restructure the system to improve structural integrity and contribute to higher degrees of maintenance. Refactoring emphasizes improving structure without incorporating any new behaviors.
Pair programming	All programmers work in pairs, and no production-quality code is written individually.
Collective ownership	Specialization is discouraged, and developers are encouraged to change and improve code anywhere at any time.
Continuous integration	The system is continuously integrated and built many times daily, after each task is completed.
Forty-hour week	Overtime is discouraged over consecutive weeks.
On-site customer	Changing requirements demand that a customer be constantly involved with the direction of the system.
Coding standards	All code is written in accordance with coding guidelines. An emphasis should be placed upon writing code that is concise, correct, and emphasizes communication.

While XP advocates adherence to these 12 practices, these practices themselves don't constitute a software development process. In explaining how we adhere to these practices and the relationships between them, the true value of XP is revealed because each of these best practices helps reinforce some other practice. For instance, refactoring without testing is rather dangerous because we are modifying our code base. If we modify the code and don't perform tests, we can't ensure that the modified code functions exactly as the previous version.

In addition to the practices reinforcing each other, other aspects of XP are important. XP emphasizes adaptability throughout the entire software development effort, and in the spirit of this, the main tenet of XP is its ability to rapidly and effectively respond to change. XP recommends focusing only on areas of the system that are of immediate need. XP uses user stories that represent system features, and the current user story under development should receive our immediate attention.

XP also emphasizes managing risk and does so in the context of its user stories. Instead of predicting the future direction of the system, XP advocates incorporating the functionality of only today. Attempting to accommodate the predicted functionality of tomorrow is error prone because that functionality may never reach fruition. Consequently, worrying about risks associated with features that ultimately may not be implemented isn't recommended in XP. The most interesting aspect of this, however, is the XP challenge of the cost of change curve.

A.1.2   Is It XP or Isn't It?

Because of some of the unique, and rather unconventional, principles of XP, it may not be applicable to all development teams. However, XP proponents are clear on one issue. If a team isn't using and judiciously adhering to all 12 of the best practices, team members shouldn't make claims as to the success or failure of XP. Keep in mind that, unlike RUP, XP isn't a process framework. While tailoring XP is certainly allowed (after all, who is going to stop you?), should your development team decide to tailor XP, the success or failure of the development effort may not necessarily be the direct result of XP.

A.2   Similarities and Differences

After discussing the characteristics of both RUP and XP, we can make some conclusions as to the similarities and differences between them. Superficially, they may look as different from each other as black does from white. Some similarities are apparent, such as the promotion of iterative development. However, examining each approach a bit further, we find some amazing, more subtle, similarities.

Many developers unfamiliar with XP view it as a glorified hacking scheme, but the multiple best practices refute this view. The metaphor promotes establishing a common theme for a system enabling developers to communicate key system mechanisms more effectively. These metaphors commonly are represented as architectural patterns. Continuous testing promotes more robust designs because individual test cases simulate how various objects in our system are used by others, which not only tests system function but also validates our interfaces. This emergent approach to design complements nicely the more active approach provided by visual modeling.

Other similarities between the two processes exist as well. The presence of an on-site customer advocated by XP enables us to more effectively elicit and manage requirements. The planning game emphasizes risk mitigation, and verifying quality is done constantly through continuous testing.

Some striking differences between the two processes are apparent. Whereas RUP advocates modeling visually to specify a software system's architecture, XP doesn't. No mention of pair programming is made in RUP, and many of the artifacts recommended by RUP aren't present in XP.

Regardless of the similarities and differences between XP and RUP, one major difference and one major similarity are apparent. First, RUP is a process framework, whereas XP is a software development process. Consequently, we should tailor RUP and devise a development case that fits our organization prior to using it. XP, on the other hand, is a process to which we should adhere if we are planning to apply it.

Based on the similarities between RUP and XP at the conceptual level, and because of the adherence of XP to RUP's best practices, XP should be considered a minimal instance of RUP.

A.3   Conclusion

RUP and XP are two popular and highly successful software development processes. Whereas RUP takes an all-encompassing approach to software development by formulating an extensive suite of software development best practices, XP takes a minimalistic approach, promoting only those 12 principles it deems absolutely necessary. While each approach has advantages and disadvantages, the underlying truth is that XP can be viewed as a minimal instance of RUP. Finally, possessing knowledge of and gleaning necessary information from each approach results in our ability to develop better software.

APPENDIX B

J2EE and the UML

You may be surprised, or even disappointed, that we didn't spend more time discussing J2EE technologies such as Servlets, JavaServer Pages (JSP), and Enterprise JavaBeans (EJB). These technologies are certainly very prominent, and it's likely that the majority of Java applications we develop will utilize at least one, if not all, of them. However, there was good reason for their omission. We view these technologies as advanced Java technologies that are constantly evolving. While their importance can't be questioned, the material we've discussed in this book is applicable regardless of future evolution. The concepts presented in this book are applicable with all Java technologies. Solid design practices are omnipresent and are independent of Java-specific implementations.

A more compelling reason for the omission is the fact that these technologies impose a certain amount of design restrictions. For instance, if we wish to create a Java Web application, we most likely would use a Servlet or JSP to process Hypertext Transport Protocol (HTTP) requests. The design of a JSP or Servlet isn't interesting nor is it very complex. However, everything that's used by the Servlet or JSP is of interest, and we've spent the majority of our discussion on these topics.

In addition, attempting to discuss in-depth J2EE technologies in conjunction with the many topics we've already discussed would require a volume of books, not a single one. Consequently, J2EE was beyond the scope of our discussion. However, for those interested in a brief overview, we provide a discussion on J2EE technologies, and how we can use the information presented in this appendix to develop more robust J2EE applications. For more information, refer to one of many excellent books, such as *Designing Enterprise Applications with the Java 2 Platform, Enterprise Edition* [KASSEM00].

We would be somewhat remiss if we didn't provide at least some discussion of how J2EE fits into everything that we've discussed throughout this book, which we discuss in the following section.

B.0 J2EE: A Brief Overview

The primary offerings of J2EE are Servlets, JavaServer Pages (JSP), and Enterprise JavaBeans (EJB). Each of these technologies serves a different purpose in the context of application development. However, Servlets and JSP are quite similar, whereas EJB is rather different. We'll point out the primary elements of each of these technologies. Our discussion in this section isn't intended to be an in-depth introduction but instead a high-level overview.

B.0.1 Servlets

In the following sections, we first discuss Servlets from a Java perspective. Then, we discuss how Servlets can be represented and mapped to the UML.

B.0.1.1 Java

A Java Servlet responds and replies to requests from clients. The most common type of request is an HTTP request that's sent from a browser to the Web server when someone clicks on one of the links on a Web page. Therefore, Servlets enable us to respond to certain actions of the user while interacting with a Web page, and they provide some sort of response to the requested action.

A common use of Servlets was to enable developers to dynamically generate the content of a Web page. Early in the life of J2EE, Servlets enabled us to create Web applications that could dynamically process user requests. Prior to Servlets, many Web sites contained only static information. Those sites that did generate dynamic content typically did so by using other server-side technologies, such as CGI (Common Gateway Interface) scripts. Servlets have a number of advantages over these more traditional technologies. The advantages include better scalability, improved performance, and a consistent programming model.

All Java Servlets must conform to the Java Servlet API. This API consists of a set of classes that enable our Java code to be run within the context of a server, commonly a Web server, and respond to requests. The most significant class in this package is the `javax.servlet.Servlet` interface, which defines the operations that all Servlets must implement. Those Servlets that respond to HTTP requests extend `javax.servlet.http.HttpServlet`, which is an adapter class that provides default implementation helping to ease Servlet development. The more significant classes composing the Servlet API are shown in Figure B.1.

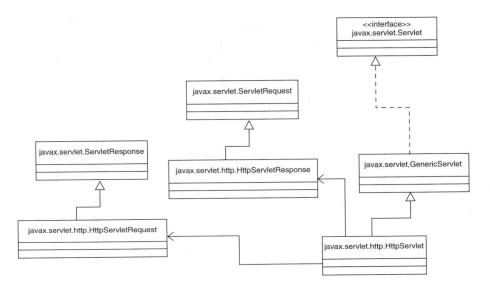

Figure B.1   Java Servlet API

B.0.1.2   The UML

Servlets are represented in the UML in the exact same manner as any other Java class by using the class notation. To differentiate between a typical Java class and a Java Servlet that can respond to HTTP requests, we attach the <<Http_Servlet>> stereotype to the class. Another alternative is to explicitly inherit our Servlet from the javax.servlet.http.HttpServlet class, but doing so would become cumbersome. Using a stereotype shown in Figure B.2 has the same meaning and is easier to model.

B.0.2   JavaServer Pages (JSPs)

In the following sections, we first discuss JSP from a Java perspective. Then, we discuss how JSP can be represented and mapped to the UML.

Figure B.2   HttpServlet Represented in the UML

B.0.2.1 *Java*

JSP is an extension of the Servlet specification. Developers came to realize that placing Hypertext Markup Language (HTML) generation code in Servlets didn't fit well with the development lifecycle. Many project teams consist of individuals filling certain roles. One such role was usability or HTML expert who typically wasn't well versed in Java technologies, nor was the Java developer typically well versed in HTML or usability. However, because Servlets combined both presentation generation and the ability to process the request, separation of responsibilities wasn't consistent with the technologies being used. Thus, JSP was introduced.

JSPs enable the HTML designer to do what he or she is best at; design robust Web pages because JSPs enable the HTML designer to specify HTML directly in the JSP, which is something that couldn't be done using Servlets. Recall that with Servlets, we need to generate HTML using quite a bit of string concatenation in conjunction with the response object. With JSP, we can focus entirely on HTML development.

When a Uniform Resource Locator (URL) is requested that maps to a JSP, however, the JSP is compiled into a Servlet, which is something our application server does for us. In this regard, a JSP is simply an extension to the Servlet API. Thus, JSP enables us to embed Java code within the JSP, which, however, was viewed as a quick and dirty solution that was difficult to maintain. The combination of Java code with HTML presented architectural challenges in that our presentation logic became tightly coupled to our business logic. We'll talk about this a bit in Section B.1.

B.0.2.2 **The UML**

Similar to Servlets, JSPs can be represented in the UML by using the <<jsp>> stereotype. This simplicity negates the need for any further discussion.

B.0.3 **Enterprise JavaBeans (EJB)**

In the following section, we first discuss EJB from a Java perspective. Then, we discuss how EJB can be represented and mapped to the UML.

B.0.3.1 *Java*

Whereas JSP and Servlets are similar in nature, EJB are entirely different from both. EJB are a server-side component architecture focused on distributed business components. EJB fall into two different categories:

- **Session Beans:** These are transient beans in that they rarely must maintain state-related information between requests. Essentially, once a session bean fulfills what was requested of it, the bean no longer needs to exist.
- **Entity Beans:** Entity beans represent persistent data. As such, they typically do maintain state across requests.

The bean specification dictates the classes that we must create and extend, regardless of whether we're creating session or entity beans. Two primary components of EJB are the remote and home interface, implemented by `EJBHome` and `EJBObject`, respectively. The purpose of the home interface is to provide a factory for creating beans. Clients use the home interface to find out how to find the bean, create it, and do other things. The remote interface handles the rest. `EJBObject` knows the business methods that are on the bean and delegates them when the methods are called. As such, when we work with beans, we don't call the methods on the bean itself, instead opting to call methods on the interfaces.

While the EJB specification is quite complex and beyond the scope of our discussion, the complexity exists for a reason. First, it allows our beans to be distributed physically among machines, which is transparent to any client because of its interaction with only the interfaces. Second, the implementation of these interfaces, which are provided by the bean container, can perform other services, such as security. Further discussion on the EJB specification is beyond the scope of this section. Further research is encouraged, and quality material is available that can help. For those readers interested, we recommend *Applying Enterprise JavaBeans: Component-Based Development for the J2EE Platform* [MATENA00].

B.0.3.2 The UML

JSR-26 is a formal specification produced as part of the Sun Community Process that defines a UML-to-EJB mapping. This document, titled "UML/EJB

Message Beans

Java 1.3 defines a new type of bean named a *message-driven bean*. A message-driven bean is an EJB that allows J2EE applications to process requests asynchronously. Message-driven beans work closely with the Java Message Service (JMS); message-driven beans can respond to JMS requests.

Table B.1   UML-to-EJB Mapping Stereotypes

Stereotype	Description
EJBEntity	Represents an entity bean.
EJBHomeInterface	Represents the home interface.
EJBPrimaryKey	Represents the primary key class, which is useful when container-managed persistence is used. Container-managed persistence is useful in that the EJB container provides all of the Create/Read/Update/Delete (CRUD) persistence mechanisms for our bean.
EJBRemoteInterface	Represents the remote interface.
EJBSession	Represents a session bean.

Mapping Specification" is more than 70 pages and quite detailed. It's meant primarily for tool vendors. An understanding of the various stereotypes that map to the primary elements of a bean is pertinent to this discussion. Table B.1 describes these stereotypes. When representing a bean on a UML class diagram, we need only the class with the appropriate stereotype. While certainly more than just that one class composes any bean, these similar details can be suppressed because all beans are architecturally similar.

B.1   Designing with J2EE

Each of the three main components of J2EE discussed previously is run in the confines of a container. For JSP and Servlets, this container may be a Web server. For EJB, it's an EJB container (possibly also a Web server). The container is responsible for instantiating and invoking the operations on the classes of each of the J2EE components. For instance, the `javax.servlet.Servlet` interface defines various methods that the Servlet container will invoke, but the container actually invokes our realization of this interface, albeit indirectly. This is a prime example of J2EE compliance with the Open-Closed Principle.

If we were to attempt to develop a Servlet that didn't adhere to the Servlet API, we couldn't use it within a Web server. Thus, the design of our system is dictated by the respective APIs. As such, the design of our Servlets always is the same. The different exists in the underlying collaboration of objects to which the Servlet delegates its work. This underlying society of objects is the focus of this book. However, important decisions must be made when using J2EE, as we must decide which J2EE technology to use in a given situation. First, however, let's discuss some general design guidelines.

Whether we are working with Servlets, JSPs, or EJB, good design principles imply that each technology simply is a facade for our underlying application classes. As such, none of the classes fulfilling these roles within our application should contain complex business logic. They should serve only as a means through which our application communicates with the container housing the J2EE components. The following list discusses our alternatives when architecting a J2EE application and where behaviors can be placed.

In general, we can put our logic in the following types of classes:

- **Servlets:** A Servlet can play a couple of different roles in a J2EE application. It can be a presentation component that generates HTML that is sent to clients. It also can respond to other HTTP requests that might not come directly from a client but instead come from other classes, such as JSP. In this regard, a Servlet typically is produced from either a controller or boundary class.
- **JSP:** JSP is responsible for generating HTML. As such, it's part of our presentation tier and maps nicely from boundary classes.
- **JFC/Swing/AWT client:** This class is a heavyweight presentation tier that isn't Web enabled.
- **Session bean:** Because of the transient nature of session beans, they're good candidates for controller classes.
- **Entity bean:** Entity beans typically are produced from entity classes.
- **Business object:** We've spent the majority of our time discussing this type of Java class in this book. Servlets, JSPs, and beans commonly delegate their work to business objects.
- **Fine-grained entities:** Fine-grained entities are entity beans that are highly cohesive. As such they have a specific purpose. Fine-grained entities are preferred when we have complex logic. Create fine-grained entities with small methods, which makes it easier to avoid duplication and to show intention, and provides more extension points for variant functionality. It's likely that fine-grained entities will result in performance problems, especially in a physically distributed environment.
- **Coarse-grained entities:** Coarse-grained entities are session or entity beans that handle process behavior and typically delegate to either a fine-grained entity or a business object. We should use coarse-grained entities in a distributed environment where method invocation between processes is slow. This helps minimize the round-trips but results in large objects with large methods. Most EJB typically should be

coarse-grained entities. Out-of-process clients can access these coarse-grained entities, which forward the request onto fine-grained entities or business objects.

B.2   Conclusion

We avoided discussing J2EE technology throughout this book for good reason. Most J2EE components are simply facades that serve as gateways to some underlying object model. This underlying collaboration of objects has been our focus throughout this book. Inevitably, however, the strength and flexibility offered by J2EE components can simplify and empower our systems. This appendix has served to provide a very high-level introduction to how these J2EE components fit into most enterprise Java applications. Further reading on J2EE architectures is encouraged.

APPENDIX C

Code Listing for UML Exercise

The following code represents the classes that have been derived from the UML diagrams in Section 3.5 in Chapter 3. This code has been produced by first analyzing the structure specified in Figure 3.5 and then the behavior specified in Figure 3.4. For simplicity, we have omitted using the eventhandler package from Figure 3.6.

```
/**
TimeChangeListener.java
This is the interface which the TimeEventSource objects "know how
to talk to." In our example, TimePrinter objects which implement
this interface are registered with the TimeEventSource.


*/
public interface TimeChangeListener extends java.util.EventListener
{

    public void timeChange(TimeChangeEvent t);
}


/**
TimeChangeEvent.java
This is our event object. It is the object which is passed from the
TimeEventSource object to our Event Handler object. Recall, the
Event Handler object is the object which implements the TimeChange-
Listener interface.


*/

public class TimeChangeEvent extends java.util.EventObject {
```

```
        public TimeChangeEvent(Object source) {
            super(source);
        }

}

/**
This class is our event handler. It implements the listener inter-
face and will respond to Time Change Event generated by the Event
Source object.


*/

public class TimePrinter implements TimeChangeListener {

    private int seconds;
    private String name;

    public TimePrinter(String s) {
        seconds = 0;
        name = s;
    }

    public void timeChange(TimeChangeEvent t) {
      System.out.println("TimePrinter - Seconds that have gone by "
+
            name + ": " + seconds);
        seconds ++;
    }
}
/**
This class is the event source. It is responsible for generating
TimeChangeEvents. Upon a TimeChangeEvent, it notifies all of its
Listeners.


*/

import java.util.*;
import java.lang.*;

public class TimeEventSource {

    private Vector listeners = new Vector();

    public void addTimeChangeListener(TimeChangeListener o) {
        listeners.addElement(o);
    }

    public void removeTimeChangeListener(TimeChangeListener o) {
        listeners.removeElement(o);
    }
```

```java
        private void notifyTimeChange() {
            Enumeration e = listeners.elements();
            TimeChangeEvent tce = new TimeChangeEvent(this);
            while (e.hasMoreElements()) {
                TimeChangeListener tcl = (TimeChangeListener)
e.nextElement();
                tcl.timeChange(tce);
            }
        }

    public void start() {
        try
        {
            boolean done = false;
            //infinite loop.
            while (!done)
            {
                //notify the current thread to sleep for 1 second.
                Thread.sleep(1000);
                notifyTimeChange();
            }
        }
        catch (Exception e)
        {
            System.out.println("start : " + e);
        }
    }
}

/**
This class serves as the entry point to the event application.


*/

public class EventExample {

    public static void main(String args[]) {

        TimePrinter p1 = new TimePrinter("PrinterOne");
        TimePrinter p2 = new TimePrinter("PrinterTwo");

        MyTimeFrame f = new MyTimeFrame("Frame 1");

        TimeEventSource timer = new TimeEventSource();
        timer.addTimeChangeListener(p1);
        timer.addTimeChangeListener(p2);
        timer.addTimeChangeListener(f);

        timer.start();
    }
}
```

BIBLIOGRAPHY

[ALEXANDER79] Alexander, Christopher. *The Timeless Way of Building*. Oxford University Press, 1979.

[BOOCH98] Booch, Grady. "The Visual Modeling of Software Architecture for the Enterprise." Rose Architect, 1998.http://www.therationaledge. com/rosearchitect/mag/archives/9810/f1.html.

[BOOCH99] Booch, Grady, James Rumbaugh, and Ivar Jacobson. *The Unified Modeling Language User Guide*. Addison-Wesley, 1999.

[BROOKS95] Brooks, Frederick P., Jr. *The Mythical Man-Month, Anniversary Edition: Essays On Software Engineering*. Addison-Wesley, 1995.

[COMP97] Szyperski, Clemens. *Component Software: Beyond Object-Oriented Programming*. Addison-Wesley, 1997.

[FOWLER97] Fowler, Martin, and Kendall Scott. *UML Distilled: Applying the Standard Object Modeling Language*. Addison-Wesley, 1997.

[FOWLER99] Fowler, Martin, Kent Beck, John Brant, William Opdyke, and Don Roberts. *Refactoring: Improving the Design of Existing Code*. Addison-Wesley, 1999.

[GOF95] Gamma, Erich, Richard Helm, Ralph Johnson, and John Vlissides. *Design Patterns: Elements of Reusable Object-Oriented Software*. Addison-Wesley, 1995.

[KASSEM00] Kassem, Nicholas. *Designing Enterprise Applications with the Java 2 Platform, Enterprise Edition*. Addison-Wesley, 2000.

[KRUCHTEN95] Kruchten, Philippe. "Architectural Blueprints—The 4 + 1 View Model of Software Architecture." *IEEE Software* 12, no. 6 (1995): 42–50.

[MARTIN00] Martin, Robert C. "Design Principles and Design Patterns." White paper, objectmentor.com, 2000. http://www.objectmentor.com.

[MATENA00] Matena Vlada and Beth Stearns. *Applying Enterprise JavaBeans: Component-Based Development for the J2EE Platform.* Addison-Wesley, 2000.

[OOSC97] Meyer, Betrand. *Object-Oriented Software Construction.* Prentice Hall, 1997.

[PLOP98] Martin, Robert, Dirk Riehle, and Frank Buschmann. *Pattern Language of Program Design 3.* Addison-Wesley, 1998.

[POSA96] Buschmann, Frank, Regine Meunier, Hans Rohnert, Peter Sommerlad, Michael Stal. *Pattern Oriented Software Architecture.* Wiley & Sons, 1996.

[RUP00] Rational Unified Process. Rational Software Corporation, 2000.

[SEM01] *OMG Unified Modeling Language Specification.* Object Management Group, September 2001. http://www.omg.org.

[SUB99]Allamaraju, Subrahmanyam. "Architecture Paradox." White paper, 1999. http://www.subrahmanyam.com/articles/architecture/Paradox.html.

[WR00] Royce, Walker. "Next-Generation Software Economics." *The Rational Edge.* December 2000. http://www.therationaledge.com/content/dec_00/f_softecon.html.

Additional Resources

Ahmed, Kwahar. *Developing J2EE applications with the UML.* Addison-Wesley, 2001.

Beck, Kent. *Extreme Programming Explained: Embrace Change.* Addison-Wesley, 2000.

Fowler, Martin, Alan Knight, and Kai Yu. *Integrating Business Objects into the J2EE Platform.* JavaOne Conference, 2000, http://java.sun.com/javaone/javaone00/.

Jacobson, Ivar, Grady Booch, and James Rumbaugh. *The Unified Software Development Process.* Addison-Wesley, 1999.

Martin, Robert C. "The Process." objectmentor.com, 2000. http://www.objectmentor.com.

INDEX

- (minus sign), 61, 132
+ (plus sign), 132
# (pound sign), 61, 132

A

Abstract classes, 9, 10, 11–12. *See also* Classes
Abstract coupling, 13, 175, 183. *See also* Coupling
Abstract Windowing Toolkit (AWT), 67, 69, 70
Accessor methods, 160–162
Activities. *See also* Activity diagrams
  separation of, 136
  use of the term, 75
Activity diagrams. *See also* Activities
  basic description of, 56
  specifying use case behavior with, 126–127
Actors
  basic description of, 59, 83, 117
  boundary classes and, 138
  notation for, 116–117
  requirements modeling and, 116–117
  three types of, 117
Acyclic dependencies, 27–29, 176
Adoption strategy, xxi
ADP (Acyclic Dependencies Principle), 27–29, 36, 176, 236
Aggregation, 64

Algorithms, 7, 20, 33–34
Alternate flows, use of the term, 85, 127, 128
Analysis
  design versus, 86
  problem, 131–144
  robustness, 138
  stage, 86–90
Ancestor, use of the term, 119
Annotations, 66
Applying Enterprise JavaBeans: Component-Based Development for the J2EE Platform, 257
Architectural modeling. *See also* Architecture
  basic description of, 201–228
  class libraries and, 217, 224–225
  establishing architecture for, 202–203
  frameworks and, 217–219
  mechanisms for, 204–211
  MVC (Model-View-Controller) pattern and, 208–209
  Observer pattern and, 207–208
  partitions and, 209–211
Architecture. *See also* Architectural modeling
  -centric software processes, 77
  complexity of, 45, 203
  component, 225–227
  document, 86–87

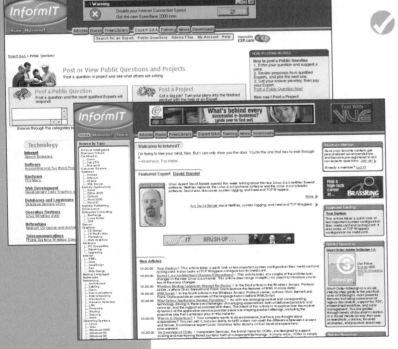

Register
Your Book
at www.aw.com/cseng/register

You may be eligible to receive:

- Advance notice of forthcoming editions of the book
- Related book recommendations
- Chapter excerpts and supplements of forthcoming titles
- Information about special contests and promotions throughout the year
- Notices and reminders about author appearances, tradeshows, and online chats with special guests

Contact us

If you are interested in writing a book or reviewing manuscripts prior to publication, please write to us at:

Editorial Department
Addison-Wesley Professional
75 Arlington Street, Suite 300
Boston, MA 02116 USA
Email: AWPro@aw.com

Addison-Wesley

Visit us on the Web: http://www.aw.com/cseng